GERMAN
STEP BY STEP

GERMAN
STEP BY STEP

CHARLES BERLITZ

Charles Berlitz, world-famous linguist and author of more than 100 language teaching books, is the grandson of the founder of the Berlitz Schools. Since 1967, Mr. Berlitz has not been connected with the Berlitz Schools in any way.

Wynwood
A DIVISION OF
Baker Book House Co
Grand Rapids, MI

Library of Congress Cataloging-in-Publication Data

Berlitz, Charles, 1914–
    German step-by-step / Charles Berlitz.
       p.   cm.
    German and English.
    1. German language—Textbooks for foreign speakers—
English.
    I. Title.
    PF3129.E5B4   1990
    438.3'421—dc20   90-32659
                                                     CIP

Copyright © 1990, 1979 by Charles Berlitz
Published by Wynwood ® Press
a division of Baker Book House Company
P.O. Box 6287, Grand Rapids, MI 49516-6287

ISBN: 0-922066-43-4

Second printing, August 1996

Printed in the United States of America

INTRODUCTION

Here's your passport to travel pleasure. Charles Berlitz, whose grandfather founded the internationally acclaimed Berlitz Language Schools, now offers a new and simplified learning technique to foreign language.

Using Berlitz's method, you'll be conversant in the language; you'll be able to read signs and newspapers with ease; and most important, you'll be comfortable and knowledgeable speaking or hearing the language.

How often have we not risked speaking a foreign tongue for fear of making a mistake or "doing it wrong"? With GERMAN STEP-BY-STEP, accent and pronunciation problems are solved forever. There will be no need to fear appearing gauche before a waiter or salesperson, no terror at buying a train ticket or sending back a steak cooked rare instead of medium. You will discover the music and rhythm of language as spoken by those born into the culture and tradition of a nation.

Charles Berlitz has determined that we use approximately 2,000 words in daily speech in *any* language. So he includes in his program a vocabulary of 2,600 words chosen especially for their frequency of use.

By familiarizing yourself with these words, accompanied by the easily understood methods of pronunciation described herein, you will come to feel at ease in a new tongue, in the context of everyday life situations.

Make sure your travel—whether it's business, vacation, or the trip of a lifetime—isn't spoiled by an inability to savor the pleasures of the native tongue.

GERMAN STEP-BY-STEP will be your personal guide to an unforgettable, truly satisfying journey to a welcoming, accessible land.

CONTENTS

Contents

in verbs — idiom — clauses — "to know" and "to be familiar with"

Contents

HOW TO PRONOUNCE GERMAN

Every sentence in the lessons and dialogues of this book is written three times — first in German, then in easy-to-read syllables that show you how to pronounce it, and finally in English, so you can understand the meaning.

To read the German correctly, say the second line out loud, pronouncing the separate syllables as if they were English and, as you will see when you try it on a German-speaking person, it comes out in understandable German.

Here is an example. Note that the syllables in capital letters are to be stressed:

Wie geht es Ihnen?
Vee gate ess EE-nen?
How are you?

As you progress you should try to pronounce the German without looking at the second line — but it will still be there if you need it.

The German pronunciation of many letters and combinations of letters differs considerably from English. The following list will help you to remember the differences.

IN GERMAN	ENGLISH SOUND
a	ah
e	eh
i	ee (or) ih
o	oh
u	oo
b	b, or at end of a syllable, p
d	d, or at end of a syllable, t
g	k at end of a syllable, otherwise a hard g as in "get"
ch	kh (a guttural sound, deep in

IN GERMAN	ENGLISH SOUND
	the throat, similar to Scottish word "loch")
au	ow as in "cow"
ei	eye
eu	oy
ie	ee
j	y
qu	kv
s	z at beginning or within a word; ss at end of word
ß (a special letter)	ss
sp	shp at beginning of word
st	sht
sch	sh
th	t
v	f
w	v
z	ts

In addition to the above differences, the vowels a, o, and u are given radically different pronunciations when they have an umlaut (¨). The ä (called a-umlaut) has the sound "eh" and äu is pronounced "oy." The o-umlaut is pronounced something like "er" but with "r" barely pronounced. The ü has the sound "ee" but made with the lips rounded in a tight circle. To remind you of this we have used a small circle over the u-umlaut in the phonetic rendition where this occurs.

Although you may not believe it at first, German is really easier to pronounce than English, since the sounds of the letters, according to their position and combination, always have the same pronunciation. Therefore, if you remember the above information you need not hesitate to say any German word, no matter how long it is. (Incidentally, the so-called long words are merely short words run together.)

A word of advice: after reading each lesson for the first time it is most important that you read the text and the instant conversation aloud. Read it slowly at first, and then gradually increase your speed to a normal conversational speed, reading the German line instead of the pronunciation line. This is an excellent and proven technique, not only to help your pronunciation but also to imprint the key expressions firmly in your mind.

Whether you are studying alone or with someone else, try reading the different roles within the lesson, and especially the instant conversations, aloud, with expression and even gestures, and with increasing speed. By accustoming yourself to speaking naturally and easily you will attain a natural flow and rhythm which is the essence of speaking German like the Germans.

GERMAN
STEP BY STEP

INSTANT CONVERSATION: IN A CAFÉ

The following phrases can be of immediate use in a café in any German-speaking country. A dash before a sentence indicates a change of speakers.

— Guten Tag!
GOO-ten Tahk!
Good Day!

A useful greeting
Guten Tag — "good day" — can be used from late morning to late afternoon. It is by no means an antiquated expression of greeting as is the English "good day."

Ist dieser Tisch frei?
Isst DEE-zer tish fry?
Is this table free?

— Jawohl, mein Herr.
Ya-VOHL, mine hehr.
Yes indeed, sir.

Herr, Frau, Fräulein
The word for "Mr." is *Herr*. However, when the waiter uses *Herr* without the name he says *mein Herr.* "Mrs." is *Frau* and when addressing a lady without her name you say *gnädige Frau* — meaning "Gracious Lady." "Miss" is *Fräulein* and this latter is proper to use by itself, but preferably followed by the young lady's name. As yet, German has no term for Ms.

Bitte, nehmen Sie Platz.
BIT-teh, NAYM'en zee plahts.
Please take a seat.

— Ach, Verzeihung, gnädige Frau.

Ahkh, fair-TS'Y-oong, G'NAY-dee-geh fr'ow.

Oh, pardon, Madam.

> **Ach!**
> *Ach* means "Oh" in the sense of surprise, disappointment, admiration, wonder, or any fairly strong emotion. (The speaker uses it to preface an apology for having bumped into a lady's table.)

— Aber bitte.

AH-ber BIT-teh.

That's all right.

> **The many uses of "bitte"**
> *Bitte* can mean "Please," "You are welcome," "It's all right," "Have some," or "Go right ahead," depending on the context. The final *-te* has been phoneticized as *teh* but is not strong. *Bitte* should be pronounced more or less like the English bitter without the r.

— Herr Ober! Ein Glas Bier, bitte.

Hehr OH-ber! Ine glahss beer, BIT-teh.

Waiter! A glass of beer, please.

> **For good service**
> "Waiter" is *Kellner;* "headwaiter" is *Oberkellner.* When you address a waiter you usually call him *Herr Ober* — "Mr. head (waiter)." This flatters him and gets you better service than if you simply call him "waiter" — *Kellner.* A "waitress" is called just *Fräulein.*

— Jawohl, mein Herr. Sofort.

Ya-VOHL, mine hehr. Zo-FORT.

Yes indeed, sir. Right away.

— Ah, Herr Strauß!

Ah, Hehr Shtr'owss!

Ah, Mr. Strauss!

Wie geht es Ihnen?
Vee gate ess EE-nen?
How are you?

— Danke, gut. Und Ihnen?
DAHN-keh, goot. Oont EE-nen?
Fine, thanks. And you?

— Nicht schlecht. Nehmen Sie Platz, bitte.
Nikht shlekht. NAYM'en zee plahts, BIT-teh.
Not bad. Take a seat, please.

Hier ist ein Stuhl.
Here isst ine shtool.
Here is a chair.

— Mit Vergnügen.
Mit fehr-GNÜ-gen.
With pleasure.

The "Umlaut"
The "¨" over the *u*" in *Vergnügen* is called the umlaut and changes the pronunciation of the "u." To get the correct pronunciation say "ee" through your nose with your lips tightly rounded.

Herr Ober! Noch ein Bier, bitte.
Hehr OH-ber! Nohkh ine beer, BIT-teh.
Waiter! Another beer, please.

— Danke schön.
DAHN-keh shern.
Thank you very much.

Das Bier ist sehr gut, nicht wahr?
Dahss beer isst zehr goot, nikht vahr?
The beer is very good, isn't it?

— Ja, es ist nicht schlecht.
Ya, ess isst nikht shleckht.
Yes, it is not bad.

"Ch" — a guttural sound
Whenever you see *kh* in the phonetics, pronounce it like a guttural "h." That is, say an "h" somewhat as if you were clearing your throat.

— Herr Ober, die Rechnung, bitte!
Hehr OH-ber, dee REKH-noong, BIT-teh!
Waiter, the bill, please!

— Danke sehr, mein Herr!
DAHN-keh zair, mine Hehr!
Thank you very much, sir!

— Und vielen Dank für das Bier!
Oont FEEL'en dahnk für dahss beer!
And many thanks for the beer!

— Auf Wiedersehen!
Ow'f VEE-dehr-zay'n!
Goodbye!

Capitalization of nouns
You will have noticed that all nouns are capitalized in German, making it easier to identify what is a noun and what isn't. (If you see the word "bear" by itself in English you cannot tell if it is "to carry" or the eating kind.)

6

TEST YOUR GERMAN

Match these phrases. Score 10 points for each correct answer. See answers below.

1. Good day.

2. Please sit down.

3. With pleasure.

4. Pardon, madam.

5. Here is a chair.

6. Waiter, a beer please.

7. Yes sir, right away.

8. How are you?

9. Very well, thank you. And you?

10. Goodbye.

A. Mit Vergnügen.

B. Verzeihung, gnädige Frau.

C. Guten Tag.

D. Auf Wiedersehen.

E. Nehmen Sie Platz, bitte.

F. Wie geht es Ihnen?

G. Sehr gut, danke. Und Ihnen?

H. Herr Ober, ein Bier, bitte.

I. Jawohl, mein Herr, sofort.

J. Hier ist ein Stuhl.

Answers: 1-C; 2-E; 3-A; 4-B; 5-J; 6-H; 7-I; 8-F; 9-G; 10-D.

SCORE _____%

NAMES OF OBJECTS AND PLACES

Das ist ein Haus.
Dahss isst ine house.
This is a house.

A question of gender
In German not only males and females but everything has a gender. There are three genders, masculine, feminine and neuter. The word "a" or "an" is *ein* for masculine and neuter and *eine* for feminine. You will see the grammatical importance of this division of all nouns into gender in later steps. In German all nouns are written with capital letters.

Das ist eine Straße.
Dahss isst INE-eh SHTRA-seh.
This is a street.

Das ist ein Hotel,
Dahss isst ine ho-TEL,
This is a hotel,

ein Restaurant,
ine rest-oh-RAHN,
a restaurant,

eine Bank.
INE-eh BAHNK.
a bank.

— Ist das ein Restaurant?
Isst dahss ine rest-oh-RAHN?
Is this a restaurant?

Was ist das?
Das, translated here as "this," is also equivalent to "that." *Was ist das?* can mean either "what is this?" or "what is that?".

— Ja, das ist ein Restaurant.
Ya, dahss isst ine rest-oh-RAHN.
Yes, this is a restaurant.

— Ist das nicht ein Hotel?
Isst dahss nikht ine ho-TEL?
Isn't this a hotel?

— Nein, das ist kein Hotel.
Nine, dahss isst kine ho-TEL.
No, this is not a hotel.

A negative article
Kein (for masculine and neuter) and *keine* (for feminine) is a negative article meaning "not a" or "no."

— Was ist das?
Vahss isst dahss?
What is that?

— Das ist ein Restaurant,
Dahss isst ine rest-oh-RAHN,
This is a restaurant,

ein Wagen, ein Taxi, ein Autobus.
ine VA-gen, ine TAHK-see, ine OW-toh-booss.
a car, a taxi, a bus.

Achtung!
The *g* is always pronounced like the g in go.

— Ist das ein Taxi oder ein Autobus?
Isst dahss ine TAHK-see OH-der ine OW-toh-booss?
Is this a taxi or a bus?

— Das ist kein Taxi, das ist ein Autobus.
Dahss isst kine TAHK-see, dahss isst ine OW-toh-booss.
This is not a taxi, it is a bus.

9

Hier ist ein Taxi,
Here isst ine TAHK-see,
Here is a taxi,

ein Theater, ein Laden,
ine tay-AH-ter, ine LAHD'en,
a theater, a store,

ein Museum, eine Kirche.
ine moo-ZAY-oom, INE-eh KEER-kheh.
a museum, a church.

— Ist das ein Laden?
Isst dahss ine LAHD'en?
Is this a store?

Diminishing stress

You will frequently note in the phonetics the use of *'en*. The apostrophe means you should not pronounce it as a separate syllable but rather deemphasize its stress.

— Ja, das ist ein Laden.
Ya, dahss isst ine LAHD'en.
Yes, this is a store.

— Ist das eine Kirche?
Isst dahss INE-eh KEER-kheh?
Is this a church?

— Nein, das ist keine Kirche.
Nine, dahss isst kine-eh KEER-kheh.
No, this is not a church.

— Was ist das?
Vahss isst dahss?
What is this?

— Das ist ein Museum.
Dahss isst ine moo-ZAY-oom.
This is a museum.

Der Platz, die Straße, das Denkmal.
Dehr plahts, dee SHTRA-seh, dahs DENK-mahl.
The square, the street, the monument.

Three words for "the" — "der," "die," "das"
Der, die and *das* are the masculine, feminine
and neuter words for "the." If you wish to know
whether a noun is masculine, feminine or neuter, consult the vocabulary at the end of this
book and you will find *der, die* or *das* before the
word.

— Welcher Platz ist das?
VEL-kher plahts isst dahss?
What square is this?

— Das ist der Bahnhofsplatz.
Dahss isst dehr BAHN–hohfs-plahts.
This is the Railroad Station Square.

— Welche Straße ist das?
VEL-kheh SHTRA-seh isst dahss?
What street is this?

The ß
The "double s" is sometimes written ß: This is
the only unfamiliar letter you will see in German.
Formerly German used to be written in the
Gothic alphabet (see Step 24) but fortunately
for the student almost everything is now written
in the Latin alphabet.

— Das ist die Goethestraße.
Dahss isst dee GHER-teh-SHTRA-seh.
This is Goethe Street.

— Welches Denkmal ist das?
VEL-khes DENK-mahl isst dahss?
What monument is this?

Which? (or) what?
"What" or "which" is expressed by *welcher*
(masculine), *welche* (feminine) or *welches*
(neuter).

— Das ist das Schillerdenkmal.
Dahss isst dahss SHIL-ler-DENK-mahl.
This is the Schiller Monument.

11

— Wie heißt dieses Restaurant?
Vee hy'st DEE-zess rest-oh-RAHN?
What's the name of this restaurant?

> **Wie heißt das?**
> "What is the name of" or "What is it called?" is
> expressed by *Wie heißt. . .?* This is a useful ex-
> pression when visiting a new place.

— Das ist das Restaurant Rumpelmayer.
Dahss isst dahss rest-oh-RAHN ROOM-pel-my-er.
This is the Rumpelmayer Restaurant.

— Wie heißt dieses Gebäude?
Vee hy'st DEE-zess geh-BOY-deh?
What's the name of this building?

> **The three genders of "this"**
> The word for "this" is *dieser* (masculine), *diese*
> (feminine), and *dieses* (neuter).

— Ist das das Hotel Siegfried?
Isst dahss dahss ho-TEL ZEEG-freet?
Is that the Hotel Siegfried?

— Nein, das ist nicht das Hotel Siegfried.
Nine, dahss isst nikht dahss ho-TEL ZEEG-freet.
No, that is not the Hotel Siegfried.

Das ist das Hotel Kaiserhof.
Dahss isst dahss ho-TEL KY-zer-hohf.
That is the Hotel Kaiserhof (Kaiser Palace).

INSTANT CONVERSATION: A RIDE IN A TAXI

— Taxi, sind Sie frei?
TAHK-see, zint zee fry?
Taxi, are you free?

— Ja, wohin, bitte?
Ya, vo-HIN, BIT-teh?
Yes, where to, please?

— Zum Hotel Rheinland. Ist es weit?
Ts'oom ho-TEL RINE-lahnt. isst ess vite?
To the Hotel Rhineland. Is it far?

— Nein, nicht weit. Es ist ganz nahe.
Nine, nikht vite. ess isst gahnts NA-heh.
No, not far. It is quite near.

— Entschuldigen Sie. Wo ist das Hotel Bismarck?
ent-SHOOL-dee-ghen zee. vo isst dahs ho-TEL BISS-mark?
Excuse me. Where is the Hotel Bismarck?

— Dort — links.
Dort — links.
Over there — to the left.

— Wie ist dieses Hotel? Gut oder schlecht?
Vee ist DEE-sess ho-TEL? goot OH-der shlekht?
How is this hotel? Good or bad?

— Sehr gut . . . und sehr teuer.
Zair goot . . . oont zair TOY-er.
Very good . . . and very expensive.

— Wo ist das Nationalmuseum?
Vo isst dahss nahts-yo-NAHL-moo-ZAY-oom?
Where is the National Museum?

— Um die Ecke — rechts.
Oom dee EHK-eh — rekhts.
Around the corner — on the right.

Dort drüben.
Dort DRŮ-ben
Right over there.

Das große Gebäude dort drüben.
Dahss GRO-seh gheh-BOY-deh dort DRŮ-ben.
The big building, over there.

Da sind wir schon.
Da zint veer shone.
Here we are already.

Inverted word order

Up to now you have been able to follow the German and English meanings more or less word for word. But when a phrase or a sentence starts with an adverb or a preposition the word order is frequently reversed. "we are" — *wir sind* is inverted and becomes *sind wir* because the sentence begins with *da* — "here."

Das ist das Hotel Rheinland.
Dahss isst dahss ho-TEL RINE-lahnt.
This is the Hotel Rheinland.

— Sehr gut. Danke. Wieviel bitte?
Zair goot. DAHN-keh. Vee-feel BIT-teh?
Very good. Thanks. How much please?

A choice for "How much?"

An idiomatic way to ask the fare would be *Was macht das?* — "What does that make it?" For a store pointing to an object, one might say *Was kostet das?* — "How much does this (or that) cost?"

— Vier Mark.
Feer mark.
Four marks.

— Einen Moment, bitte — eins, zwei, drei, vier — und fünf.

INE mo-MENT, BIT-teh — ine'ts, ts'vye, dry, feer — oont fünf.

One moment, please — one, two, three, four — and five.

— Danke schön.

DAHN-keh shern.

Thank you very much.

— Bitte.

BIT-teh.

You are welcome.

TEST YOUR GERMAN

Insert *ein* or *eine* in the space before each noun. Score 10 points for each correct answer. When there are two spaces in a sentence, score 5 points for each. See answers below.

1. Ist das _____ Kirche?

2. Ist das _____ Laden oder _____ Restaurant?

3. Das ist _____ Straße.

4. Ist das _____ Taxi oder _____ Autobus?

Insert *der, die* or *das* in each blank space.

5. Ist _____ Restaurant gut?

6. Das ist _____ Schillerdenkmal.

7. Wo ist _____ Goethestraße?

8. Das ist nicht _____ Nationalmuseum.

9. Das ist _____ Bahnhofsplatz.

10. Wo ist _____ Hotel Metropol?

Answers: 1. eine 2. ein . . . ein 3. eine 4. ein . . . ein 5. das 6. das 7. die 8. das 9. der 10. das

SCORE _____%

step 2

HOW TO USE THE PRESENT TENSE OF VERBS

Das Zeitwort *sein.*
Dahss TS'ITE-vort zine.
The verb *sein* ("to be").

— Wer ist hier?
  Vehr isst here?
  Who is here?

Related but different

Although German and English are related languages, words that sound the same or almost the same do not necessarily have the same meaning. *Wer* sounds like the English "where" but it means "who" and *nein* ("no") is said exactly like the English number 9.

— Ich bin hier.
  Ikh bin here.
  I am here.

Und Sie sind auch hier.
Oont zee zint ow'kh here.
And you are also here.

Wir sind beide hier.
Veer zint BY-deh here.
We are both here.

— Ist Herr Bauer hier?
  Isst hair BOW-er here?
  Is Mr. Bauer here?

— Nein, er ist nicht hier.
  Nine, ehr isst nikht here.
  No, he is not here.

— Wo ist er?
Vo isst ehr?
Where is he?

— Er ist in Bremen.
Ehr isst in BRAY-men.
He is in Bremen.

— Ist Frau Bauer auch in Bremen?
Isst fr'ow BOW'er ow'kh in BRAY-men?
Is Mrs. Bauer also in Bremen?

— Nein, sie sind nicht zusammen in Bremen.
Nine, zee zint nikht ts'oo-ZAHM'en in BRAY-men.
No, they are not together in Bremen.

Frau Bauer ist zu Hause, in Hamburg.
Fr'ow Bow'er isst ts'oo HOW'zeh, in HAHM-boork.
Mrs. Bauer is at home, in Hamburg.

— Sind Sie Deutscher?
Zint zee DOYT-cher?
Are you German?

The capital "S"
The capital s in *Sie* indicates that it means
"you." *Sie* with a small s means "she" or
"they," depending on the context. The "i" in
ich is not capitalized.

— Ja, ich bin Deutscher.
Ya, ikh bin DOYT-cher.
Yes, I am German.

Nationalities
Nationalities are expressed in their masculine or
feminine forms:

	MALE	FEMALE
German	*ein Deutscher*	*eine Deutsche*
English	*ein Engländer*	*eine Engländerin*
French	*ein Franzose*	*eine Französin*
American	*ein Amerikaner*	*eine Amerikanerin*
Russian	*ein Russe*	*eine Russin*

Swiss	ein Schweizer	eine Schweizerin
Austrian	ein Österreicher	eine Österreicherin
Japanese	ein Japaner	eine Japanerin
Chinese	ein Chinese	eine Chinesin
Italian	ein Italiener	eine Italienerin
Spaniard	ein Spanier	eine Spanierin

— Ist Ihre Frau auch Deutsche?
Isst EE-reh fr'ow OW'kh DOYT-cheh?
Is your wife also German?

— Nein, meine Frau ist Amerikanerin.
Nine, MY-neh fr'ow isst ah-may-ree-KA-neh-rin.
No, my wife is American.

— Ist das Ihr Sohn?
Isst dahss eer zohn?
Is that your son?

Possessives
The possessive pronouns vary according to whether the object *possessed* is masculine, feminine or neuter.

	MAS.	FEM.	NEUTER
my	mein	meine	mein
our	unser	unsere	unser
your	Ihr	Ihre	Ihr
his, its	sein	seine	sein
her, their	ihr	ihre	ihr

Masculine and neuter forms are the same, and the same form is used for "his" and "its" and for "her" and "their"; "your" is also the same as the her/their form, but capitalized. (You have fewer forms to learn than if you were a German studying English.)

— Ja, das ist unser Sohn Fritz.
Ya, dahss isst OON-zer zohn, Fritz.
Yes, this is our son, Fritz.

— Und das ist Ihre Tochter?
Oont dahss isst EER-reh TOHK-ter?
And is that your daughter?

19

"This" or "that"
Das can mean "this" or "that" according to context as the daughter is standing, evidently, some distance away.

— Ja, das ist unsere Tochter Liesl.
Ya, dahss isst OON-zeh-rer TOHK-ter, Leesl.
Yes, this is our daughter, Liesl.

— Wie hübsch sie ist!
— **Vee hûbsh zee isst!**
— How pretty she is!

Das Zeitwort „sprechen."
Dahss TS'ITE-vohrt SHPREKH'en.
The verb "to speak" (or "to talk").

Sprechen
When you look up a German verb you will find that the infinitive form, that listed in the dictionary, always ends in -n. But some of the other forms change. Here are the most important forms of *sprechen* — "to speak":

I speak   — *ich spreche*
he (she, it) speaks   — *er (sie, es) spricht*
we (you, they) speak — *wir (Sie, sie) sprechen*

Remember this:
The present tense forms for *Sie, wir* and *sie* are the same as the infinitive for all verbs except *sein*, which you already know. The form for *ich* generally ends in -e and the form for *er, sie* or *es* usually ends in -t.

There is no progressive mood in German, no difference between "I speak" and "I am speaking." The same form — *ich spreche* — is used for both.

The imperative or command form for *Sie* ("you") is the same as the infinitive, with the *Sie* following:

Speak! — *Sprechen Sie!*

— Ich spreche Deutsch.
Ikh SHPREH-kheh doytch.
I speak German.

Sprechen Sie Englisch?
SHPREKH'en zee EHNG-lish?
Do you speak English?

— Ja, ich spreche Englisch.
Ya, ikh SHPREH-kheh EHNG-lish.
Yes, I speak English.

— Sprechen Sie Deutsch?
SHPREKH'en zee doytch?
Do you speak German?

No word for "do"
There is no word like "do" in German to ask a question. You simply invert the order. "Does he speak English?" — *Spricht er Englisch?*

— Ja, aber meine Frau spricht nicht sehr gut Deutsch.
Ya, AH-ber MINE-eh fr'ow shprikht nikht zehr goot doytch.
Yes, but my wife doesn't speak German very well.

The negative for verbs
There is no equivalent word for does not or don't for the negative. To make the negative for a verb, simply use *nicht, after* the verb.

Bitte, sprechen Sie langsam.
BIT-teh, SHPREKH'en zee LAHNK-zahm.
Please, speak slowly.

— Wir sprechen Deutsch mit Karl und Greta.
Veer SHPREKH'en doytch mit Karl oont Gray-ta.
We speak German with Karl and Greta.

Aber sie sprechen sehr schnell.
AH-ber zee SHPREKH'en zehr shnel.
But they speak very fast.

21

INSTANT CONVERSATION:
BEING INTRODUCED TO PEOPLE

Eine kurze Unterhaltung.
INE-eh KOOR-ts'eh oon-ter-HAHL-toong.
A brief conversation.

— Mein Name ist Müller.
Mine NA-meh isst MŮL-ler.
My name is Müller.

— Freut mich sehr. Ich bin Gustav Schmidt.
Froy't mikh zair. ikh bin GOO-stahf shmit.
Glad to meet you. I am Gustav Smith.

Sind Sie Amerikaner?
Zint zee ah-may-ree-KA-ner?
Are you American?

— Ja, ich bin Amerikaner.
Ya, ikh bin ah-may-ree-KA-ner.
Yes, I am American.

— Aber Ihr Name ist deutsch, nicht wahr?
AH-ber eer NAH-meh isst doytch, nikht vahr?
But your name is German, isn't it?

A high frequency expression
Nicht wahr? ("Not true?") is an easy way of
asking agreement, equivalent to "isn't it?,"
"aren't you?," "don't you think so," etc. depending on the context.

Und Sie sprechen sehr gut Deutsch.
Oont zee SHPREKH'en zehr goot doytch.
And you speak German very well.

— Sie sind sehr liebenswürdig.
Zee zint zair LEE-bens-vůr-dikh.
You are very kind.

Meine Eltern sind Deutsche.
MINE-eh EL-tern zint DOYT-cheh.
My parents are German.

Plural of possessive pronouns
Eltern, a collective plural noun, means "parents." The possessive plurals add an *e* for all genders when they refer to the plural, becoming *meine, unsere, ihre,* etc. (The plural of nouns will be taken up in Step 5).

Sie sind beide aus München.
Zee zint BY-deh ow'ss MÜNT-yen.
They are both from Munich.

— Wirklich? München ist eine schöne Stadt!
VEERK-likh? MÜN-khen isst INE-eh SHER-neh shtaht!
Really? Munich is a beautiful city!

— Ja, das stimmt.
Ya, dahss shtimt.
Yes, that is correct.

— Sprechen Sie zu Hause in Amerika Deutsch?
SHPREKH'en zee ts'oo HOW-zeh in ah-MAY-ree-ka doytch?
Do you speak German at home in America?

— Ja. Oft. Meine Eltern sprechen nur Deutsch zu Hause.
Ya. Offt. MINE-eh EL-tern SHPREKH'en noor doytch ts'oo HOW-zeh.
Yes. Often. My parents speak only German at home.

— Ist Ihre Frau auch hier?
Isst EER-eh fr'ow owkh here?
Is your wife also here?

— Ja. Meine Frau kommt bald.
Ya. MINE-eh fr'ow kohmt bahlt.
Yes. My wife is coming soon.

To come — kommen
"To come" is *kommen,* a word that should be easy to remember since it resembles English. Here are its important forms:

> *ich komme* — I come (or) I am coming
> *er (sie, es) kommt* — he (she, it) comes
> *wir (Sie, sie) kommen* — we (you, they) come

Ach, da ist sie schon!
Akh, da isst zee shone!
Oh, here she is already!

Greta, das ist Herr Schmidt.
GRAY-ta, dahss isst hair shmit.
Greta, this is Mr. Smith.

Herr Schmidt — meine Frau.
Hair shmit — MINE-eh fr'ow.
Mr. Smith — my wife.

— Sehr angenehm, Herr Schmidt!
Zehr AHN-geh-naym, hehr shmit!
A pleasure, Mr. Smith!

— Freut mich sehr, gnädige Frau!
Froyt mikh zehr, GNAY-dee-geh fr'ow!
Glad to meet you, Madam!

Sind Sie hier auf Urlaub?
Zint zee here ow'f OOR-l'owp?
Are you here on vacation?

— Mein Mann ist hier auf einer Geschäftsreise,
Mine mahn isst here owf ine-er geh-SHEHFTS-rye-zeh,
My husband is here on a business trip,

Coming events
Einer is *eine* (fem.) in the dative case. (see Step 3) used after most prepositions. It is given here simply as a set phrase since it is a question one is constantly asked when traveling.

aber ich bin hier zum Vergnügen.
AH-ber ikh bin here ts'oom fehrg-NÜ-ghen.
but I am here for pleasure.

TEST YOUR GERMAN

Match these phrases. Score 10 points for each correct answer. See answers below.

1. Do you speak English?

2. I speak German.

3. I am from Munich.

4. He is on a business trip.

5. My parents are German.

6. You speak German very well.

7. Here comes my wife.

8. Are you an American?

9. Do you speak German at home?

10. This is my wife.

A. Das ist meine Frau.

B. Sprechen Sie zu Hause Deutsch?

C. Ich bin aus München.

D. Meine Eltern sind Deutsche.

E. Er ist auf einer Geschäftsreise.

F. Ich spreche Deutsch.

G. Sprechen Sie Englisch?

H. Da kommt meine Frau.

I. Sie sprechen sehr gut Deutsch.

J. Sind Sie Amerikaner?

Answers: 1-G; 2-F; 3-C; 4-E; 5-D; 6-I; 7-H; 8-J; 9-B; 10-A.

SCORE _____%

HOW TO SAY WHERE THINGS ARE

Der Wagen, die Straße, das Haus.
Dehr VA-gen, dee SHTRA-seh, dahss HOUSE.
The car, the street, the house.

Der Wagen ist auf der Straße vor dem Haus.
Dehr VA-gen isst ow'f dehr SHTRA-seh for dem house.
The car is in the street in front of the house.

The dative case

The three articles *der, die, das,* change when they are put into the dative case. In this step, we introduce an easy aspect of the dative; that is, after such words as *in* ("in") *auf* ("on") *über* ("over") *unter* ("under") *vor* ("in front of") *von* ("from") *an* ("at") *zu* ("to") etc. When they refer to location, that is, to where something *is.* In this case the masculine, feminine and neuter words for "the" change as follows:

> *der* becomes *dem*
> *die* becomes *der*
> *das* becomes *dem.*

— Ist der Wagen in der Garage?
Isst dehr VA-ghen in dehr ga-RA-zheh?
Is the car in the garage?

— Nein, dort ist er nicht.
Nine, dort isst ehr nikht.
No, it is not there.

Er ist auf der Straße.
Ehr isst ow'f dehr SHTRA-seb
It is in the street.

— Wer sitzt im (in dem) Wagen?
Vehr zitst imm (in dem) VA-gen?
Who is sitting in the car?

Combinations of prepositions + articles
Certain dative combinations form contractions:

in + dem = im
an + dem = am
zu + dem = zum
zu + der = zur
von + dem = vom

— Herr Peters sitzt im Wagen.
Hehr PAY-ters zitst imm VA-gen.
Mr. Peters is sitting in the car.

Frau Peters sitzt nicht im Wagen.
Frow PAY-ters zitst nikht imm VA-gen.
Mrs. Peters is not sitting in the car.

Sie steht vor der Tür, vor dem Hause.
Zee shtat for dehr Tür, for dem HOW-zeh.
She is standing before the door, in front of the house.

Ein Hund sitzt unter dem Wagen.
Ine hoont zitst OON-ter dem VA-ghen.
A dog is sitting under the car.

Sitzen, stehen, sagen
Three verbs used here resemble English
words — *sitzen* — "to sit," *stehen* — "to
stand," and *sagen* — "to say." Here are the
important forms:

ich	*sitze*	*stehe*	*sage*
er, (sie, es)	*sitzt*	*steht*	*sagt*
wir, (Sie, sie)	*sitzen*	*stehen*	*sagen*

Frau Peters sagt:
Frow PAY-ters zahkt:
Mrs. Peters says:

„Vorsicht! Der Hund ist unter dem Wagen!"
„FOR-zikht! Dehr hoont isst OON-ter dem VA-ghen!"
"Careful! The dog is under the car!"

Ein Tisch, eine Flasche, ein Glas, ein Aschenbecher.
Ine TISH, ine-eh FLA-sheh, ine GLAHSS, ine AH-shen-beh-kher.
A table, a bottle, a glass, an ashtray.

Die Flasche, das Glas und der Aschenbecher stehen auf dem Tisch.
Dee FLA-sheh, dahss GLAHS oont dehr AH-shen-beh-kher shtay'en
ow'f dem tish.
The bottle, the glass, and the ashtray stand on the table.

Das Glas steht neben der Flasche.
Dahss glahs shtayt NAY-ben dehr FLA-sheh.
The glass stands next to the bottle.

Das Glas steht zwischen dem Aschenbecher und der Flasche.
Dahss glahs shtayt TS'VISH'en dem AH-shen-beh-kher oont dehr
FLA-sheh.
The glass stands between the ashtray and the bottle.

Der Wein ist in der Flasche
Dehr vine isst in dehr FLA-sheh
The wine is in the bottle

und auch im Glas.
oont ow'kh imm glahs.
and also in the glass.

Die Zigarette liegt im Aschenbecher.
Dee ts'ig-ah-RET-teh leegt imm AH-shen-beh-kher.
The cigarette is laying in the ashtray.

Ein Schlüssel.
Ine SHLÛS-sel.
A key.

Ich öffne die Tür mit einem Schlüssel.
Ikh ERF-neh dee tûr mit INE-em SCHLÛS-sel.
I open the door with a key.

Aber wo ist mein Schlüssel?
AH-ber vo isst mine SHLÛS-sel?
But where is my key?

Ach, hier ist er —
Akh, here isst ehr —
Oh, here it is —

in meiner Hosentasche.
in MINE-er HO-zen-TA-sheh.
in my trouser pocket.

> **Achtung! (Attention!)**
> The possessives and other adjectives also take
> the dative endings.

— Mit wem spricht diese Dame?
Mit vaym shprikht DEE-zeh DA-meh?
With whom is this lady talking?

> **The dative with "mit"**
> *Wer* ("who") becomes *wem* in the dative, nec-
> essary here because of *mit* ("with").

— Die Dame spricht mit einem Taxichauffeur.
Dee DA-meh shprikht mit INE-em TAHK-see-sho-FUR.
The lady is talking with a taxi driver.

> *Ein* ("a" masculine and neuter) becomes *einem*
> in the dative, while *eine* ("a" feminine) becomes
> *einer.*
>
> The same change of ending occurs with the
> possessives, *mein,* etc. *In seinem Koffer* — "In
> his suitcase."

— Mit wem spricht dieser Herr?
Mit vay'm shprikht DEE-zer hehr?
With whom is this gentleman talking?

— Der Herr spricht mit seinem Freund.
Dehr hair shprikht mit ZINE-em froy'nt.
The gentleman is talking with his friend.

— Mit wem spricht dieses Mädchen?
Mit vay'm shprikht DEE-zess MAYT-yen?
With whom is this girl talking?

— Das Mädchen spricht mit seiner Mutter.
Dahss MAYT-yen shprikht mit zine-er MOOT-ter.
The girl is talking with her mother.

— Sprechen Sie Deutsch mit Ihrer Frau?
SHPREKH'en zee doytch mit EE-rer fr'ow?
(Do) you speak German with your wife?

— Ja, aber wir sprechen Englisch
Ya, AH-ber veer SHPREKH'en EHNG-lish
Yes, but we speak English

mit unserem Sohn.
mit OON-zeh-rem zone.
with our son.

Er geht in England zur (zu der) Schule.
Ehr gay't in EHNG-lahnt ts'oor (ts'oo dehr) SHOO-leh.
He goes to school in England.

INSTANT CONVERSATION: IN AN OFFICE

Herr Schindler ist Amerikaner.
Hehr SHIND-ler isst ah-may-ree-KA-ner.
Mr. Schindler is (an) American.

Er ist in Bonn auf einer Geschäftsreise.
Ehr isst in Bonn ow'f INE-er geh-SHEFTS-rye-zeh.
He is in Bonn on a business trip.

Jetzt spricht er mit einer Sekretärin in einem Büro.
Yetst shprikht ehr mit INE-er zek-reh-TAY-rin in INE-em bû-ROH.
Now he is talking with a secretary in an office.

— Entschuldigen Sie,
　Ent-SHOOL-dee-gen zee,
　Pardon (me),

　ist Herr Hofer in seinem Büro?
　isst hehr HO-fer in ZINE-em bû-ROH?
　is Mr. Hofer in his office?

— Ja, aber er ist momentan beschäftigt.
　Ya, AH-ber ehr isst mo-men-TAHN beh-SHEF-tikht.
　Yes, but he is busy right now.

　Er ist am (an dem) Telefon.
　Ehr isst ahm (ahn dem) teh-leh-FOHN.
　He is on the phone.

　Ihr Name, bitte . . .
　Eer NA-meh, BIT-teh . . .
　Your name, please . . .

— Ich heiße Schindler — Ruprecht Schindler.
　Ikh HI-seh SHIND-ler — ROOP-rekht SHIND-ler.
　My name is Schindler — Ruprecht Schindler.

Wie heißen Sie?
Ich heiße. — *I am called (or) My name is.*
Wie heißen Sie? — *What are you called? (or)*
What is your name?

Ich bin ein Freund von Herrn Hofer.
Ikh bin ine froy-nt fohn hehrn HO-fer.
I am a friend of Mr. Hofer's.

Herrn
Herrn is the dative form of *Herr.* Just a few
nouns have a special dative case. Another is
Haus:
zu Hause — at home

Herrn is also used before the name on the envelope in writing a letter to a man to indicate
"to" him. (*Frau* and *Fräulein* do not have a special dative case.)

Ich komme aus New York.
Ikh KOHM-meh ow'ss New York.
I come from New York.

— Eine Minute, bitte.
INE-eh mee-NOO-teh, BIT-teh.
One minute, please.

Hallo! Herr Hofer?
Ha-LO! Hehr HO-fer?
Hello! Mr. Hofer?

Sind Sie jetzt frei?
Zint zee yetst fry?
Are you free now?

Ein Herr Schindler ist hier im Büro.
Ine hehr SHIND-ler isst here im bů-RO.
A Mr. Schindler is here in the office.

— Ach, ja! Natürlich. Sehr gut!
Akh, ya! na-TŮR-likh. Zair goot!
Oh, yes! Of course. Fine!

— Gehen Sie direkt hinein, Herr Schindler.
GAY-en zee dee-REKT hin-INE, hehr SHIND-ler.
Go right in, Mr. Schindler.

Verbs are easy in German
The present tense verb form for "you," "we,"
and "they" is also the form of infinitive. This will
make it easy for you in conversation since, from
hearing a new verb used, you automatically can
apply the other forms in the present tense according to the table on page 27.

Sein Büro ist dort:
Zine bŭ-ROH isst dort:
His office is over there:

im Gang — ganz am Ende.
im gahng — gahnts ahm EN-deh.
in the hall — completely at the end.

— Danke sehr, Fräulein.
DAHN-keh zehr, FROY-line.
Thanks a lot, miss.

— Bitte sehr, Herr Schindler.
BIT-teh zair, hehr SHIND-ler.
You are welcome, Mr. Schindler.

33

TEST YOUR GERMAN

Fill in the correct dative singular form of the — *dem* (mas.) *der* (fem) *dem* (neuter) or "a" — *einem* (mas.), *einer* (fem.), *einem* (neuter). Do not use contractions in the first seven sentences. Score 10 points for each correct sentence. See answers below.

1. Der Wage ist auf _____ Straße
   "the"

2. Frau Peters steht vor _____ Haus.
   "the"

3. Sitzt der Hund unter _____ Wagen?
   "the"

4. Das Glas steht neben _____ Flasche.
   "the"

5. Ich öffne die Tür mit _____ Schlüssel.
   "a"

6. Der Wein ist in _____ Flasche.
   "a"

7. Er spricht mit _____ Sekretärin.
   "the"

Now use contractions where applicable.

8. Er ist _____ Telefon.
   "on the"

9. Herr Schindler ist _____ Büro.
   "in the"

10. Das Bier ist _____ Glas.
    "in the"

ANSWERS: 1. der 2. dem 3. dem 4. der 5. einem 6. einer 7. der 8. am 9. im 10. im

SCORE ____%

step 4

NUMBERS AND HOW TO USE THEM

Von null bis zehn.
Fohn NOOL biss TS'AYN.
From zero to ten.

0	1	2	3	4	5
null	eins	zwei	drei	vier	fünf
nool	**ine'ts**	**ts'vye**	**dry**	**feer**	**fûnf**

6	7	8	9	10
sechs	sieben	acht	neun	zehn
zeks	**ZEE'ben**	**akht**	**noy'n**	**ts'ayn**

Von elf bis zwanzig.
Fonn elf biss TS'VAHN-ts'ikh.
From eleven to twenty.

11	12	13
elf	zwölf	dreizehn
elf	**ts'verlf**	**DRY-ts'ayn**

14	15	16
vierzehn	fünfzehn	sechzehn
FIR-ts'ayn	**FÛNF-ts'ayn**	**ZEKH-ts'ayn**

17	18	19
siebzehn	achtzehn	neunzehn
ZEEP-ts'ayn	**AKHT-ts'ayn**	**NOYN-ts'ayn**

20
zwanzig
TS'VAHN-ts'ikh

Von zwanzig bis dreißig.
Fonn TS'VAHN-ts'ikh biss DRY-sikh.
From twenty to thirty.

21	22
einundzwanzig	zweiundzwanzig
INE-oont-ts'vahn-ts'ikh	**TS'VYE-oont-ts'vahn-ts'ikh**
23	24
dreiundzwanzig	vierundzwanzig
DRY-oont-ts'vahn-ts'ikh	**FEER-oont-ts'vahn-ts'ikh**
25	26
fünfundzwanzig	sechsundzwanzig
FÜNF-oont-ts'vahn-ts'ikh	**ZEKS-oont-ts'vahn-ts'ikh**
27	28
siebenundzwanzig	achtundzwanzig
ZEE'ben-oont-ts'vahn-ts'ikh	**AKHT-oont-ts'vahn-ts'ikh**
29	30
neunundzwanzig	dreißig
NOYN-oont-ts'vahn-ts'ikh	**DRY-sikh**

Die anderen wichtigen Zahlen sind:
Dee AHN-deh-ren VIKH-tee-ghen TSAH-len zint:
The other important numbers are:

40	50	60
vierzig	fünfzig	sechzig
FIR-ts'ikh	**FÜNF-ts'ikh**	**ZEKH-ts'ikh**

70	80	90
siebzig	achtzig	neunzig
ZEEP-ts'ikh	**AKHT-ts'ikh**	**NOYN-ts'ikh**

100	101	und so weiter
		(abbrv. usw.)
einhundert	hunderteins	oont zo v'ye-ter
INE-HOON-dert	**hoon-dert-INE'S**	**and so forth**

1.000	100.000
eintausend	einhunderttausend
INE-tow-zent	**INE-hoon-dert-TOW-zent**

Achtung!
In writing large figures, a period is used instead of a comma — and vice versa.

1.000.000	2.000.000	1.000.000.000
eine Million	zwei Millionen	eine Milliarde
INE-eh mill-YOHN	**ts'vye mill-YOHN'en**	**INE-eh mill-YAR-deh**

Zählen ist wichtig —
TSAYL'en isst VIKH-tikh —
Counting is important —

In einem Laden:
In INE-em LA-den:
In a store:

Der Kunde: Wieviel kostet das?
Dehr KOON-deh: VEE-feel KOS-tet dahss?
The customer: How much does this cost?

The Feminine Form
Kunde and *Verkäufer* are "customer" and "salesman." The feminine forms are *Kundin* and *Verkäuferin:*
   -in is a feminine suffix.

Die Verkäuferin: Zehn Mark fünfzig, mein Herr.
Dee fehr-KOY-feh-rin: ts'ayn mark FÜNF-ts'ikh mine hehr.
The saleswoman: Ten marks fifty, sir.

Und am Telefon:
Oont ahm teh-leh-FOHN:
And on the telephone:

Eine Stimme: Hallo! Wer spricht?
INE-eh SHTIM-eh: ha-LO! vehr shprikht?
A voice: Hello! Who is speaking?

Zweite Stimme: Ist das Nummer
TS'VITE-eh SHTIM-eh: Isst dahss NOOM-er
Second voice: Is this number

zwo-acht-fünf-sechs-drei (28563)?
ts'vo-akht-fünf-zeks-dry?
two-eight-five-six-three?

Zwo
Zwei has an alternate form, *zwo* — often used, especially on the telephone, when the pronunciation of *zwei* could be confused with *drei*.

Erste Stimme: Dies ist Nummer
EHRS-teh SHTIM-eh: dees isst NOOM-er
First voice: This is number

Ordinal numbers
The ordinal numbers, "first," "second," "third" etc., are formed by adding -*te* to the cardinal number, except in the special cases of "first" which is *erster* (mas.), *erste* (fem.) and *erstes* (neuter); and "third" — *dritter* (mas.), *dritte* (fem.) and *drittes* (neuter).

zwo -acht-fünf-null-vier.
ts'vo -akht-fûnf-nool-feer.
two-eight-five-zero-four.

Zweite Stimme: Ach, Verzeihung, bitte!
TS'VYE-teh SHTIM-eh: Akh, fehr-TS'Y-oong, BIT-teh!
Second voice: Oh, pardon me, please!

Falsch verbunden!
Fahlsh fehr-BOON-den!
Wrong number! (lit. wrongly connected)

Zählen ist auch wichtig für
TS'AY-len isst ow'kh VIKH-tikh fûr
Counting is also important for

die Auskunft über eine Adresse.
dee OW'SS-koonft ûh-ber INE-eh ah-DRESS-eh
(the) information about an address.

Ein Mann: Wie ist Ihre Adresse?
INE mahn: vee isst EER-eh ah-DRESS-eh?
A man: What's your address?

EINE DAME: Friedensstraße 14 —
INE-eh DA-meh: FREE-dens-shtra-seh FEER-ts'ayn —
A lady: Peace Street 14 —

dritter Stock.
DRIT-ter shtohk.
Third floor.

Adjective before nouns without "der-die-das"
When adjectives are used alone in front of a
noun, they have the endings -er, -e, -es in the
nominative (subject) case according to whether
the noun is masculine, feminine, or neuter.

Und wenn man fragt: Wie spät ist es?
Oont ven mahn frahkt: vee shpayt isst ess?
And when one asks: What time is it?

Es ist ein Uhr.
Ess isst ine oor.
It is one o'clock.

Es ist zwei Uhr.
Ess isst ts'vye oor.
It is two o'clock.

Es ist zwei Uhr zehn.
Ess isst ts'vye oor ts'ayn.
It is two ten.

Es ist viertel nach zwei.
Ess isst FEER-tel nahkh ts'vye.
It is a quarter past two.

Wieviel Uhr ist es?
Telling time in German resembles the English
construction in some ways but in others is quite
different. "Past" the hour uses *nach* and "to"
the next hour is expressed by *vor*.

Zehn nach sechs. — Ten past six.
Zwanzig vor sieben. — Twenty to seven.

When asking the time you may use either of two
expressions:

Wie spät ist es? — How late is it?
Wieviel Uhr ist es? — Literally:
How many is it according to the clock?

Both are idiomatic and quite correct.

39

Es ist zwanzig nach zwei.
Ess isst ts'vahn-ts'ikh nakh ts'vye.
It is twenty past two.

Es ist halb drei.
Ess isst hahlp dry.
It is half past two.

Es ist drei Uhr dreiundzwanzig.
Ess isst DRY oor DRY-oont-TS'VAHN-ts'ikh.
It is three twenty-three.

Es ist viertel vor drei.
Ess isst feer-tel for dry.
It is a quarter to three.

Es ist zehn vor drei.
Ess isst ts'ayn for dry.
It is ten to three.

Es ist drei Uhr.
Ess isst dry oor.
It is three o'clock.

Für Verabredungen:
Für fehr-AHP-ray-doong'en:
For making appointments:

— Um wieviel Uhr?
oom VEE-feel oor?
At what time?

— Morgen nachmittag dann, um fünf Uhr.
MORE-ghen NAKH-mit-tahk dahn, oom fünf oor.
Tomorrow afternoon then, at five o'clock.

— Jawohl. Aber wo?
Ya-VOHL. AH-ber VO?
Very well. But where?

— Am Bahnhofsplatz, vor der Turmuhr.
Ahm BAHN-hohfs-plahts, for dehr TOORM-oor.
At the Railroad Station Square, in front of the clock tower.

40

—Einverstanden. Aber wenn ich um Punkt fünf nicht dort bin,
INE-fehr-shtahn-den. AH-ber venh ikh oom poonkt fůnf nikht dort bin,
Agreed. But if I am not there at five sharp,

warten Sie bitte noch fünf oder zehn Minuten.
VART'en zee bit-teh nokh fůnf OH-der ts'ayn mee-NOO-ten.
please wait another five or ten minutes.

Der Verkehr ist sehr stark
Dehr fehr-KEHR isst zehr shtark
The traffic is very heavy

Achtung
When an adjective follows the verb *sein* ("to be") it does not change its form.

um diese Zeit.
oom DEE-zeh ts'ite.
at this hour.

INSTANT CONVERSATION: AT A UNIVERSITY

Ein junger Mann spricht mit einem Mädchen:
Ine YOONG-er mahn shprikht mit INE-em MAYT-yen:
A young man speaks to a young woman:

— Guten Morgen, gnädiges Fräulein!
GOO-ten MOR-gen, GNAY-dig-ess FROY-line!
Good morning, Miss!

> **Greetings**
> *Guten Morgen!* is used only in the morning,
> "Good evening" is *Guten Abend,* and "good
> night" is *Gute Nacht.*
>
> *Gnädiges* here makes the use of *Fräulein* more
> formal and polite, as is the case for *Gnädige,* in
> *Gnädige Frau*

Sie sind neu hier, nicht wahr?
Zee zint noy here, nikht vahr?
You are new here, aren't you?

— Ja, dies ist mein erstes Jahr hier.
Ya, deess isst mine EHR-stess yahr here.
Yes, this is my first year here.

— Ich bin vom Studentenanmeldungsbüro.
Ikh bin fohm shtoo-DEN-ten-AHN-mel-doongs-bů-RO.
I am from the student registrar's office.

> **Compound words**
> German has a trend to running several words
> together to make a very long one. Do not be in-
> timidated by this peculiarity of the language, but
> separate the words for meaning and they be-
> come understandable.

Mein Name ist Heinrich Dorn.
Mine NA-meh isst HINE-rikh Dorn.
My name is Heinrich Dorn.

— Sehr angenehm.
Zair AHN-geh-name.
Very pleased (to meet you).

— Und Ihr Name bitte?
Oont eer NA-meh BIT-teh?
And your name, please?

— Ich heiße Marlene Kern.
Ikh HY-seh Mar-LAY-neh Kehrn.
My name is Marlene Kern.

— Sehr erfreut.
Zair er-FROYT.
Very happy (to meet you).

A pleasure to meet you
Both *Sehr erfreut* and *Sehr angenehm* are used
to acknowledge introductions.

Und wie ist Ihre Telefonnummer?
Oont vee isst EE-reh teh-leh-FOHN-noo-mer?
And what is your telephone number?

— Meine Telefonnummer ist 346272.
MY-neh teh-leh-FOHN-noo-mer isst dry-feer-zeks-tsvo-ZEE-bents'vo.
My telephone number is 346272.

— Danke, und Ihre Adresse?
DAHN-keh, oont EE-reh ah-DRESS-seh?
Thank you, and what is your address?

— Wagnerstraße 25,
VAHG-ner-shtra-seh, funf-oont-TS'VANT-sik,
25 Wagner Street,

vierter Stock.
FEER-tehr shtohk.
fourth floor.

— Ausgezeichnet. Das ist alles.
Owss-geh-TSIKH-net. Dahs isst AHL-less.
Excellent. That's all.

Danke sehr, und bis bald.
DAHN-keh zehr, oont biss bahlt.
Thanks very much, and see you soon.

Ein anderer junger Mann kommt. Er fragt:
Ine AHN-deh-rer YOONG-er mahn kohmt. Ehr frahgt:
Another young man arrives. He asks:

— Woher kennen Sie ihn?
Vo-hair KEN-nen zee een?
From where do you know him?

— Er ist jemand vom Studentenanmeldungsbüro.
Ehr isst YEH-mahnt fohm shtoo-DEN-ten-AHN-mel-doongs-bû-ro.
He is someone from the student registrar's office.

— Ach Unsinn! Das ist nicht wahr.
Ahkh OON-zinn! Dahs isst nikht vahr.
Oh, nonsense! That isn't true.

Er ist ein Student, genau wie wir alle.
Ehr isst ine stoo-DENT, gheh-NOW vee veer AHL-leh.
He is a student, just like all of us.

Also Vorsicht, verstehen Sie?
AHL-zo FOR-zikht, fehr-SHTEH'en zee?
So (be) careful, you understand?

> **"Also" is not also**
> As you progress from step to step you will notice the resemblance, except in accent, between many German and English words, such as *Mann, Student, Telefonnummer, Adresse,* etc. But some words look the same and have a different meaning — *also,* for example, does not mean "also" but "therefore" or "so."

— Ach, jetzt verstehe ich. Danke.
Ahkh, yetst fehr-SHTEH-eh ikh. DAHN-keh.
Oh, now I understand. Thanks.

TEST YOUR GERMAN

Translate these sentences into English. Score 10 for each correct answer. See answers below.

1. Wieviel kostet das? _____

2. Sechs Mark fünfzig, mein Herr. _____

3. Wer spricht? _____

4. Wie ist Ihre Adresse? _____

5. Wie spät ist es? _____

6. Es ist dreiviertel vier. _____

7. Um fünf Uhr nachmittags. _____

8. Und Ihr Name, bitte? _____

9. Wie ist Ihre Telefonnummer? _____

10. Ich verstehe sehr gut. _____

Answers: 1. How much is it? 2. Six Marks fifty, Sir. 3. Who is speaking? 4. What is your address? 5. What time is it? 6. It is a quarter to four. 7. At five o'clock in the afternoon. 8. And your name, please? 9. What is your telephone number? 10. I understand very well.

SCORE _____%

step 5

TRAVEL SITUATIONS

Für Ihre Reise
Fur EE-reh RYE-seh
For your trip

der Paß	das Geld	die Brieftasche	die Schlüssel
dehr Pahss	**dahss gelt**	**dee BREEF-ta-sheh**	**dee shlûs-sel**
the passport	the money	the wallet	the keys

die Armbanduhr	die Aktentasche	der Handkoffer
dee ARM-bant-oor	**dee AHK-ten-ta-sheh**	**dehr HAHNT-kof-fair**
the wristwatch	the briefcase	the suitcase

das Gepäck	die Flugkarten	der Platz
dahss geh-PECK	**dee FLOOG-kar-ten**	**dehr Plahtz**
the baggage	the flight tickets	the seat

The plural of nouns

The singular of *Flugkarten* is *die Flugkarte*. The adding of the *-n* has made it plural. German forms the plural of nouns, not in "s," but by a final *-n, -en, -r, -er, -e,* or an umlaut within the word sometimes followed by a final *-e*. Other nouns, however, do not change at all for the plural, with just the article changing to the plural form.

Some examples of the plural:

singular	plural
die Flugkarte	*die Flugkarten*
die Armbanduhr	*die Armbanduhren*
der Paß	*die Pässe*
der Schlüssel	*die Schlüssel*
der Handkoffer	*die Handkoffer*
der Platz	*die Plätze*

46

der Mann	*die Männer*
die Frau	*die Frauen*
das Fräulein	*die Fräulein*
das Kind	*die Kinder*

In any case, to help you find the plural of German nouns, each noun in the dictionary at the end of this book is given with its plural ending or umlaut modification. When nothing follows, then it does not change for the plural.

Herr von Heldt fährt
Hehr fonn helt fairt
Mr. von Heldt is traveling

mit seiner Frau and seinem Kind
mit ZINE-er fr'ow oont ZINE-em kint
with his wife and his child

nach Wien.
nahkh Veen.
to Vienna.

Sein Paß, sein Geld und seine Schlüssel
Zine pahss, zine gelt oont ZINE-eh SHLÛS-sel
His passport, his money and his keys

The nominative plural for possessives
The possessives add an -e when the noun they refer to is in the nominative plural.

liegen auf dem Tisch.
LEEG'en ow'f dem tish.
are laying on the table.

Er nimmt den Paß und steckt ihn
Ehr nimmt den pahss oont shtekt een
He takes the passport and puts it

The accusative case
Der Paß becomes *den Paß* when it is a direct object, or what Germans refer to as the accusative case. Nouns are in the accusative when someone or something is doing something to them. When the passport, money and keys

47

were lying on the table they were in the nominative case, but when Herr von Heldt starts to take them and put them in various places they become accusative. In the accusative case *der* becomes *den*, but *die* and *das* do not change. *Ein* becomes *einen* but *eine* and *ein* (for the neuter) do not change. The accusative for *der*, *die*, *das* are all *die* in the plural.

The only accusative change for *ein* (''a'') is that it becomes *einen* for the masculine. *Eine* (fem.) and *ein* (neuter) do not change. The object form of *er* (''he'' or ''it'' for a masculine object) is *ihn*. *Sie* (''she'' or ''it'' for a feminine object) or *es* (''it'' for a neuter object) do not change. *Sie* is the accusative plural for all three. Example:

I'm taking them. — *Ich nehme sie.*

in seine Aktentasche.
in ZINE-eh AHK-ten-ta-sheh.
in his briefcase.

Er nimmt sein Geld
Ehr nimmt zine gelt
He takes his money

und steckt es in die Brieftasche.
oont shtekt ess in dee BREEF-ta-sheh.
and puts it in the wallet.

Er steckt die Brieftasche in seine Rocktasche.
Ehr shtekt dee BREEF-ta-sheh in ZINE-eh ROHK-ta-sheh.
He puts the wallet in his coat pocket.

Aber er findet die Flugkarten nicht.
AH-ber ehr FIN-det dee FLOOK-karten nikht.
But he doesn't find the plane tickets.

„Wo sind die Flugkarten?" ruft er.
„Vo zint dee FLOOK-karten?" rooft ehr.
"Where are the plane tickets?" he calls.

„Einen Moment," sagt seine Frau —
„INE-en mo-MENT," zahkt ZINE-eh fr'ow —
"One moment," his wife says —

Einen Moment, bitte!
Einen Moment is in the accusative because von
Heldt's wife is telling him — to "wait a moment," putting *moment* into the accusative case.

„Ich finde sie sofort . . ."
„Ikh FIN-deh zee zo-FORT . . ."
"I'll find them right away . . ."

The present for the future
The present tense can be used colloquially for the future tense:

Ich komme um sechs Uhr. Can be translated as "I'm coming at six," "I come at six" or "I'll come at six."

Sie nimmt den Schlüssel
Zee nimmt den SHLÜS-sel
She takes the key

und macht seinen Koffer auf.
oont makht ZINE-en KOF-fer ow'f.
and opens his bag.

„Da sind sie — unter den Hemden
„Da zint zee — OON-ter den HEM-den
"There they are — under the shirts

The dative and the accusative
Der, die and *das* become *den* in the dative plural. The dative (see Step 3) is used here with *unter* because it denotes location. However, if a direct action is involved, such as placing the keys under the shirts, the *unter* would be followed by *die,* the accusative plural.

im Koffer."
imm KOF-fer."
in the bag."

49

Dann machen sie alle Koffer zu
Dahn MA'khen zee AHL-leh KOF-fer ts'oo
Then they close all the bags

> **Verbs that split — "separable prefixes"**
> Many verbs have separable prefixes, which
> means that, although they are written as one
> word in the infinitive, they separate in use, with
> the separable prefix following the main verb.
> This corresponds to the English "Put the cat
> out," "Lock the house up," etc. The infinitives
> for the verbs given here — "to open" and "to
> close" are **auf***machen* and **zu***machen*, literally
> "to make open" and "to make closed."

und rufen ein Taxi.
oont ROOF'en ine TAHK-see.
and call a taxi.

Sie tragen die Koffer
Zee TRAHG'en dee KOHF-fer
They carry the bags

zum Taxi, und der Taxichauffeur
ts'oom TAHK-see oont dehr TAHK-see-sho-FUR
to the taxi and the taxi driver

stellt sie in den Wagen.
shtelt zee in den VA-gen.
places them in the car.

Dann fahren sie zum Flugplatz.
Dahn FAR'en zee ts'oom FLOOK-plahts.
Then they drive to the airport.

> **Zu and nach — take the dative only**
> Preposition indicating direction "to" take the
> accusative except *zu* and *nach*, which always
> take the dative.
> Note:
>   *zu + dem = zum*
>   *zu + der = zur*
> *Nach* does not contract with the article.

Am Flugplatz gehen sie
Ahm FLOOK-plahts GAY'en zee
At the airport they go

an den Lufthansaschalter
ahn dehn LOOFT-hahn-za-shahl-ter
to the Lufthansa counter

und geben ihr Gepäck auf.
oont GAYB'en eer gay-PEHK ow'f.
and check their baggage.

Aufgeben — another separable prefix
This is another separable prefix verb — *aufgeben* — "to check." Verbs with separable prefixes have the separable prefix underlined in the dictionary section at the end of the book.

Das Fräulein gibt ihnen
Dahss FROY-line gibt EEN-en
The young lady gives them

Wie geht es Ihnen?
Ihnen means "to them" or "to you" according to whether it begins with a small or a capital letter. The basic German greeting *"Wie geht es Ihnen?"* Literally means "How goes it to (with) you."

eine Platznummer im (in dem) Flugzeug.
INE-eh PLAHTS-noomer imm FLOOK-ts'oyk.
a seat number on the plane.

Dann gehen sie durch
Dahn gay'en zee doorkh
Then they go through

die Sicherheitskontrolle
dee ZIKH-ehr-hites-kohn-TRO-leh
the security check

und steigen ins Flugzeug.
oont shtye-gen inss FLOOK-ts'oyg.
and get on the airplane.

INSTANT CONVERSATION: CUSTOMS INSPECTION — HOTEL ARRANGEMENTS

REISENDER:
RY-zend-er:
TRAVELER:

> Da sind unsere Koffer.
> **Da zint OON-zehr-eh KOF-fer.**
> There are our bags.

> Träger! Bringen Sie diese Koffer
> **TRAY-ger! BRING'en zee DEE-zeh KOF-fer**
> Porter! Bring those bags

> hierher, bitte.
> **HERE-her, BIT-teh.**
> here, please.

> Den großen schwarzen
> **Den GRO-sen SH'VAR-ts'en**
> The big black one

> und den kleinen blauen.
> **oont den KLINE-en BL'OW'en.**
> and the little blue one.

ZOLLBEAMTER:
TS'OHL-beh-ahm-ter:
CUSTOMS OFFICIAL:

> Machen Sie bitte den großen Koffer auf.
> **MA'khen zee BIT-teh den GRO-sen KOHF-fer ow'f.**
> Open the big bag, please.

> Gut. Was haben Sie
> **Goot. Vahs HAHB'en zee**
> Good. What have you

in der Aktentasche?
in dehr AHK-ten-ta-sheh?
in the briefcase?

REISENDER:
Ich habe nur Dokumente darin.
Ikh HA-beh noor doh-koo-MEN-teh da-RIN.
I have only documents in it.

ZOLLBEAMTER:
Und in diesem blauen Koffer?
Oont in DEE-zem BL'OW'en KOF-fer?
And in this blue bag?

> **In**
> *Diesem* is dative after *in*, indicating location, without action.

REISENDER:
Der gehört meiner Frau.
Dehr geh-HURT MINE-er fr'ow.
That belongs to my wife.

Sie hat nur Kleider
Zee haht noor KLY-der
She has only dresses

und persönliche Dinge darin.
oont pair-ZERN-likh-eh DING-eh da-RIN.
and personal things in it.

> **The plural of adjectives**
> When an adjective in the nominative case is used alone in front of a noun, without *der, die, das* or *ein, mein*, etc., then its accusative plural ends in *-e*, as here.

ZOLLBEAMTER:
Keine Zigaretten oder Alkohol?
KINE-eh ts'ig-ah-RET-ten oh-dehr ahl-ko-OHL?
No cigarettes or alcohol?

REISENDER:

Nur ein paar Päckchen
Noor ine par PEK-khen
Only a couple of packs

und ein bißchen Schnaps
oont ine BISS-khen shnahps
and a little bit of liquor

für die Reise.
für dee RY-zeh.
for the trip.

Im Hotel
Imm ho-TEL
In the hotel

REISENDER:
Haben Sie ein Doppelzimmer mit Bad?
HAHB'en zee ine DO-pel-TS'IM-mer mit baht?
Do you have a double room with bath?

Wir haben eine Reservierung.
Veer HAHB'en INE-eh ray-zehr-VEER-oong.
We have a reservation.

Mein Name ist von Heldt.
Mine NA-meh isst fohn helt.
My name is von Heldt.

HOTELANGESTELLTER:
Ho-TEL-ahn-geh-shtel-ter:
DESK CLERK:
Ah — Herr von Heldt aus Flensburg.
Ah — hehr fohn helt ow's FLENS-boorg.
Ah — Mr. von Heldt from Flensburg.

Jawohl. Sie haben Zimmer Nummer
Ya-VOHL. Zee HAHB'en TS'IM-mer NOO-mer
Yes indeed. You have room number

vierundvierzig im vierten Stock.
FEER-oont-FEER-ts'ikh im FEER-ten shtok.
44 on the 4th floor.

Page! Bringen Sie das Gepäck
PA-zheh! BRING'en zee dahss geh-PEHK
Bellboy! Bring this baggage

auf Zimmer vierundvierzig.
ow'f TS'IM-mer FEER-oont-FEER-ts'ikh.
to room 44.

REISENDER:
Herein!
Hehr-INE!
Come in!

ZIMMERMÄDCHEN:
TS'IM-mer-MAYT-yen:
CHAMBERMAID:
Sie wünschen, mein Herr?
Zee VŮNSH'en, mine hehr?
You wish, sir?

> **Wünschen — "to wish"**
> *Wünschen* means "to wish" or "to desire." The three important forms to remember are:
>
> *ich wünsche; er (sie, es) wünscht; wir, (Sie, sie) wünschen.*

REISENDER:
Bitte nehmen Sie
BIT-teh NAYM'en zee
Please, take

diese zwei Anzüge
DEE-zeh ts'vye AHN-ts'ů-geh
these two suits

und lassen Sie sie reinigen.
oont LA-sen zee zee RINE-ee-gen.
and have them cleaned.

To have something done
Lassen means "to allow" (*lasse, läßt, lassen*) and, combined with a following infinitive, conveys the meaning of having something done. In other words, "allow them to be cleaned."

Und nehmen Sie auch diese Hemden
oont NAYM'en zee ow'kh DEE-zeh HEM-den
And take these shirts too

und lassen Sie sie waschen.
oont LAHS'en zee zee VA-shen.
and have them washed.

Sagen Sie — wann kommen die Sachen zurück?
ZA-gen zee — vahn KOHM'en dee ZA-khen ts'oo-RŮK?
Tell me — when will the things be back?

Ist es möglich bis morgen?
Isst ess MER-glikh MOR-gen?
Is it possible for tomorrow?

ZIMMERMÄDCHEN:
Morgen bringe ich die Anzüge
MOR-gen BRING-eh ikh dee AHN-ts'ů-geh
Tomorrow I'll bring the suits

und die Hemden in zwei Tagen.
oont dee HEM-den in ts'vye TA-gen.
and the shirts in two days.

TEST YOUR GERMAN

Fill in correct accusative forms of "the" — *den* (mas.), *die* (fem.), *das* (neuter) or *die* (plural); "it" — *ihn* (mas.), *sie* (fem.), *es* (neuter); or "them" — *sie*, or "his" — *seinen, seine, sein* or "her" — *ihren, ihre, ihr*. Score 10 points for each correct sentence. See answers below.

1. Er nimmt _____ Paß.
    ("the")

2. Er steckt _____ in _____ Aktentasche.
    ("it")   ("his")

3. Sie nimmt _____ Geld
    ("the")

4. und steckt _____ in _____ Handtasche.
    ("it")   ("her")

5. Sie rufen _____ Taxi.
    ("a")

6. Der Taxichauffeur nimmt _____ Koffer,
    ("the") (plural)

7. und stellt _____ in _____ Wagen.
    ("them")   ("the")

8. Das Fräulein gibt ihnen _____Platznummer.
    ("a")

9. Bringen Sie _____ Gepäck auf _____ Zimmer!
    ("the")   ("the")

10. Ich bringe _____ Anzüge und _____ Hemden morgen.
    ("the") (plural)   ("the") (plural)

SCORE _____%

57

Das ist ein Büro.
Dahss isst ine bû-RO.
This is an office.

— Ist jemand in diesem Büro?
Isst YEH-mahnt in DEE-zem bû-RO?
Is there anyone in this office?

— Ja, ein paar Leute.
Ya, ine pahr LOY-teh.
Yes, several people.

> **The difference of a capital letter**
> *ein paar* — several
> *ein Paar* — a pair

— Wie viele Personen sind im Büro?
VEE-fee leh pair-ZONE-en zint imm bû-RO?
How many people are in the office?

— Sieben Personen.
ZEE-ben pair-ZONE-en.
Seven people.

— Wie viele Männer und wie viele Frauen?
VEE feeleh MEN-ner oont VEE-feeleh FROW'en?
How many men and how many women?

> **Achtung, bitte!**
> Men and women — *Männer und Frauen*
> Ladies and gentlemen — *Damen und Herren*

— Drei Männer und vier Frauen.
Dry MEN-ner oont feer FROW'en.
Three men and four women.

— Wie viele Schreibtische sind im Büro?
VEE feeleh SHRYP-tish-eh zint imm bû-ROH?
How many desks are there in the office?

— Vier.
Feer.
Four.

— Was hängt an der Wand?
Vahss henkt ahn dehr vahnt?
What is hanging on the wall?

— Einige Bilder und eine Uhr
INE-ee-geh BILL-der oont INE-eh oor
Some pictures and a clock

hängen an der Wand.
heng'en ahn dehr vahnt.
are hanging on the wall.

— Jetzt ist es halb sechs.
Yetst isst ess hahlp zeks.
Now it is half past five.

Und ist jetzt jemand im Büro?
Oont isst yetst YEH-mahnt imm bû-RO?
And is anyone in the office now?

— Nein, jetzt ist niemand im Büro.
Nine, yetst isst NEE-mahnt im bû-RO.
No, there is nobody in the office now.

— Ist etwas auf dem Tisch?
Isst ET-vahss ow'f dem tish?
Is there anything on the table?

— Ja, es ist etwas auf dem Tisch.
Ya, ET-vahss isst ow'f dem tish.
Yes, something is on the table.

— Was ist es?
Vahss isst ess?
What is it?

— Verschiedene Dinge:
Fer-SHEE-den-eh DING-eh:
Different things:

Blumen, Früchte, Bücher und eine Lampe.
BLOO-men, FRÜKH-teh, BÜ-kher oont EYE-neh LAHM-peh.
flowers, fruits, books, and a lamp.

— Ist etwas auf dem Stuhl?
Isst ET-vahss ow'f dem shtool?
Is there anything on the chair?

— Nein, es ist nichts auf dem Stuhl — gar nichts.
Nine, ess isst nikhts ow'f dem shtool — gahr nikhts.
No, there is nothing on the chair — absolutely nothing.

Die Ausdrücke *wo ist* und *gibt es* sind nützliche Fragen auf Reisen.
**Dee OW'SS-drük-eh *vo isst* oont *gipt ess* zint NÜTS-likh-eh FRAH-ghen
ow'f RISE-en.**
The expressions "where is" and "is there" ("are there") are useful questions while travelling.

Es gibt

Es gibt means "there is," "there are"; and *gibt es?* means "is there?," "are there?" in the sense of "is there available?" or "does it exist?" — in other words, less precise than *wo ist?* — ("where is?") *Es gibt* is the *es* form of the verb *geben* — "to give," so *gibt es?* literally means "gives it?" followed by the accusative form.

Zum Beispiel:
T'oom BY-shpeel:
For example:

— Wo ist die Bank?
Vo isst dee bahnk?
Where is the bank?

— Wo ist hier die Apotheke?
Vo isst here dee ah-po-TAY-keh?
Where is the drugstore here?

— Wo ist ein Briefkasten?
Vo isst ine BREEF-kahs-ten?
Where is there a mailbox?

— Entschuldigen Sie, mein Herr,
Ent-SHOOL-dee-gen zee, mine hehr,
Excuse me, sir,

gibt es ein gutes Restaurant
gipt ess ine GOO-tess rest-oh-RAHN
is there a good restaurant

hier in der Nähe?
here in dehr NAY-eh?
around here?

— Gibt es eine Garage in diesem Dorf?
Gipt ess INE-eh ga-RA-zheh in DEE-zem dorf?
Is there a garage in this village?

— Gibt es ein Münztelefon in diesem Gebäude?
Gipt ess ine MÜNTS-teh-leh-fohn in DEE-zem geh-BOY-deh?
Is there a coin telephone in this building?

Im Hotel:
Imm ho-TEL:
In the hotel:

EIN REISENDER: Haben Sie ein Zimmer frei?
Ine RISE-en-der: HAHB'en zee ine TS'IM-mer fry?
A TRAVELER: Do you have a room free?

Haben
Haben — is the linguistic ancestor of the English "to have." The forms to remember are *ich habe,* ("I have"), *er hat* ("he has"), *wir haben* ("we have"). In the future we will give only these three forms, since *sie* and *es* ("she" and "it") are always the same as *er* and *Sie* ("you") and *sie* ("they") are always the same as *wir*.

DER HOTELANGESTELLTE: Es gibt leider keines mehr.
Dehr ho-TEL-ahn-geh-shtel-teh: Ess gipt LY-der KINE-ehs mehr.
THE HOTEL EMPLOYEE: There are, unfortunately, no more left.

German Step by Step

Kommen Sie etwas später wieder.
KOHM-men zee ET-vahss SHPAY-ter VEE-der.
Come back a little later.

Zu Hause:
Ts'oo HOW-zeh:
At home:

DER JUNGE: Gibt es etwas zu essen?
Dehr YOON-gheh: Gipt ess ET-vahss ts'oo ESS'en?
THE BOY: Is there anything to eat?

> **Zu = to**
> *Zu* is used with verbs like the English "to" with
> a verb:
>
> > *nichts zu essen* — nothing to eat
> > *etwas zu tun* — something to do
> > *etwas zu trinken* — something to drink
>
> The *zu* is not used with the infinitive in the dic-
> tionary because the basic form of the verb it-
> self — *sprechen, essen, trinken,* etc. is the
> infinitive.

Ich habe Hunger.
Ikh HA-beh HOONG-er.
I am hungry.

> **Achtung**
> The usual way to express "to be" hungry or "to
> be" thirsty is to use the verb *haben*, literally,
> "to have" hunger, "to have" thirst.

DIE MUTTER: Ja, es gibt Brot, Butter und Wurst.
Dee MOO-ter: Ya, ess gipt broht, BOOT-ter oont voorst.
THE MOTHER: Yes, there is bread, butter and cold cuts.

Sie sind auf dem Tisch in der Küche.
Zee zint ow'f dem tish in dehr KÜ-kheh.
They are on the table in the kitchen.

DER MANN: Gibt es etwas zu trinken?
Dehr mahn: gipt ess ET-vahss ts'oo TRINK'en?
THE HUSBAND: Is there anything to drink?

Ich habe Durst.
Ikh HA-beh doorst.
I am thirsty.

DIE FRAU: Das Bier ist im Kühlschrank.
Dee fr'ow: Dahss beer isst im KÜL-shrahnk.
THE WIFE: The beer is in the refrigerator.

Im Büro:
Imm bů-ROH:
At the office:

DER CHEF: Gibt es etwas Wichtiges
Dehr shehf: Gipt ess ET-vahss VIKH-tee-gess
THE BOSS: Is there anything important

Etwas Wichtiges
Adjectives do not change when they are at the
end of a sentence or a phrase, but they change
when they are used before the noun according
to whether they are preceded by *der, die, das*
or *ein, eine, ein.*

The letter is important. — *Der Brief ist wichtig.*
The important letter — *Der wichtige Brief*
An important letter — *Ein wichtiger Brief*
Something important — *Etwas Wichtiges*

The last example has the neuter ending since
the gender of "something" is not known, and
therefore must be neuter. And *Wichtiges,* becoming a noun, begins with a capital letter.

in der Post?
in dehr post?
in the mail?

DIE SEKRETÄRIN: Nein, nichts Wichtiges.
Dee zek-reh-TAY-rin: Nine, nikhts VIKH-tee-gess.
THE SECRETARY: No, nothing important.

In einer Unterhaltung zwischen Freunden:
In INE-er oon-ter-HAHL-toong TS'VISH'en FROYN-den:
In a conversation between friends:

FRITZ: Hallo, Otto! Was gibt's Neues?
Fritz: Ha-lo, OH-toh! Vahss gibts NOY-yess?
FRITZ: Hello, Otto! What's new?

> **Dropping the "e"**
> An apostrophe is frequently used, especially in informal speech, to replace the *e* of *es*.

OTTO: Ach, nichts Besonderes.
OHT-toh: Akh, nikhts beh-ZONE-deh-ress.
OTTO: Oh, nothing special.

Alles in Ordnung.
AH-lehs in ORD-noong.
Everything (is) in order.

INSTANT CONVERSATION:
GETTING MAIL AND MESSAGES

EIN HERR:
Ine hehr:
A GENTLEMAN:

Sagen Sie bitte —
zahgh'en zee BIT-teh —
Tell me please —

ist Post für mich da?
isst post fůr mikh da?
is there any mail for me?

EIN ANGESTELLTER:
Ine AHN-geh-shtel-ter:
AN EMPLOYEE:

Jawohl. Hier sind zwei Briefe für Sie
Ya-VOHL. Here sint ts'vye BREE-feh fůr zee
Yes. Here there are two letters for you

und eine Postkarte für Ihren Sohn.
oont INE-eh POST-kart-eh fůr EER-en zohn.
and a postcard for your son.

Die Postkarte kommt aus dem Ausland.
Dee POST — kart-eh kohmt ow'ss dem OW'SS-land.
The postcard comes from abroad.

Die Marken sind sehr interessant, nicht wahr?
Dee MAR-ken zint zair in-ter-ess-AHNT, nikht vahr?
The stamps are very interesting, aren't they?

— Verzeihung. Ich bin in Eile.
Fair-TS'Y-oong. Ikh bin in ILE-eh.
Excuse me. I am in a hurry.

Ist das alles?
Isst dahss AH-lehs?
Is that all?

— Einen Augenblick.
INE-en OW'GH-en-blik.
One second.

Wir haben noch ein paar Pakete
Veer HAHB'en nokh ine par pa-KEH-teh
We also have several packages

für Ihre Frau
für EE-reh frow
for your wife

und einen Telefonanruf für Sie
oont INE-en tel-eh-FOHN-ahn-roof für zee
and a telephone message for you

von Ihrer Frau.
fonn EE-rer fr'ow.
from your wife.

Sie ist beim Einkaufen
Zee isst bime INE-kowf'en
She is shopping

und kommt etwas später.
oont kohmt ET-vahss SHPAYT-er.
and is coming a little later.

— Danke. Sagen Sie,
DAHN-keh. ZAHG'en zee:
Thanks. Tell me:

haben Sie Briefmarken hier?
HA-ben zee BREEF-mar-ken here?
Do you have any postage stamps here?

— Sicher. Marken, Postkarten, Schreibpapier und Umschläge.
ZIKH-er. MAR-ken, POST-kart-en, SHRIPE-pa-peer oont
                                                      OOM-shlay-geh.
Certainly. Stamps, postcards, writing paper, and envelopes.

— Gut. Geben Sie mir
Goot. GAYB'en zee meer
Good. Give me

> **Geben Sie mir . . .**
> *Mir* — "me" or "to me" is the dative case of
> *ich.* Note the other forms of the dative with the
> following pronouns:
>
> > Give (to) him . . . ! Geben Sie ihm. . . . . !
> > Give (to) her. . . . ! Geben Sie ihr. . . . . . !
> > Give (to) us. . . . . ! Geben Sie uns. . . . . !
> > Give (to) them. . . ! Geben Sie ihnen. . . . !
> > and "I give (to) you" is *ich gebe Ihnen.*

drei Luftpostmarken für Amerika.
dry LOOFT-post-mark-en für ah-MAY-ree-ka.
three airmail stamps for America.

TEST YOUR GERMAN

Translate these sentences into English. Score 10 points for each correct translation. See answers below.

1. Wie viele Personen sind im Büro? _____

2. Niemand ist im Büro. _____

3. Wo ist hier die Apotheke? _____

4. Wo ist ein Briefkasten? _____

5. Gibt es eine Garage hier in der Nähe? _____

6. Kommen Sie etwas später wieder. _____

7. Alles in Ordnung. _____

8. Ist Post für mich da? _____

9. Wir haben einen Telefonanruf für Sie. _____

10. Haben Sie Marken hier? _____

Answers: 1. How many people are in the office? 2. There is nobody in the office. 3. Where is the drugstore here? 4. Where is there a mailbox? 5. Is there a garage around here? 6. Come back a little later. 7. Everything is O.K. 8. Is there mail for me there? 9. We have a telephone message for you. 10. Do you have any stamps here?

SCORE _____%

68

step 7 FAMILY RELATIONSHIPS

Die verschiedenen Mitglieder der Familie
Dee fair-SHEE-den-en MIT-glee-der dehr fa-MEEL-yeh
The different members of the family

Der Mann und die Frau
Dehr mahn oont dee fr'ow
The husband and the wife

Die Eltern und ihre Kinder
Dee El-tern oont EE-reh KIN-der
The parents and their children

Der Vater und sein Sohn
Dehr FA-ter oont zine zone
The father and his son

Die Mutter und ihre Tochter
Dee MOO-ter oont EE-reh TOHKH-ter
The mother and her daughter

Der Bruder und seine Schwester
Dehr BROO-der oont ZINE-eh SHVESS-ter
The brother and his sister

Der Großvater und seine Enkelin
Dehr GROHS-fa-ter oont ZINE-eh EHN-keh-lin
The grandfather and his granddaughter

Die Großmutter und ihr Enkel
Dee GROHS-moo-ter oont eer EHN-kel
The grandmother and her grandson

The genitive case.
In this Step we learn the genitive case, the fourth (and last) of the cases of nouns, pronouns and adjectives you must recognize and use in speaking correct German. The genitive corresponds to the English "of" or the " 's" denoting possession. *Der Wagen des Vaters* can be translated either as "the father's car" or "the car of the father." In the genitive *der* and *das* become *des*, die becomes der, while *ein*

becomes *eines* and *eine* changes to *einer*. *Wer* (who) becomes *wessen* (whose). The plural of "the" — *die* becomes *der*. As for the nouns themselves, some add *-s* or *-es* or *-n* or an umlaut, while some do not change at all, as you will note in the following examples.

Der Wagen des Vaters
Dehr VA-gen dess FA-ters
The father's car

Der Schreibtisch der Mutter
Dehr SHRYP-tish dehr MOO-ter
The mother's writing desk

Die Kinder der Familie Braun
Dee KIN-der dehr fa-MEEL-yeh Brown
The children of the Brown family

Der Fußball des Jungen
Dehr FOOSS-bahl dess YOONG'en
The boy's football

Das Fahrrad des Mädchens
Dahss FAR-raht dess MAYT-yens
The girl's bicycle

Die Freunde des Bruders und der Schwester
Dee FROYN-deh dess BROO-ders oont dehr SHVESS-ter
The friends of the brother and of the sister

Der Hund des Großvaters
Dehr hoont dess GROHS-fa-ters
The grandfather's dog

Die Katze der Großmutter
Dee KAHT-seh dehr GROHS-moo-ter
The grandmother's cat

In einer Familie finden wir auch
In INE-er fa-MEEL-yeh FINND'en veer ow'kh
In a family we also find

Onkeln und Tanten, Neffen und Nichten und
OHN-keln oont TAHN-ten, NEF-fen oont NIKH-ten oont
uncles and aunts, nephews and nieces, and

Vettern und Kusinen.
FET-tern oont koo-ZEE-nen.
cousins (male) and cousins (female).

> The singular forms of the other members of the family are *der Onkel, die Tante, der Neffe, die Nichte, der Vetter, die Kusine.*

Herr Schmidt ist Kaufmann.
Hehr schmit isst KOWF-mahn.
Mr. Smith is a businessman.

> **Vergessen Sie nicht! (Don't forget)**
> In describing jobs, positions or vocations the indefinite article (*ein, eine*) is usually dropped.

Er hat sein Büro in Bremen.
Ehr haht zine bû-RO in BRAY-men
He has his office in Bremen.

Die Schmidts haben zwei Kinder,
Dee shmits HAHB'en ts'vy KIN-der,
The Smiths have two children,

einen Sohn und eine Tochter.
INE-en zone oont INE-eh TOKH-ter.
a son and a daughter.

Ihr Sohn Wilhelm geht zur Schule.
Eer zone VILL-helm gayt ts'oor SHOO-leh.
Their son William goes to school.

Helga, Wilhelms Schwester, ist Kunststudentin.
HELL-ga, VILL-helms SHVESS-ter, isst KOONST-shtoo-DEN-tin.
Helga, William's sister, is an art student.

> **No apostrophe**
> The genitive case of names and of many nouns is expressed by *s*, just as in English, but without the apostrophe.

71

Sie ist verlobt.
Zee isst fehr-LOHBT.
She is engaged.

Ihr Verlobter ist Rechtsanwalt.
Eer fehr-LOHB-ter isst REKHTS-ahn-vahlt.
Her fiance is a lawyer.

Herrn Brauns Vater,
Hehrn browns FA-ter,
Mr. Brown's father,

Wilhelms und Helgas Großvater,
VILL-helms oont HELL-gahs GROHS-fa-ter,
William's and Helga's grandfather,

ist pensioniert.
isst pahns-yo-NEERT.
is retired.

— Wessen Vater ist pensioniert?
VES-sen FA-ter isst pahns-vo-NEERT?
Whose father is retired?

— Der Vater von Herrn Brown.
Dehr FA-ter fohn Hehrn Brown.
The father of Mr. Brown.

Sehr wichtig (very important)
Now that you have had the fourth of the four cases, which we have presented in the order of nominative, dative, accusative, and genitive, we suggest that you consult the appended table on how the definite article *der, die, das* changes for each case as well as the adjective ending of an adjective placed in front of the noun.

the small car *der kleine Wagen (nom.)*
des kleinen Wagens (gen.)
dem kleinen Wagen (dat.)
den kleinen Wagen (acc.)

the small cat *die kleine Katze (nom.)*
der kleinen Katze (gen.)
der kleinen Katze (dat.)
die kleine Katze (acc.)

the small village *das kleine Dorf* (*nom.*)
des kleinen Dorfes (*gen.*)
dem kleinen Dorf (*dat.*)
das kleine Dorf (*acc.*)

Note that the genitive ending of the noun changes as well for the masculine and neuter.

— Wessen Verlobter ist Rechtsanwalt?
VES-sen Fair-LOHB-ter isst REKHTS-ahn-vahlt?
Whose fiance is a lawyer?

— Helgas Bräutigam.
HELL-gahs BROY-tee-gahm.
Helga's fiance.

INSTANT CONVERSATION:
TALKING ABOUT ONE'S FAMILY

— Sind Sie verheiratet?
Zint zee fair-HY-ra-tet?
Are you married?

— Ja — dieser Herr dort ist mein Mann.
Ya, DEE-zer hair dort isst mine mahn.
Yes, that gentleman there is my husband.

> **This and that**
> *Dieser, diese, dieses* is generally used to mean
> either "this or "that." But another more specific
> word for "that" is *jener, jene, jenes.*

— Der mit dem kurzen Bart?
Dehr mit dem KOORTS'en bart?
The one with the short beard?

> **Another use for der, die, das**
> *Der, die, das* besides meaning "the" can func-
> tion as a demonstrative "the one" as it does
> here.

— Nein, der mit dem Schnurrbart
Nine. Dehr mit dem SHNOOR-bart
No, the one with the moustache

und mit der Brille.
oont mitt der BRIL-leh.
and with the glasses.

> **Singular in German — Plural in English**
> Some words are plural in English but singular in
> German. "Eyeglasses" — *die Brille* is one of
> these.

— Haben Sie Kinder?
HAHB'en zee KIN-der?
Do you have any children?

— Ja, wir haben vier Kinder.
Ya, veer HAHB'en feer KIN-der.
Yes, we have four children.

Drei Söhne und eine Tochter.
Dry ZER-neh oont INE-eh TOKH-ter.
Three sons and one daughter.

Und Sie...?
Oont zee?
And you...?

— Ich habe keine Kinder.
Ikh HA-beh KY-neh KIN-der.
I have no children.

Ich bin Junggeselle.
Ikh bin YOONG-geh-ZEL-leh.
I am a bachelor.

Sind Ihre Kinder hier?
Zind EE-reh KIN-der here?
Are your children here?

— Nein. Einer unserer Söhne
Nine. INE-er OON-zeh-rer ZER-neh
No. One of our sons

> **Einer — eine — eines**
> When "one" is used by itself it becomes *einer,
> eine, eines* according to the gender of whatever
> is referred to. *Unser* becomes *unserer* because
> the genitive plural of possessive adjectives ends
> in *-er*.

ist mit einer Engländerin verheiratet.
isst mit INE-er EHNG-lehn-der-in fair-HY-ra-tet.
is married to an English girl.

Die anderen Jungen und das Mädchen
Dee AHN-der-en YOONG'en oont dahss MAYT-yen
The other boys and the girl

gehen noch zur Schule.
gay'en nokh ts'oor SHOO-leh.
still go to school.

Hier ist ein Bild von allen.
Here isst ine bilt fohn AH-len.
Here is a picture of all of them.

> **Von**
> *Von* means "by," "of," or "from" depending
> on the context and governs the dative case

— Was für reizende Kinder!
Vahss für RY-ts'en-deh KIND'er!
What charming children!

> **Was für . . . what a**
> *Was für* followed by the person or thing referred
> to means "what a," "what," or "what sort of"
> in the sense of admiration, surprise or other
> emotion, or question. *Was für* literally means
> "what for" but remember that you cannot trans-
> late a language word for word but that you must
> consider it by its complete expressions.

Wie alt sind sie?
Vee ahlt zint zee?
How old are they?

— Kurt ist fünfzehn und Hans ist zwölf.
Koort isst FÜNF-ts'ayn oont Hahnss isst ts'verlf.
Kurt is fifteen and Hans is twelve.

Und dies ist Hilda.
Oont deess isst HIL-da.
And this is Hilda.

Sie ist fast siebzehn.
Zee isst fahsst ZEEP-ts'ayn.
She is almost seventeen.

— Was für ein schönes Mädchen!
Vahss fûr ine SHER-ness MAYT-yen!
What a beautiful girl!

Und so schöne Augen.
Oont zo SHER-neh OW-ghen.
And such beautiful eyes.

Sie sieht aus wie Sie.
Zee zeet ow'ss vee zee.
She looks like you.

> **Aussehen**
> The compliment that has just been offered illus-
> trates a use of **aus**sehen *wie* — "to look
> like" — a separable prefix verb composed of
> *sehen* and *aus* followed by *wie.*

Wo gehen sie zur Schule?
Vo gay'en zee ts'oor SHOO-leh?
Where do they go to school?

— Die Jungen hier,
Dee YOONG'en here,
The boys here,

und das Mädchen ist in einem
oont dahs MAYT-yen isst in INE-em
and the girl is in a

Internat für Mädchen
Innter-NAHT fûr MAYT-yen
boarding school for girls

in der Schweiz.
in dehr shvy'ts.
in Switzerland.

Verwandte meines Mannes —
Fair-VAHNT-eh MY-nes MAHN-nes —
Relatives of my husband —

77

seine Schwester und sein Schwager —
ZY-neh SHVESS-ter oont zine SHVA-ger —
his sister and his brother-in-law —

In-laws

Other in-laws include:

der Schwiegervater — the father-in-law
die Schwiegermutter — the mother-in-law
der Schwiegersohn — the son-in-law
die Schwiegertochter — the daugher-in-law
die Schwägerin — the sister-in-law

wohnen in der Nähe.
VOHN'en in dehr NAY-heh.
live nearby.

— Hat sie nicht Heimweh —
Haht zee nikht HIME-veh —
Isn't she homesick —

Die Übersetzung — (the Translation)

Literally — "Hasn't she homesickness?"

so weit weg von Ihnen?
zo vite vek fohn EE-nen?
so far away from you?

— Im Gegenteil — sie hat sehr
Im GAY-ghen-tile — zee haht zehr
On the contrary — she is having

viel Spaß.
feel shpahss.
lots of fun.

Sie geht reiten,
Zee gate RITE'en,
She goes riding,

schwimmen und tanzen.
SHVIM'en oont TAHNTS'en.
swimming and dancing.

Use of the infinitive
You will note that the infinitive — *tanzen* — is used here, although in English we would use the present participle. The present participle is relatively little used in German and will be dealt with at a later step.

— Lernt sie auch Französisch?
Lehrnt zee ow'kh frahnt-ZERR-zish?
Is she also learning French?

— Hoffentlich!
HOHF-fent-likh!
I hope so!

Hoffentlich!
Hoffentlich is not a verb but an adverb, literally "hopefully," which can also be translated as "I hope so."

Man spricht nur Französisch
Mahn shprikht noor frahnt-ZERR-zish
They speak only French

Man spricht Deutsch
Man is an impersonal pronoun, using the same verb form as *er* (*he*). It is equivalent to the impersonal "one," "we," "you" or "they" used in a general sense, as in the expressions *man sagt* — "they say" and *man spricht Deutsch* — "German spoken" — a sign one often sees in shops in Europe and America.

in ihrer Schule.
in EE-rer SHOOL-leh.
at her school.

Oh — Hier kommt mein Mann.
Oh — here kohmt mine mahn.
Oh — Here comes my husband.

Es ist wahrscheinlich Zeit zu gehen.
Ess isst vahr-SHINE-likh ts'ite ts'oo GAY'en.
It is probably time to go.

79

TEST YOUR GERMAN

Translate these phrases into German. Score 10 points for each correct translation. See answers below.

1. The father and his daughter. _____

2. The mother and her son. _____

3. The parents and their children. _____

4. The boy's dog. _____

5. The girl's cat. _____

6. The uncle's house. _____

7. Are you married? _____

8. Do you have any children? _____

9. Yes, here is a picture of all of them. _____

10. What charming children! _____

SCORE _____%

step 8 THE ALPHABET, READING, WRITING, TELEPHONING

Das deutsche Alphabet hat
Dahss DOYTH-eh ahlfa-BEHT haht
The German alphabet has

sechsundzwanzig Buchstaben wie das englische.
SEKHS-oont-ts'vahn-ts'ikh BOOKH-shta-ben vee dahss ENG-lish-eh
twenty-six letters like the English one.

Learn German through German
You will notice that in the first part of each step
we frequently use German to explain verbs or
other constructions. While this information is re-
peated more fully in the English notes, seeing it
first in German is a more natural and direct ap-
proach and you will be learning German
through the use of German, which will be of
special value when you review without following
the English text. After you go through each lesson several times, we suggest you cover the
two bottom lines of each sentence and read the
German aloud.

Aber die Aussprache
AH-ber dee OWS-shpra-kheh
But the pronunciation

der deutschen Buchstaben ist anders.
dehr DOYTCH'en BOOKH-shta-ben isst AHN-ders
of the German letters is different.

Zum Beispiel:
Ts'oom BY-shpeel:
For example:

A	B	C	D	E	F	G	H	I
ah	**bay**	**t'say**	**day**	**eh**	**ef**	**gay**	**hah**	**ee**
J	K	L	M	N	O	P	Q	R
yoht	**kah**	**el**	**em**	**en**	**oh**	**pay**	**koo**	**ehr**
S	T	U	V	W	X	Y		Z
ess	**tay**	**oo**	**f'ow**	**vay**	**eeks**	**Ůp-see-lohn**		**ts'et**

For messages
When you know the names of the letters of the alphabet an immediate use is for spelling your name over the telephone when leaving a message (*eine Nachricht*).

In der deutschen Sprache
In dehr DOYTCH-en SPRA-kheh
In the German language

haben wir außerdem
hahb'en veer OW-sir-dem
we have in addition

den Umlaut.
den OOM-l'owt.
the umlaut.

The use of the umlaut
The umlaut is often used in plurals — *Buch* (*book*), *Bücher* (*books*) and sometimes its use designates two different words otherwise spelled alike, such as the rather important difference between

zahlen — to pay
zählen— to count

Der Umlaut macht
Dehr OOM-l'owt mahkt
The umlaut makes

aus a, o, u,
ow'ss ah, o, oo
from a, o, u,

die neuen Buchstaben
dee NOY-en BOOKH-shtah-ben
the new letters

ä, ö, ü.
a (umlaut), o (umlaut), u (umlaut)

Pronunciation of the umlaut
The pronunciation of the umlaut, especially the ö and the ü can be rendered only approximately by phonetics. In general the ä is said like the ea in "bear," ö is like the er sound in English, while ü is said with the lips tightly rounded, and has a nasal quality. To check the exact way they should sound ask a German speaking person to pronounce words like *schön, Tür,* and *zählen.*

Ein kurzes Telefongespräch:
Ine KOOR-ts'ess teh-leh-FOHN-geh-shprekh:
A short telephone conversation:

— Hallo, ist Herr Schönberg da?
Ha-LO, isst hehr SHERN-berg da?
Hello, is Mr. Schönberg there?

— Nein, er ist nicht da.
Nine ehr isst nikht da.
No, he is not here.

— Wann kommt er zurück?
Vahn kohmt ehr ts'oo-RŮK?
When is he coming back?

— Ich weiß nicht.
Ikh vice nikht.
I don't know.

Wer spricht, bitte?
Vehr sprikht BIT-teh?
Who is speaking, please?

— Ich bin Herbert Kühner.
Ikh bin HEHR-behrt KŮ-ner.
I am Herbert Kuhner.

83

German Step by Step

— Verzeihung, wie schreibt man
Fehr-TS'Y-oong, vee shrypt mahn
Excuse me, how does one spell

Ihren Namen?
EER-en NA-men?
your name?

— Man schreibt ihn:
Mahn shrypt een:
It is spelled:

K — Ü — H — N — E — R.
ka — oo OOM-l'owt — ha — en — eh — air.
K — U — H — N — E — R.

Das Lesen:
Dahs LAYZ'en:
Reading:

— Lesen Sie deutsche Bücher?
LAYZ'en zee DOYTCH-eh BŮ-kher?
Do you read German books?

— Ja, oft. Wir lesen auch deutsche Zeitungen
Ya oft. Veer LAYZ'en ow'kh DOYTCH-eh TSY-toong-en
Yes, often. We also read German newspapers

und einige der Illustrierten.
oont INE-ig-eh dehr ee-loo-STREER-ten.
and a few of the magazines.

> **Die Illustrierte**
> *Illustrierte* means "illustrated" and is used for "magazines."

— Welche Zeitung lesen Sie?
VELK-heh TS'Y-toong LAYZ'en zee?
What newspaper do you read?

— Ich lese die *Frankfurter Allgemeine*
Ikh LAY-zeh dee FRAHNK-foo-ter AHL-gay-my neh
I read the *Frankfurt General* (*News*)

und meine Frau liest *das Abendblatt.*
oont MY-neh fr'ow leest *dahss AH-bent-blaht.*
and my wife reads the Evening Press.

To read — to write
The key forms of *lesen* ("to read") and *schreiben* ("to write") are:

ich lese	*ich schreibe*
er liest	*er schreibt*
wir lesen	*wir schreiben*

Von den Illustrierten lesen wir
FONN den ee-loo-STREER-ten LAYZ'en veer
Among magazines we read

beide den *Spiegel* und den *Stern.*
BY-deh den SHPEE-ghel oont den shtairn.
both the *Mirror* and the *Star.*

Das Schreiben:
Dahss SHRYB'en:
Writing:

Wir schreiben Briefe
Veer SHRYB'en BREE-feh
We write letters

an unsere Freunde.
ah OON-zeh-reh FROYN-deh.
to our friends.

Wir schreiben den Namen unseres Freundes
Veer SHRYB'en den NA-men OON-zeh-ress FROYN-dess
We write the name of our friend (male)

oder unserer Freundin
OH-der OON-zeh-rer FROYN-din
or our friend (female)

und die Adresse auf den Umschlag.
oont dee ah-dress-eh ow'f den OOM-shlahk.
and the address on the envelope.

The direction of the action
Umschlag is in the accusative case because
when we write an address "on" the envelope
we are performing an action on it — therefore it
becomes accusative in case.

Danach kleben wir Briefmarken darauf
Da-NAKH KLAYB'en veer BREEF-mar-ken da-ROWF
Then we stick stamps on it

und stecken den Brief
oont SHTEK'en den breef
and put the letter

A choice of words for "put"
There are several words for put depending on
how the object you are putting normally stands.

If it stands by itself — like a chair — use
stellen.
If it normally lies — like a book — use *legen.*
If it goes into something — like a letter into an
envelope — use *stecken.*

in den Briefkasten.
in den BREEF-ka-sten.
in the mailbox.

INSTANT WRITING:
A THANK-YOU LETTER AND A
POSTCARD

Ein kurzer Brief an einen Freund:
Ine KOOR-ts'er breef ahn INE-en froynt:
A short letter to a (male) friend:

Lieber Kurt,
LEE-ber koort,
Dear Kurt,

vielen Dank für die Blumen.
FEEL'en dahnk für dee BLOO-men.
Many thanks for the flowers.

Sie sind wirklich schön.
Zee zint veerk-likh shern.
They are really beautiful.

Gelbe Rosen sind meine Lieblingsblumen.
GHEL-beh RO-zen zint MINE-eh LEEB-lings-BLOO-men.
Yellow roses are my favorite flowers.

> **Liebling**
> *Favorite* is expressed by prefixing *Lieblings* to what the favorite is.
>
> "Her favorite painter" — *ihr Lieblingsmaler.*
> *Liebling* by itself is a term of endearment — literally "little love."

Nochmals vielen Dank!
NOKH-mahls FEEL'en dahnk!
Once more, many thanks!

Alles Gute!
AHL-lehs GOO-teh!
All the best!

Herzlichst,
HEHRTS-likhst,
Most sincerely,

Greta.

Herzlichst ("most heartily") is a good way to close a personal letter or a card. Business letters usually end with *hochachtungsvoll* — literally "full of high esteem."

Eine Postkarte an eine Freudin:
INE-eh POST-kar-teh ahn INE-eh FROYN-din:
A postcard to a (female) friend:

Liebe Helga,
LEE-beh HEL-ga,
Dear Helga,

Grüße aus München.
GRÜ-seh owss MÜNT-yen.
Greetings from Munich.

Hier ist es wunderschön.
Here isst ess VOON-dehr-shern.
It is wonderful here.

Die Stadt ist interessant,
Dee shtaht isst in-teh-reh-SAHNT,
The city is interesting,

und die Leute sind sehr amüsant.
oont dee LOY-teh zint zehr ah-mü-ZAHNT.
and the people are very entertaining.

Schade, daß Sie nicht hier sind!
SHA-deh, dahss zee nikht here zint!
Too bad you are not here!

Auf baldiges Wiedersehen.
Ow'f BAHL-dee-ghess VEE-dehr-zay'n.
See you soon.

Die Übersetzung (The Translation)
The adverb *bald* means "soon," while *baldiger*
(-e) (-es) "early," is the adjective form when
used before the noun. *Auf baldiges Wiederse-*
hen literally means "To an early seeing
again" — a good example of why idiomatic
translations must be preferred over word-by-
word renditions.

Herzlichst,
HAIRTS-likhst,
Most sincerely,

Karl

TEST YOUR GERMAN

Translate the following phrases into German. Score 10 points for each correct answer. See answers below.

1. When is he coming back? _____

2. Who is speaking, please? _____

3. Do you read German books? _____

4. What newspaper do you read? _____

5. Many thanks for the flowers. _____

6. All the best! _____

7. Greetings from Munich! _____

8. It is wonderful here. _____

9. The city is very interesting. _____

10. The people are very entertaining. _____

Answers: 1. **Wann kommt er zurück?** 2. **Wer spricht, bitte?** 3. Lesen Sie deutsche Bücher? 4. Welche Zeitung lesen Sie? 5. Vielen Dank für die Blumen. 6. Alles Gute! 7. Grüße aus München! 8. Hier ist es wunderschön. 9. Die Stadt ist sehr interessant. 10. Die Leute sind sehr amüsant.

SCORE _____%

step 9
PROFESSIONS AND OCCUPATIONS

Um zu erfahren, was jemand ist
Oom ts'oo ehr-FAR'en, vahss YEH-mahnt isst
In order to find out what someone is

> **For the purpose of**
> *Um zu* followed by the infinitive of a verb means "in order to" do something, or "for the purpose of" doing it.
>
> I am going to Germany to study German. — *Ich gehe nach Deutschland, um Deutsch zu studieren.*

oder tut, fragen wir:
OH-der toot, FRAHG'en veer:
or does, we ask:

> **Tun**
> *Tun* is equivalent to "to do" but only in the sense of "perform."
>
> *Was tun Sie hier?* — What are you doing here?
>
> *Ich tue nichts.* — I'm not doing anything.

„Wo arbeiten Sie?" oder
„Vo AR-bite'en zee," OH-der
"Where do you work?" or

„Was sind Sie von Beruf?"
„Vahss zint zee fohn beh-ROOF?"
"What is your profession?" (Literally: "What are you by profession?")

Hier sind ein paar Beispiele für Berufe.
Here zint ine pahr BY-shpee-leh für beh-ROO-feh.
Here are some examples of professions.

Ein Geschäftsmann arbeitet in einem Büro.
Ine geh-SHEFTS-mahn AR-bite-tet in INE-em bů-RO.
A businessman works in an office.

Arbeiter arbeiten in einer Fabrik.
AR-bite-er AR-bite'en in INE-er fa-BREEK.
Workers work in a factory.

Ärzte behandeln die Kranken.
AIRST-teh beh-HAHN-deln dee KRAHN-ken.
Doctors treat the sick.

Schauspieler und Schauspielerinnen
SH'OW-shpee-ler oont SH'OW-shpee-ler-in-nen
Actors and actresses

> **Actors and actresses**
> *Schauspieler* — actor — is an example of a
> word that does not change for the plural. To
> make it feminine, *-in* is added, and the feminine
> plural adds an additional *-nen*.

arbeiten im Theater oder im Filmstudio.
AR-bite'en im tay-AH-ter OH-der im film shtood-yo.
work in the theater or in films.

Ein Maler malt Bilder.
Ine MA-ler mahlt BILL-der.
A painter paints pictures.

Ein Schriftsteller schreibt Bücher.
Ine SHRIFT-shtel-ler shry'pt BŮ-kher.
A writer writes books.

Ein Musiker spielt Klavier
Ine MOO-zeek-er shpeelt kla-VEER
A musician plays the piano

oder ein anderes Instrument.
OH-der ine AHN-der-ess in-stroo-MENT.
or another instrument.

Ein Autoschlosser repariert Wagen.
Ine OW-toh-shloss-er ray-pa-REERT VA-ghen.
An auto mechanic repairs cars.

Der Briefträger bringt die Post.
Dehr BREEF-tray-gher brinkt dee post.
The mailman brings the mail.

Der Autobusfahrer fährt einen Bus,
Dehr OW-toh-boos-far-er fehrt INE-en boos.
The bus driver drives a bus,

> As all verbs add -e to their stem for *ich*, -t or -et
> for *er*, *sie* or *es* and -en or -n for *wir*, *Sie* and
> *sie* (pl.), we will supply the key forms only for
> special verbs that change their *interior* spelling,
> that is, vowel or umlaut changes, as in the case
> of *fahren* — "to ride in" or "to drive" a vehicle.
>
> *ich fahre* —
> *er fährt* —
> *wir fahren* —

und der Taxichauffeur fährt ein Taxi.
oont dehr TAHK-see-sho-fur fehrt ine TAHK-see.
and the taxidriver drives a taxi.

Feuerwehrleute löschen Feuer.
FOY-er-vehr-loy-teh LERSH'en FOY-er.
The firemen put out fires.

Polizisten regeln den Verkehr
po-lits-ISS-ten RAY-gheln den fehr-KEHR
The policemen direct traffic

und verhaften Verbrecher.
oont fehr-HAHFT'en fehr-BREH-ker.
and arrest criminals.

93

INSTANT CONVERSATION:
AT A PARTY

— Was für eine nette Gesellschaft!
Vahss für INE-eh NET-teh gheh-ZELL-shahft!
What a pleasant party!

— Ja, es ist sehr interessant
Ya, ess isst zehr in-teh-reh-SAHNT
Yes, it is very interesting

hier heute abend.
here HOY-teh AH-bent.
here this evening.

> **Heute = today**
> Expressions such as:
>
> > This morning — *heute morgen*
> > this afternoon — *heute nachmittag*
> > this evening — *heute abend*
>
> are not written with capitals when they are used
> as adverbial expressions.

— Das stimmt. Frau von Waldeck
Dahss shtimt. Fr'ow fohn VAHL-dek
That's right. Mrs. von Waldeck

> **Das stimmt**
> *Das stimmt* is a colloquial expression meaning
> "correct," "exactly," or "that is right." The
> basic meaning of *stimmen* is "to tune" (a musi-
> cal instrument).

hat reizende Freunde.
haht RYE-ts'en-deh FROYN-deh.
has charming friends.

In dieser Gruppe beim Fenster
In DEE-zer GROO-peh bime FEN-ster
In that group by the window

sehen Sie einen Rechtsanwalt,
ZAY'en zee INE-en REKHTS-ahn-wahlt,
you see a lawyer,

einen Komponisten, einen Ingenieur,
INE-en kom-pon-ISS-ten, INE-en in-jay-N'YEHR,
a composer, an engineer,

einen Architekten, einen Zahnarzt
INE-en ar-khee-TEK-ten, INE-en TS'AHN-arts't
an architect, a dentist,

und einen bekannten Fußballspieler.
oont INE-en beh-KAHN-ten FOOSS-bahll-SHPEEL-er.
and a well-known football player.

> **Vergessen Sie nicht!**
> Note that all of the above people or professions
> are preceded by *einen* the accusative form of
> *ein* because they are the direct object of *sehen*.

— Was für eine buntgewürfelte Gruppe!
Vahss fûr INE-eh BOONT-geh-vûr-felt-eh GROO-peh!
What a varied group!

Wer weiß, worüber sie reden?
Vehr vice vo-RÛ-behr zee RAYD'en?
Who knows what they are talking about?

Architektur, Musik, Medizin . . . ?
Ar-khee-tek-TOOR, moo-ZEEK, mehd-ee-T'SEEN . . . ?
Architecture, music, medicine . . . ?

— Fußball, natürlich.
FOOSS-bahl, na-TÛR-likh.
Football (*soccer*), naturally.

— Wissen Sie, wer die hübsche Dame dort ist?
VISS-en zee, vehr dee HÛP-sheh DA-meh dort isst?
Do you know who the attractive lady is over there?

— Welche? Hier sind so viele.
VEL-kheh? Here zint so FEEL-eh.
Which one? There are so many here.

— Die mit dem roten Kleid da, am Fenster.
Dee mit dem Ro-ten kly't da, ahm FEN-ster.
The one with the red dress over there, by the window.

— Sie ist Opernsängerin
Zee isst OH-pairn-zeng-gher-in
She is an opera singer

und heißt Inge Dietrich.
oont hy'st IN-geh DEE-trikh.
and her name is Inge Dietrich.

— Und die Herren, die bei ihr stehen?
Oont dee HEHR-en, dee by eer SHTAY'en?
And the men who are standing next to her?

> **Der, die, das as "who" "which," or "that"**
> *Der, die, das* can also be used relatively — as
> "the one who," "who," "what," "that" etc.

> **Pronouns with the dative**
> Pronouns used as objects of prepositions that
> take the dative are as follows. Their subject
> form is in parenthesis.
>
> (*ich*) — *mir*
> (*er*) — *ihm*
> (*sie*) — *ihr*
> (*es*) — *ihm*
> (*wir*) — *uns*
> (*Sie*) — *Ihnen*
> (*sie*) (pl.) — *ihnen*

— Der ältere Herr ist Kunstkritiker
Dehr ELT-eh-reh hehr isst KOONST-krit-ee-ker
The older man is an art critic

und der Junge, der mit den langen Haaren,
oont dehr YOONG-eh, dehr mit den LAHNG-en HAR'en,
and the young one, the one with the long hair,

ist Dichter.
isst DIKH-ter.
is a poet.

— Aber sehen Sie, wer jetzt kommt?
AH-ber ZAY'en zee, vehr yetst kohmt?
But do you see who is coming in now?

Use of the comma
When you write German, remember that relative sub-clauses, that is, those starting with *wer, wo, wie, der,* etc. are always introduced by a comma, as here.

Das ist Lotte Hesse,
Dahss isst LOT-teh HEH-seh,
That is Lotte Hesse,

die berühmte Schlagersängerin.
dee beh-RÜHM-teh SHLA-ger-zeng-er-in.
the famous hit singer.

— Wirklich? Sie ist sehr gut.
VEERK-likh? Zee isst zehr goot.
Really? She is very good.

Finden Sie nicht auch?
FIN-den zee nikht ow'kh?
Don't you think so too?

Finden = "to find" or "to think"
Finden — "to find" is generally used to express "to think" in terms of giving an opinion.

— Sicher. Wissen Sie, ich kenne sie.
ZIKH-er. VISS'en zee, ikh KEN-neh zee.
Certainly. You know, I know her.

Kennen und wissen
Wissen is "to know" a fact and *kennen* is "to know" a person or to be familiar with something.

The forms of *wissen* are:
ich weiß
er weiß
wir wissen

Gehen wir mal hinüber.
GAY'en veer mahl hin-Ů-ber.
Let's just go over.

"Mal" — ein wichtiges Wort (an important word)
Mal means "sign," "mark," or "point in time."
einmal — one time, once

> *das zweite Mal* — the second time
> *zweimal* — twice (also used for "round trip")

Mal is one of the short but useful words so important in speaking a language idiomatically. Generally speaking, it gives an intensive or persuasive meaning to what is said.

> *Sehen wir mal!* — Now let's see!"
> *Hören Sie mal!* — Listen, will you!"

In this special use, *mal* is short for *einmal*, so what you are really saying is: "Look once!" or "Listen once!"

Ich stelle Sie ihr vor.
Ikh SHTELL-eh zee eer for.
I'll introduce you to her.

TEST YOUR GERMAN

Match these people to the work they do. Score ten points for each correct answer. See answers below.

1. Ein Geschäftsmann —————— A. fährt einen Bus.

2. Ärzte —————— B. löschen Feuer.

3. Ein Maler —————— C. bringt die Post.

4. Arbeiter —————— D. verhaften Verbrecher.

5. Ein Musiker —————— E. malt Bilder.

6. Der Briefträger —————— F. spielt Klavier.

7. Feuerwehrleute —————— G. arbeiten im Theater.

8. Der Autobusfahrer —————— H. arbeitet in einem Büro.

9. Polizisten —————— I. arbeiten in einer Fabrik.

10. Schauspieler und Schauspie-
    lerinnen —————— J. behandeln Kranke.

Answers: 1-H; 2-J; 3-E; 4-I; 5-F; 6-C; 7-B; 8-A; 9-D; 10-G.

SCORE _____%

step 10

HOW TO ASK FOR AND GIVE DIRECTIONS: TRAVEL BY CAR

Der Autofahrer hält an einer Straßenecke.
Dehr OW-toh-far-er hehlt ahn INE-er STRA-sen-eh-keh.
The motorist stops at a corner.

> **Halten Sie!**
> *Halten* — "to stop" ("to halt") — has an umlaut over the third person form *ich halte, er hält, wir halten.*

Er fragt einen Fußgänger:
Ehr frahgt INE-en FOOS-geng-er:
He asks a pedestrian:

„Ist das die richtige Straße nach Stuttgart?"
„Isst dahss dee RIKH-tig-eh SHTRA-seh nahk SHTOOT-gart?"
"Is this the right way to Stuttgart?"

Der Fußgänger antwortet ihm:
Dehr FOOS-geng-er AHNT-vor-tet eem:
The pedestrian answers him:

„Nein. Sie sind auf der falschen Straße.
„Nine. Zee zint ow'f dehr FAHL-shen SHTRA-seh.
"No. You are on the wrong road.

> **Erinnern Sie sich (Remember)**
> When an adjective follows *der, die, das* before a noun it ends in *-n* in all cases except the nominative singular (all three genders) and the feminine and neuter accusative singular — when it ends in *-e.*

Fahren Sie geradeaus bis
FAR'en zee geh-RA-deh-OW'SS biss
Go straight ahead up to

zur zweiten Querstraße.
t'soor TS'VY-ten KVEHR-shtra-seh.
the second cross road.

Dann biegen Sie links ab.
Dahn BEEGH'en zee links ahb.
Then turn left.

Ab
Ab-biegen means "to turn in" and is a separable prefix verb, separating in the present tense and in the imperative.

Fahren Sie weiter bis zur
FAR'en zee VY-ter biss ts'oor
Drive on until the

nächsten Straßenampel.
NEKHS-ten SHTRA-sen-ahm-pel.
next traffic light.

Dort biegen Sie rechts ab.
Dort BEEGH'en zee rekhts ahp.
Then turn right.

Dann geradeaus.
Dahn geh-RA-deh-OW'SS.
Then straight ahead.

Bleiben Sie auf dieser Straße.
BLYB'en zee ow'f DEE-zer SHTRA-seh.
Stay on that street.

Sie führt direkt dorthin.
Zee fûrt di-REKT dort-HIN.
It leads right there.

Aber Vorsicht vor der Polizei!
AH-ber FOR-zikht for dehr po-lee-TS'Y!
But, careful with the police!

Sie sind hier sehr streng
Zee zint here zehr shtreng
They are very strict here

101

mit Schnellfahrern."
mit SHNEL-far-ern."
with speeders."

Der Fahrer dankt ihm
Dehr FAR-er dahnkt eem
The driver thanks him

und folgt seinem Rat.
oont fohlgt ZY-nem raht.
and follows his advice.

> **Folgen = "to follow"**
> *Folgen* is a special verb that automatically puts
> the following object into the dative case even
> though logically "to follow" would seem to take
> the direct object. (Even German is not logical all
> the time.)

Aber als er aus der Stadt fährt,
Ah-ber ahls ehr ow'ss dehr shtaht fehrt,
But as he travels out of town

folgt ihm ein Polizist auf einem Motorrad.
fohlgt eem ine po-leet-SIST ow'f INE-em mo-TOR-raht.
a policeman is following him on a motorcycle.

Er hält ihn an.
Ehr helt een ahn.
He stops him.

Er ruft: „Halt!"
Er rooft: „hahlt!
He calls, "Stop!"

Dann sagt der Polizist zu ihm:
Dahn zahkt dehr po-leet-SISTts'oo eem:
Then the policeman says to him:

„Was ist los?
„Vahss isst lohs?
"What's the matter?

Was ist los?
Was ist los? literally "What's loose?" is an expression meaning "What's wrong?" or "What's the matter?"

Wohin fahren Sie in solcher Eile?"
Vo-HIN FAR-en zee in ZOHL-kher ILE-eh?"
Where are you driving in such a hurry?"

Der Fahrer antwortet ihm:
Dehr FAR-er AHNT-vor-tet eem:
The driver answers him:

„Entschuldigen Sie, Herr Wachtmeister.
„**Ehnt-SHOOL-deeg'en zee, hehr VAHKT-my-ster.**
"Excuse me, officer.

A bit of diplomacy
Herr Wachtmeister, a polite and diplomatic way of addressing a policeman, has echoes of medieval times. It literally means "Mr. Master of the Watch."

Ich bin verspätet.
Ikh bin fehr-SHPAYT-et.
I am late.

Man wartet auf mich in Stuttgart."
Mahn VAR-tet ow'f mikh in SHTOOT-gart."
They are waiting for me in Stuttgart."

Der Polizist sagt zu ihm:
Dehr po-leet-SIST zahkt ts'oo eem:
The policeman says to him:

„Zeigen Sie mir Ihren Führerschein!"
„**TS'YGH'en zee meer EER-en FÜ-rer-shine."**
"Show me your driver's license!"

Der Herr zeigt ihn ihm.
Dehr hehr ts'ygt een eem.
The man shows it to him.

The exactness of German
Notice how the meaning of the pronoun ending is clearer than in English. *Ihm* (dative) shows it is "to" him, while *ihn* is masculine singular accusative, showing that "it" (the license) is the object of the verb.

„Und auch die Zulassung!"
„Oont ow'kh dee TS'OO-la-soong!"
"And the registration also!"

Der Fahrer nimmt sie aus der Tasche
Dehr FAR-er nimt zee ow'ss dehr ta-sheh
The driver takes it out of his pocket

und gibt sie ihm.
oont gipt zee eem.
and gives it to him.

Der Polizist schaut beides an.
Dehr pò-leet-SIST shout BY-dehs ahn.
The policeman looks at both.

Use of separable prefix
Since *anschauen* — "to look at" or "to examine" is a verb with a separable prefix, the word *beides* — "both" comes between the verb and its prefix.

Er gibt sie ihm zurück und sagt:
Ehr ghipt zee eem ts'oo-RŮK oont zahkt:
He gives them back and says:

Similar construction-English and German
"To give" — *geben* and "back" — *zurück* shows how closely German and English concepts resemble each other. However, in German *zurückgeben* is one word, which separates when used in the present tense, as here.

„Naja — Sie sind Ausländer.
„Na-ya — zee zint OW'SS-lend-er.
"Well — you're a foreigner.

Diesmal lasse ich Sie gehen.
DEES-mahl LA-seh ikh zee GAY'en.
This time I'll let you go.

Aber fahren Sie langsamer in der Stadt!
AH-ber FAR'en zee LAHNG-za-mehr in dehr staht!
But drive more slowly in town!

Comparative form of adjectives & adverbs
Most adverbs and adjectives have the same
basic form:

good or well — *gut*
bad or badly — *schlecht*
beautiful or beautifully — *schön*
quick or quickly — *schnell*
slow or slowly — *langsam*

The comparative of adverbs or adjectives is
formed by adding *-er* to the base.

Das nächste Mal bekommen Sie
Dahss NEX-teh mahl beh-KOHM'en zee
The next time you'll get

einen Strafzettel!"
INE-en STRAHF-ts'et-tel!
a ticket!"

A "punishment note"
Strafzettel — "a ticket" (summons) is made up
from the verb *strafen* (to punish) and *Zettel*
(note, slip). It literally means a "punishment
note," a designation with which most motorists
would agree.

105

INSTANT CONVERSATION:
GIVING ORDERS

EINE FRAU:
INE-eh fr'ow:
A LADY:

Gertrud, hören Sie nicht?
GEHR-troot, HER'ren zee nikht?
Gertrude, don't you hear?

Jemand klingelt an der Tür.
YEH-mahnt KLIN-gelt ahn dehr tûr.
Someone is ringing at the door.

Machen Sie bitte auf!
MA'khen zee BIT-teh ow'f!
Open it, please.

Wer ist es?
Vehr isst ess?
Who is it?

GERTRUD:
GEHR-troot:
GERTRUDE:

Es ist der Junge
Ess isst dehr YOON-geh
It's the young man

mit den Lebensmitteln.
mit den LEH-bens-mit-teln.
with the food supplies.

Genauigheit = Exactness
German tends to be extremely precise. "Food"
is *das Essen* but a delivery of food, as here, becomes "provisions" or "supplies." *Lebensmit-*

tel (from das Leben — "life" and Mittel —
"means") is litterally "means of life."

DIE FRAU:

Gut. Legen Sie das Fleisch in den Kühlschrank!
Goot. LAYG'en zee dahss flysh in den KUL-shrahnk!
Good. Put the meat in the refrigerator.

Stellen Sie auch die Milch und die Butter hinein!
SHTEL'en zee ow'kh dee milkh oont dee BOO-ter hin-INE!
Put also the milk and the butter inside.

Legen Sie das Gemüse ins Gemüsefach!
LAYG'en dahss geh-MŮ-zeh ins gheh-MŮ-zeh-fahk!
Put the vegetables in the vegetable compartment.

Lassen Sie die Kartoffeln auf dem Tisch!
LAHS'en zee dee kar-TOHF-feln ow'f dem tish!
Leave the potatoes on the table.

Wir machen später einen Kartoffelsalat.
Veer mahk'hen shpayt'er INE-en ka-TOHF-fel-sa-laht.
Later we'll make a potato salad.

GERTRUD:

Ja. Sofort, gnädige Frau.
Ya. zo-FORT, GNAY-dee-geh fr'ow.
Yes. Right away, madam.

DIE FRAU:

Ich gehe jetzt aus.
Ikh GAY-heh yetst ow'ss.
I am going out now.

The prefix gives the clue
Ausgehen is a separable prefix verb. A useful
point to remember is that German uses prepositions like "out" — *aus*, "over" — *über*, "behind — *hinter*, "inside" — *hinein*, "back"
— *zurück* combined with verbs. In a German
dictionary they are part of the verb and are
found in the dictionary listed according to the
separable prefix.

German Step by Step

Zuerst zum Friseur
ts'oo-EHRST ts'oom free-ZERR
First to the hairdresser's

"Zu" und "bei"
Zum (*zu* and *dem*) is used for "to the" (place of) referring to a profession or establishment.

to the doctor's — *zum Arzt*
to the dentist's — *zum Zahnarzt*
to the butcher's — *zum Schlachter* (or) *zum Metzger*
to the barber's — *zum Friseur*

To express "at the" use *beim* (*bei* and *dem*).

The following expressions will be useful
beim Friseur:

Für die Damen:	For the ladies:
Waschen und Einlegen	Wash and set
Zu heiß	Too hot
Zu kalt	Too cold
Heller	Lighter
Dunkler	Darker

Für die Herren:	For the gentlemen:
Haare schneiden, bitte.	A haircut, please.
Nicht zu kurz	Not too short
Rasieren, bitte.	A shave, please.
Gesichtsmassage	A massage
Maniküre	A manicure

und dann einkaufen.
oont dahn INE-kow-fen.
and then shopping.

In der Zwischenzeit
In dehr TS'VISH-en-ts'ite
In the meantime

räumen Sie bitte auf. Wir erwarten Gäste.
ROYM'en zee BIT-teh ow'f. Veer er-VART'en GUESS-teh.
tidy up please. We are expecting guests.

Mein Gott! Schon wieder das Telefon!
Mine Gott! Shohn VEED-er dahss teh-leh-FOHN!
My God! The telephone again!

Heben Sie bitte ab! Wer ist es?
HAYB'en zee BIT-teh ahb! Vehr isst ess?
Pick it up, please. Who is it?

GERTRUD:
Es ist mein Freund Kurt.
Ess isst mine froynt Koort.
It is my friend Kurt.

Er lädt mich ins Kino ein ...
Ehr layt mikh ins KEE-no ine ...
He's inviting me to the movies ...

DIE FRAU:
Wir haben aber Gäste!
Veer HAHB'en AH-ber GUESS-teh!
But we are having guests!

Na gut. Aber zuerst servieren Sie das Essen.
Na goot. AH-ber ts'oo-AIRST zehr-VEER'en zee dahss ESS'en.
Well all right. But first serve the dinner.

Dann sind Sie frei.
Dahn zind zee fry.
Then you are free.

Commands

This step contains frequent commands, which are expressed, as you will remember from Step 5 by adding *Sie* to the basic verb, usually followed by an exclamation point. Most of the time you will give orders for daily accommodations and arrangements while orders will be given to you by various authorities and functionaries, of which there are many in Germany. When you give an order don't forget to say *bitte!*

TEST YOUR GERMAN

Translate the following phrases into German. Where pronouns are used gender is indicated. Score 5 for each correct answer. See answers on following page.

1. Drive straight ahead! _____

2. Turn left! _____

3. Stay on this street! _____

4. He thanks him. _____

5. He says to him "Stop!" _____

6. What's the matter? _____

7. Excuse me — I am late. _____

8. Show me your driver's license! _____

9. He shows it (masc.) to him. _____

10. Who is it? _____

11. He gives them to him. _____

12. He gives them back. _____

13. Drive more slowly! _____

14. Open the door, please. _____

15. Pick it up, please. _____

16. Who is it? _____

17. Serve the dinner, please. _____

18. Don't you hear? _____

19. Leave it (neuter) on the table! _____

20. Then you are free. _____

SCORE _____%

Answers: 1. Fahren Sie geradeaus! 2. Biegen Sie links ab! 3. Bleiben Sie auf dieser Straße! 4. Er dankt ihm. 5. Er sagt zu ihm: „Halt!" 6. Was ist los? 7. Entschuldigen Sie — ich bin verspätet. 8. Zeigen Sie mir ihren Führerschein! 9. Er zeigt ihn ihm. 10. Wer ist es? 11. Er gibt sie ihm. 12. Er gibt sie ihm zurück. 13. Fahren Sie langsamer! 14. Machen Sie bitte die Tür auf! 15. Heben Sie bitte ab! 16. Wer ist es? 17. Servieren Sie bitte das Essen! 18. Hören Sie es nicht? 19. Lassen Sie es auf dem Tisch! 20. Dann sind Sie frei.

step 11

HOW TO SAY "WANT," "CAN," "MAY," "MUST," AND "MIGHT"

Ein junger Mann will zum Fußballspiel gehen.
Ine YOONG-er mahn vill ts'oom FOOSS-bahl-shpeel gay'en.
A young man wants to go to the football game.

Fußball
Fußball is *soccer*, a popular game in Germany and Central Europe (*Mitteleuropa*) and increasingly popular in the U.S. (*Vereinigten Staaten*)

Aber er kann nicht.
AH-ber ehr kahn nikht.
But he cannot.

Wollen — können
"To want to" is translated by *wollen* and "can" by *können*. These are complete verbs with certain differences (such as no -*t* in their present tense. Here are the important forms:

Ich will	*Ich kann*
Er will	*Er kann*
Wir wollen	*Wir können*

When they are followed by a second verb the following verb is in the infinitive, but without *zu*. "He wants to come." — *Er will kommen.* A word of caution — although *will* looks the same as the English "will" it always means "want" or "wants." "Will" for the future will come in Step 21.

Warum nicht?
Va-ROOM nikht?
Why not?

Weil er keine Eintrittskarte hat.
Vile ehr KINE-eh INE-tritts-KAR-teh haht.
Because he has no ticket.

Warum kauft er keine?
Va-ROOM kow'ft ehr KINE-eh?
Why doesn't he buy one?

Weil er nicht genug Geld hat.
Vile ehr nikht ge-NOOK gelt haht.
Because he hasn't enough money.

Word order inversion
After introductory conjunctions, such as *weil*,
the word order is inverted, as after adverbs and
prepositions.

Ohne Geld kann er
OH-neh gelt kahn ehr
Without money he cannot

das Fußballspiel nicht sehen.
dahss FOOS-bahl-shpeel nikht ZAY'en.
see the football game.

Wenn er hineingehen will, muß er zahlen.
Ven ehr hin-INE-gay'en vill, mooss ehr TS'AHL'en.
If he wants to go in he must pay.

Wenn
"If" is translated by *wenn* and followed by inverted word order. Do not confuse *wenn* with
the English word 'when," which, in German is
wann, as you have already seen. *Wenn* means
"when" not as a question, but as a sort of future supposition.
"When he comes" — *wenn er kommt.*

Müssen
Müssen — "must," "to have to," — is another
auxiliary verb like *können* and *wollen.*
remember these forms:

Ich muß
er muß
wir müssen.

It is indicative of the close linguistic relationship between German and English that these important auxiliary verbs resemble English ones, but with an occasional change of meaning:

ich will — I want
ich muß — I must, have to
ich kann — I can
ich habe — I have
ich mag — I like

Aber da sieht er einen Bekannten.
AH-ber da zeet ehr INE-en beh-KAHN-ten.
But there he sees an acquaintance.

Er fragt ihn:
Ehr frahkt een:
He asks him:

— Ich brauche ein paar Mark,
Ikh BROW-kheh ine pahr mark,
I need a few marks

um das Fußballspiel zu sehen.
oom dahss FOOSS-bahl-shpeel ts'oo ZAY'en.
to see the game.

Können Sie mir zehn Mark leihen?
KERN'nen zee meer ts'ayn mark LY'en?
Can you lend me ten marks?

— Vielleicht . . . Wann können Sie
Fee-LY'KHT . . . vahn KERN'nen zee
Perhaps . . . when can you

sie mir zurückgeben?
zee meer ts'oo-RŮK GAYB'en?
give them back to me?

Vergessen Sie nicht!
The first *Sie* is capitalized because it means
"you." The following *sie*, in small letters, is
"them."

— Oh, morgen, bestimmt. Ehrenwort!
Oh, MOR-ghen beh-SHTIMMT. AY-ren-vort!
Oh, tomorrow, surely. Word of honor!

———————

— Ich kann den Motor nicht starten.
Ikh kahn den mo-TOR nikht SHTART'en.
I can't start the motor.

— Warum nicht?
Va-ROOM nikht?
Why not?

— Ich glaube, daß nicht
Ikh GL'OW-beh, dahss nikht
I think there isn't

genug Benzin im Tank ist.
ge-NOOK ben-TS'EEN imm tahnk isst.
enough gas in the tank.

— Natürlich. Wenn kein Benzin
Na-TÜR-likh. venn kine ben-ST'EEN
Naturally. When there is no gas

im Tank ist, kann der Wagen nicht fahren.
imm Tahnk isst, kahn dehr VA-gen nikht FA-ren.
in the tank, the car can't go.

Wir müssen Benzin kaufen.
Veer MÜSS'en ben-TS'EEN KOWF'en.
We must buy gas.

— Wo kann man Benzin kaufen?
Vo kahn mahn ben-TS'EEN KOWF'en?
Where can one buy gas?

Können Sie mir sagen,
KERN'nen zee meer ZAHG'en,
Can you tell me

wo die nächste Tankstelle ist?
vo dee NEX-teh TAHNK-shtel-leh isst?
where the nearest gas station is?

> **Für den Wagen**
> While on the subject of service stations memo-
> rize the following key expressions. They will
> help you as you speed over the *Autobahnen.*
>
> Fill it! — *Volltanken, bitte!*
> Check the oil! — *Sehen Sie nach dem Öl!*
> Check the battery! — *Prüfen Sie die Batterie!*
> This isn't working well. — *Das ist nicht in
> Ordnung.*
> This is broken. — *Das ist kaputt.*
> Can you fix it? — *Können Sie das reparieren?*
> How long will it take? — *Wie lange dauert das?*
> Check the tires! — *Prüfen Sie die Reifen!*

Zwei Mädchen haben eine Reifenpanne.
Ts'vy MAYT-yen HAHB'en INE-eh RY-fen-pa-neh.
Two girls have a flat tire.

Sie können den Reifen nicht wechseln,
Zee KERN'nen den RY'fen nikht VEK-seln,
They cannot change the tire,

weil sie keinen Wagenheber haben.
vile zee KINE-en VA-gen-HEH-ber HAHB'en.
because they don't have a jack.

Da kommt ein junger Mann in einem Sportwagen.
Da kohmt ine YOONG-er mahn in INE-em SHPORT-va-ghen.
There comes a young man in a sports car.

Er sagt: „Darf ich Ihnen helfen?"
Ehr zahkt: „Darf ikh EE-nen HEL-fen?"
He says: "May I help you?"

Dürfen, another verb of the special group explained in this Step, means "may" in the sense of asking permission. It goes: *ich darf, er darf, wir dürfen.*

„Ja, gern. Sie dürfen.
„Ya, gairn. zee DÜRF'en.
"Yes, gladly. You may.

Können Sie uns Ihren Wagenheber leihen?"
KERN'en zee oonts EE-ren VA-gen-HAY-ber LY'en?"
Can you lend us your jack?"

„Ich kann noch mehr," sagt er.
„Ikh kahn nokh mehr," zahkt ehr.
"I can (do) even more," he says.

„Ich kann den Reifen für Sie wechseln."
„Ikh kahn den RY-fen für zee VEK-zeln."
"I can change the tire for you."

INSTANT CONVERSATION:
A TV PROGRAM

— Ach, wie schade!
Akh, vee SHA-deh!
Oh, what a shame!

Heute abend ist im Fernsehen
HOY-teh AH-bent isst imm FEHRN-zay'en
Tonight on the TV

> *Fernsehen* literally means "Farseeing." "Tele-
> phone" is referred to as *das Telefon* or *der
> Fernsprecher* — "Farspeaker," and a teletype
> is *Fernschreiber* — "far writer."

ein sehr interessantes Programm.
ine zehr in-teh-reh-SAHN-tess pro-GRAHM.
there is a very interesting program.

Aber leider kann ich es nicht sehen.
AH-ber LY-der kahn ikh ess nikht ZAY'en.
But unfortunately I can't watch it.

Mein Apparat ist kaputt.
Mine ahp-pa-RAHT isst ka-POOT.
My set is out of order.

— Warum rufen Sie nicht den Reparaturdienst an?
Va-ROOM ROOF'en zee nikht den reh-pa-ra-TOOR-deenst ahn?
Why don't you call the repair service?

— Wozu? Sie wissen doch genau
Vo-TS'OO zee viss'en dohkh gen-OW
What for? You well know

daß diese Leute nie sofort kommen.
dahss DEE-zeh LOY-teh nee zo-FORT KOHM'en.
that these people never come right away.

Sie können bestimmt nicht
Zee KERN'en beh-SHTIMMT nikht
They certainly won't be able to come

vor morgen oder übermorgen kommen.
for MOR-gen OH-der ÜBER-mor-ghen KOHM'en.
before tomorrow or the day after tomorrow.

— Hören Sie! Wenn Sie an diesem Programm
HER-ren zee! Venn zee ahn DEE-zem pro-GRAHM
Listen! If you are so interested

so interessiert sind,
zo in-teh-ress-EERT zint,
in this program,

dann kommen Sie doch zu mir.
dahn KOHM'en zee dohkh ts'oo meer.
then come to my house.

— Das ist sehr nett von Ihnen,
Dahss isst zair net fohn EE-nen,
That's very nice of you,

aber ich möchte Sie nicht stören.
AH-ber ikh MERKH-teh zee nikht SHTER'ren.
but I wouldn't want to disturb you.

Would you like . . . ?
Ich möchte is a specially polite form of *mögen*
and means "I would like to." *Sie möchten*
means "You would like," and *Möchten*
Sie . . . ? "Would you like . . . ?" These expressions are so constantly used in spoken German
that they should be introduced here although
they will be dealt with more fully in Step 21.

— Im Gegenteil! Es ist mir ein Vergnügen.
Im GAY-gen-tile! Ess isst meer ine fehrg-NÜ-gen.
On the contrary! It's a pleasure for me.

— Dann können wir das Programm zusammen ansehen.
Dahn KERN'en veer dahss Pro-GRAHM ts'oo-ZAHM-men
                                          AHN-zay'en.
Then we can see the program together.

German Step by Step

— Was ist das eigentlich für ein Programm?
Vahss isst dahss I-ghent-likh für ine pro-GRAHM?
What kind of a program is it anyway?

— Es ist eine Farbsendung
Ess isst INE-eh FARB-zen-doong
It is a color broadcast

der Wiener Staatsoper.
dehr WEEN-er SHTAHTS-oper.
of the Vienna State Opera.

Es gibt „Der Rosenkavalier."
Ess ghipt „Der RO-zen-ka-vahl-eer."
They are giving "The Rosenkavalier."

— Wann beginnt die Sendung?
Vahn beh-GHINT dee ZEN-doong?
When does the show begin?

— Punkt neun.
Poonkt noyn.
Nine sharp.

— Dann können wir vorher etwas essen.
Dahn KERN'nen veer FOR-her ET-vahss ESS'en.
Then we can eat something before.

Wollen Sie mit mir essen gehen?
VOHL'en zee mit meer ESS'en GAY'en?
Do you want to go to dinner with me?

— Mit Vergnügen — aber Sie müssen mein Gast sein.
Mit fehrg-NÜ-ghen — AH-ber Zee MÜSS'en mine gahst zine.
With pleasure — but you must be my guest.

— Aber das kommt nicht in Frage!
AH-ber dahss kohmt nikht in FRA-geh!
But that's out of the question!

Die Übersetzung
Literally — "that doesn't come into the question!"

120

— Doch! Ich bestehe darauf!
Dokh! Ikh beh-SHTAY-eh da-R'OWF!
No! I insist on it!

> **Doch**
> *Doch* is a short word of many meanings, including "however," "nevertheless, "on the contrary," "at least," etc. and can be used to intensify what is being said.
>
> *Seien Sie doch ruhig!* — Do be quiet!
> *Lassen Sie es doch!* — Leave it alone then!

— In diesem Fall kann ich nicht nein sagen.
In DEE-zem FAHL kahn ikh nikht nine ZAHG'en.
In that case I can't say no.

— Einverstanden.
INE-fair-shtahn-den.
Agreed.

— Gehen wir in das kleine Lokal an der Ecke.
GAY'en veer in dahss KLINE-eh lo-KAHL ahn dehr EK-keh.
Let's go to the little place on the corner.

Das ist nicht sehr teuer,
Dahss isst nikht zehr TOY-er,
It's not very expensive

und man ißt dort ganz gut.
oont mahn isst dort gahnts goot.
and one eats very well there.

— Eine prima Idee!
INE-eh PREE-ma ee-DAY!
A first rate idea!

> **Prima!**
> *Prima* does not change its form, unlike other adjectives. It is colloquial and very frequently used either in combination or by itself, as an exclamation. It means: "great," "excellent," "wonderful," "the best," etc.

Aber wir müssen schnell machen,
AH-ber veer MÜSS'en shnell MA'khen,
But we must hurry,

wenn wir nicht zu spät
ven veer nikht ts'oo shpayt
if we don't want

kommen wollen
KOHM'en VOHL'en
to arrive too late

für die Ouvertüre.
für dee oo-ver-TU-reh.
for the overture.

TEST YOUR GERMAN

Translate the first five sentences into German and the second five into English. Score 10 points for each correct translation. See answers below.

1. He wants to see the football game.

2. Why can't he?

3. Because he hasn't enough money.

4. I need an entrance ticket.

5. Can you lend me 20 marks?

6. Wenn kein Benzin im Tank ist, kann der Wagen nicht fahren.

7. Können Sie mir sagen, wo eine Tankstelle ist?

8. Darf ich Ihnen helfen?

9. Mein Fernsehapparat ist kaputt.

10. Ich möchte Sie nicht stören.

SCORE _____%

123

step 12

HOW TO EXPRESS PREFERENCES AND OPINIONS

Wir sind am Strand.
Veer zint ahm shtrahnt.
We are at the beach.

Der Himmel ist blau.
Dehr HIM-mel isst bl'ow.
The sky is blue.

Himmel

Himmel means both "sky" and "heaven." *Himmel* is frequently used by itself as an exclamation:

Himmel! — Heavens! or *Gott im Himmel!* — God in Heaven!

Die Wolken sind weiß.
Dee VOHL-ken zint vice.
The clouds are white.

Das Wasser ist dunkelblau.
Dahss VAHS-ser isst DOON-kel bl'ow.
The water is dark blue.

Dort drüben sind drei Mädchen.
Dort DRÜ-ben zint dry MAYT-yen.
Over there are three girls.

Sie sitzen im Sand.
Zee ZITS'en imm zahnt.
They are sitting on the sand.

Sie wollen nicht schwimmen.
Zee VOHL'en nikht SHVIM'en.
They do not want to swim.

124

Das Wasser ist zu kalt zum Schwimmen.
Dahss VAHS-ser isst ts'oo kahlt tsoom SHVIM'en.
The water is too cold for swimming.

Aber die Sonne scheint. Es ist heiß.
AH-ber dee ZO-neh shint. Ess isst hice.
But the sun is shining. It is hot.

Und sie bleiben lieber in der Sonne.
Oont zee BLYB'en LEE-ber in dehr ZO-neh.
And they prefer to stay in the sun.

To prefer
Lieber is the comparative of gern which is used with a verb giving it the meaning of "to like":

Singen Sie gern? — Do you like to sing?
Ja, aber ich tanze lieber. — Yes, but I prefer (like better) to dance.

Eine von ihnen
INE-eh fohn EE-nen
One of them

Grammatically neuter — but still feminine
Although das Mädchen is technically neuter in gender (all words ending in -lein or chen are neuter), one may still refer to the girl herself by the feminine pronoun (sie) or the demonstrative pronoun-article (die).

hat einen roten Badeanzug an.
haht INE-en RO-ten BA-deh-ahn-ts'ook ahn.
is wearing a red bathing suit.

Adjective endings after -ein
In Step 7 you noted the endings of adjectives which follow der. The endings of adjectives following ein also generally end in -en in the different cases but with certain exceptions. For your convenience here are the different forms with a noun of each gender:

a small car — ein kleiner Wagen (nom.)
— eines kleinen Wagens (gen.)

125

— *einem kleinen Wagen* (dat.)
— *einen kleinen Wagen* (acc.)
a small cat — *eine kleine Katze* (nom.)
— *einer kleinen Katze* (gen.)
— *einer kleinen Katze* (dat.)
— *eine kleine Katze* (acc.)
a small bed — *ein kleines Bett* (nom.)
— *eines kleinen Bettes* (gen.)
— *einem kleinen Bett* (dat.)
— *ein kleines Bett* (accus.)

Der Badeanzug der zweiten ist grün.
Dehr BA-deh-ahn-ts'ook dehr ts'vigh-ten isst grün.
The bathing suit of the second one is green.

Die dritte trägt einen schwarzen Bikini.
Die DRIT-teh traygt INE-nen SHWART-sen bee-KEE-nee.
The third one is wearing a black bikini.

Neben den Mädchen spielen ein paar junge Männer
NAY-ben den MAYT-yen SHPEEL'en INE pahr YOONG-eh MEN-ner
Near the girls several young men

Gitarre und singen dazu.
ghee-TAR-eh oont ZING'en da T'SOO.
are playing the guitar and singing along with it.

Die Mädchen hören zu.
Dee MAYT-yen HER'en ts'oo.
The girls are listening.

Hören — zuhören
"to hear" is *hören* and "to listen to" is
zuhören. *Zuhören* is a separate prefix verb!

Sie hören gern Musik.
Zee HER'en ghern moo-ZEEK.
They like to hear music.

Und die jungen Männer
Oont dee YOONG-en MEN-ner
And the young men

spielen und singen sehr gern.
SHPEEL'en oont ZING'en zehr gehrn.
like to play and sing very much.

Das blonde Mädchen sagt zu der Braunhaarigen,
Dahss BLOHN-deh MAYT-yen zahkt ts'oo dehr BROWN-HA-ree-gen,
The blonde girl says to the brunette,

die den Bikini trägt:
dee den BEE-kee-nee traygt;
who is wearing the bikini:

„Die singen schön, nicht wahr?"
„Dee ZING-en shern, nikht vahr?"
"Those (boys) sing beautifully, don't they?"

„Gewiß," antwortet sie,
„Gheh-VISS," AHNT-vohr-tet zee,
"Certainly," she answers,

sie singen alle gut,
zee ZING'en AH-leh goot,
they all sing well,

aber der in der Mitte singt am besten."
AH-ber dehr in dehr MIT-teh zinkt ahm BESS-ten."
but the one in the middle sings best."

„Das stimmt nicht," sagt die Blonde,
„Dahss shtimmt nikht," zahkt dee BLOHN-deh,
"That isn't so," says the blonde,

der da rechts singt besser."
dehr da rekhts zinkt BESS-er."
the one there on the right sings better."

Comparison of adjectives and adverbs.
Note the comparison of *gut* which is both an adjective and an adverb — "good" and "well":
good — *gut*
better — *besser*
the best — *der (die, das) beste*

127

well — *gut*
better — *besser*
the best — *am besten*

Schnell is an example of a simple adverb and adjective which is not irregular:
quick — *schnell*
quicker — *schneller*
the quickest — *der (die, das) schnellste*
quickly — *schnell*
more quickly — *schneller*
most quickly — *am schnellsten*

Nach einer Weile
Nakh INE-er VILE-eh
After a while

hören die jungen Männer auf zu singen.
HER-ren dee YOUNG-en MEN-ner ow'f ts'oo ZING'en.
the young men stop singing.

Aufhören
aufhören, another word for ''to stop,'' is a separate prefix verb.

Einer sagt zu dem anderen:
INE-er zahkt ts'oo dem AHN-deh-ren:
One says to the other:

„Die sind hübsch, die Mädchen da drüben,
„Dee zint hůpsh, DEE MAYT-yen da DRŮB-en,
''They are pretty, those girls over there,

nicht wahr?"
nikht var?"
aren't they?''

„Mir gefällt die Dunkle am besten."
„Meer geh-FAILT dee DOONK-leh ahm BESS-ten."
''I like the dark one best.''

„Überhaupt nicht," sagt der andere,
„Ů-ber-howpt nikht," zahkt dehr AHN-deh-reh,
''Not at all,'' says the other,

„die Blonde ist hübscher als die Braunhaarige."
„dee BLOHN-deh isst HŮP-sher ahlss dee brown-HA-ree-geh."
"the blonde is prettier than the brunette."

Darauf sagt der dritte:
Da-ROWF zahkt dehr DRIT-teh:
At this the third one says:

„Das stimmt nicht;
„Dahss shtimmt nikht,
"That's not so,

die Rothaarige ist die Schönste von allen!"
dee ROHT-ha-ree-geh iss dee SHERN-steh fohn AH-len!
the red-haired one is the most beautiful of all!"

INSTANT CONVERSATION: SHOPPING

EINE TOURISTIN:
INE-eh too-RIST-in:
A LADY TOURIST:
Wir müssen noch Geschenke kaufen
Veer MŮSS'en nohkh geh-SHENK-eh KOWF'en
We must buy presents

für unsere Freunde und Verwandten.
fůr OON-zeh-reh FROYN-deh oont fehr-VAHN-ten.
for our friends and relatives.

Hier ist ein guter Laden.
Here isst ine GOO-ter LA-den.
Here is a good store.

Gehen wir hinein!
GAY-en veer hin-INE!
Let's go in!

EINE VERKÄUFERIN:
INE-eh fehr-KOY-fer-in:
A SALESLADY:
Sie wünschen, gnädige Frau?
zee VŮNSH'en, G'NAY-dee-geh fr'ow?
You wish, madam?

DIE FRAU:
Bitte zeigen Sie uns ein paar
BIT-teh TS'YGH'en zee oons ine par
Please show us some

seidene Schals.
ZIDE-eh-neh shahls.
silk scarves.

130

DIE VERKÄUFERIN:
Hier haben wir zwei
Heer HAHB'en veer ts'vye
Here we have two

besonders schöne Schals.
beh-SOHN-ders SHER-neh shahls.
especially beautiful scarves.

Einer ist schwarz und weiß
INE-er isst shvarts oont vice
One is black and white

und der andere ist
oont deh AHN-deh-reh isst
and the other is

grün und blau.
grun oont bl'ow.
green and blue.

Gefallen sie Ihnen?
Geh-FAHL'en zee EE-nen?
Do you find them attractive?

> **Gefällt es Ihnen? — Do you like it?**
> *Gefallen* (literally, "to please"), used with the dative, is another way of saying "to like."
>
> I like that. — *Das gefällt mir.*
> He likes that. — *Das gefällt ihm.*
> She likes that. — *Das gefällt ihr.*
> We like that. — *Das gefällt uns.*
> You like that. — *Das gefällt Ihnen.*
> They like that. — *Das gefällt ihnen.*
>
> As you can see, *gefällt* changes. But if what one likes is plural, the form is *gefallen*.
>
> How do you like German songs? — *Wie gefallen Ihnen deutsche Lieder?*

131

DIE FRAU:

Mir gefällt dieser hier.
Meer geh-FELT DEE-zer here.
I like this one here.

Die Farben sind lebhafter
Dee FAR-ben zint LEHP-hahft-er
The colors are more lively

und das Muster ist hübscher.
oont dahss MOOS-ter isst HÜP-sher
and the design is prettier.

Wieviel kostet er?
VEE-feel KO-stet ehr?
How much does it cost?

VERKÄUFERIN:

Vierzig Mark und fünfzig Pfennige.
FEER-ts'ig mark oont FÜNF-ts'ikh P'FEN-nee-geh.
Forty marks and fifty pfennings.

DIE FRAU:

Das ist zu teuer.
Dahss isst ts'oo TOY-er.
That is too expensive.

Haben Sie nicht etwas Billigeres?
HAHB'en zee nikht ET-vahss BIL-lee-geh-ress?
Don't you have anything cheaper?

VERKÄUFERIN:

Natürlich, gnädige Frau.
Na-TÜR-likh, GNAY-dee-gheh fr'ow.
Of course, madam.

Aber nicht aus reiner Seide.
AH-ber nikht ow'ss RYE-ner ZIDE-eh.
But not of pure silk.

Wie finden Sie die hier?
Vee FIND'en zee dee here?
How do you like the ones here?

Die sind nicht so teuer —
Zee zint nikht zo TOY-er —
They are not as expensive —

fünfzehn Mark und zwanzig Mark.
FÛNF-ts'ayn mark oont TS'VAHN-ts'ikh mark.
fifteen marks and twenty marks.

DIE FRAU:
Die sind aber nicht so hübsch
DEE zint AH-ber nikht so hûpsh
These are not as pretty

wie die teuren.
vee dee TOY-ren.
as the expensive (ones).

DER MANN:
Dehr Mann:
THE HUSBAND:
Mag sein, aber sie sind gut genug.
Mahg zine, AH-ber zee zint goot gheh-NOOK.
That may be, but they are good enough.

Ich nehme den in lila für Tante Irma.
Ikh NEH-meh dehn in LEE-la Fûr TAHN-teh EER-ma.
I'll take the one in violet for Aunt Irma.

Und jetzt, was sollen wir für Mutter kaufen?
Oont yets't, vahss ZOHL'en veer fûr MOO-ter KOW-F'en?
And now, what should we buy for mother?

> **Sollen — should, ought to**
> *Sollen* — "should," "to be supposed to," or
> "to be expected to," "shall" is another special
> auxiliary like *wollen, müssen, dürfen* and
> *mögen,* and like them, is followed directly by
> the infinitive. The key forms are: *ich soll, er soll,
> wir sollen.*

VERKÄUFERIN:
Bitte sehr, mein Herr,
BIT-teh zehr, mine hehr,
Please, sir,

schauen Sie sich diese Kette an.
SH'OW'en zee zikh DEE-zeh KET-teh ahn.
take a look at this necklace.

Sie kostet nur einhundertsechzig Mark.
Zee KO-stet noor INE-hoon-dert-ZEKH-ts'ikh mark.
It costs only 160 marks.

Sie ist sehr schön, nicht wahr?
Zee isst zehr shern, nikht var?
It is very beautiful, isn't it?

DER MANN:
Ja, das stimmt.
Ya, dahss shtimmt.
Yes, I agree.

> **Das stimmt.**
> *Das stimmt* from *stimmen* — "to tune" —
> means "That is correct" — or "That is exact,"
> and is used in conversation to mean "I agree,"
> "Yes, that's right," "Isn't it?" and even "O.K."

DIE FRAU:
Sollen wir sie kaufen, Liebling?
ZOHL'en veer zee KOWF'en, LEEP-ling?
Should we buy it, my dear?

DER MANN:
Gewiß, warum nicht?
Ghe-VISS, va-ROOM nikht?
Certainly, why not?

DIE FRAU:
Wir nehmen sie.
Veer NAYM'en zee.
We'll take it.

DER MANN:
Und jetzt möchte ich
Oont yetzt MERKH-teh ikh
And now I would like

etwas für meine Sekretärin kaufen.
ET-yahss fûr MINE-eh zek-reh-TAY-rin KOWF'en.
to buy something for my secretary.

Können Sie mir
KERN'en zee meer
Can you show me

die großen Ohrringe dort zeigen?
dee GRO-sen OR-ring-eh dort TS'Y'ghen?
those large earrings over there?

Adjectives in the plural

You have already noted that adjectives change their ending before the nouns they modify according to whether they are preceded by *der-die-das* (page 72) or *ein-eine, kein* and *mein, Ihr* and other possessives (page 125), but this was only for the singular. Here is how these changes go for the plural with *der, die, das,* starting with the large earrings (masc.) the man has just fancied for his secretary, and other examples such as "the beautiful women" (fem.) and "the new books" (neut.)

masculine plural

nom.	die großen Ohrringe
gen.	der großen Ohrringe
dat.	den großen Ohrringe n*
acc.	die großen Ohrringe

feminine plural	*neuter plural*
die schönen Damen	die neuen Bücher
der schönen Damen	der neuen Bücher
den schönen Damen	den neuen Büchern
die schönen Damen	die neuen Bücher

All these plural adjectives cases end in *-en.*

The same is true for the adjectives that follow *ein, eine* or the possessive adjectives, *mein, Ihr, sein* and also *kein.*

* The *dative plural* case of nouns ends in *-n.*

135

But in the case when the adjective stands alone in front of the noun, the ending of the adjective then is like the plural of the definite article, that is:

masc.	fem.	neut.
-e	-e	-e
-er	-er	-er
-en	-en	-en
-e	-e	-e

The correct use of these adjective endings is a mark of correct speech, but don't worry too much at first, and don't hesitate to use them, even Germans sometimes use the wrong ending!

VERKÄUFERIN:
Selbstverständlich, mein Herr.
Zelpst-fer-SHTEND-likh, mine hehr.
But of course, sir.

Sie sind aus Gold und einfach wunderbar.
Zee zint ow'ss golt oont INE-fahkh VOON-der-bar.
They are (made of) gold and simply wonderful.

DIE FRAU:
Willi, um Gotteswillen!
VIL-lee, oom GOHT-tess-vill-en!
Willi, for God's sake!

Wir können nicht so viel Geld
Veer KERN-en nikht zo feel ghelt
We cannot spend so much money

für Geschenke ausgeben.
für ghe-SHENK-eh OW'SS-gayb'en.
for presents.

Außerdem kann man diese Ohrringe
OW-sehr-dem kahn mahn DEE-zeh OR-ring-eh
In any case, these earrings cannot

nicht im Büro tragen.
nikht im bü-RO TRAHG-en.
be worn in the office.

136

Die silberne Brosche mit dem „Berliner Bär"
Dee ZIL-ber-neh BRO-sheh mit dem „Ber-LEE-ner Bear"
The silver brooch with the "Berlin Bear"

ist eine bessere Idee. Sie ist ganz praktisch
isst INE-eh BESS-er-eh ee-DAY. Zee isst gahnts PRAHK-tish
is a better idea. It is quite practical

und sehr interessant.
oont zehr in-teh-reh-SAHNT.
and very interesting.

DER MANN:
Stimmt. Ich nehme die Brosche.
Shtimmt. Ikh NAYM-eh dee BRO-sheh.
All right. I'll take the brooch.

DIE VERKÄUFERIN:
Gnädige Frau, wollen Sie
G'NAY-dee-gheh fr'ow, VOHL'en zee
Madam, do you want

diese Ohrringe ansehen?
dee-zeh OR-ring-eh AHN-zay'en?
to take a look at these earrings?

Finden Sie nicht, daß sie reizend sind?
FINN'den zee nikht, dahss zee RYE-ts'ent zint?
Don't you think that they are lovely?

DIE FRAU:
Ja, die sind wirklich großartig!
Ya, dee zint VIRK-likh GROSS-art-ikh!
Yes, they are really magnificent!

Aber wahrscheinlich auch sehr teuer!
AH-ber VAHR-shine-likh OW'kh zehr TOY-er
But probably also very expensive!

VERKÄUFERIN:
Vielleicht, aber dafür sind sie auch das Beste, was es gibt.
**Fee-lye'kt, AH-ber da-für zint zee ow'kh dahss BESS-teh, vahss ess
gipt.**
Perhaps, but that is why they are the best there is.

Sie kosten vierhundert Mark.
Zee KOHST'en FEER-hoon-dert MARK.
They cost four hundred marks.

DER MANN:

Das macht nichts.
Dahss mahkt nikhts.
It doesn't matter.

Ich kaufe diese Ohrringe für meine Frau.
Ikh K'OW-feh DEE-zeh OR-ring-eh für MY-neh fr'ow.
I'll buy these earrings for my wife.

DIE FRAU:

Ach, wie lieb! Vielen Dank, mein Schatz!
Akh, vee leep! FEEL'en dahnk, mine shahts!
Oh, how sweet! Many thanks, darling!

Love terms — and selected insults

Mein Schatz (literally "my treasure"), is equivalent to "dear," or "darling." Other terms of endearment include *Meine Liebe* — "my love" and *Liebling* or *Liebchen* — "Little Love," and obversely, not for use but for recognition only, here are some current insults:

Dummkopf! (dumb head) — idiot

Trottel — halfwit

Schwein — pig and the immortal,
   Schweinehund! (pig + dog — but one gets the idea.)

TEST YOUR GERMAN

Fill in the verb forms. Score 10 for each correct answer. See answers below.

1. Let's go in!
   _____ wir hinein!

2. You wish, madam?
   Sie _____, gnädige Frau?

3. Do you like them?
   _____ sie Ihnen?

4. I like this one.
   Mir _____ das hier.

5. Shall we buy it?
   _____ wir es kaufen?

6. We'll take it.
   Wir _____ es.

7. Can you show them to me?
   _____ Sie sie mir zeigen?

8. I like the blonde one best.
   Mir _____ die Blonde am besten.

9. I would like to buy something.
   Ich _____ etwas _____.

10. We must buy some presents.
    Wir _____ Geschenke _____.

SCORE _____%

MARKETING AND NAMES OF FOODS

Eine Hausfrau geht zum Einkaufen.
INE-eh HOUSE-fr'ow gay't ts'oom INE-kow-fen.
A housewife is going shopping in town.

Sie will Fleisch, Aufschnitt, Gemüse,
Zee vill fly'sh, OW'F-shnit, geh-MÜ-zeh,
She wants to buy meat, cold cuts, vegetables,

Brot, Butter, Käse und Bier kaufen.
Broht, BOO-ter, KAY-zeh oont beer KOWF'en.
bread, butter, cheese, and beer.

Zuerst geht sie zum Metzger.
Ts'oo-EHRST gayt zee ts'oom METS-gher.
First she goes to the butcher.

Noun endings in -er and -ei
The suffix *-er* often denotes a person who does something, as in English. The ending *-ei* generally indicates a shop or place where services are available.

die Metzgerei — the butcher's shop
die Bäckerei — the bakery
die Drogerie — shop for perfumes, soaps, etc. (not a drugstore)
die Brauerei — the brewery

Another special institution which one sees frequently in German-speaking countries is *die Konditorei* — "a special restaurant for pastry."

Sie fragt ihn:
Zee frahkt een:
She asks him:

„Haben Sie heute gute Kalbsschnitzel?"
„HAHB'en zee HOY-teh GOO-teh KAHLPS-shnits-el?"
"Have you good veal cutlets today?"

Der Metzger antwortet ihr:
Dehr METS-ger AHNT-vort-et eer:
The butcher answers her:

> Fragen/antworten
> Fragen — "to ask" — takes the direct object
> but antworten — "to answer" — takes the indirect object because you are replying "to"
> someone in answering his question.

„Aber natürlich, gnädige Frau!"
„AH-ber na-TÜR-likh, GNAY-dee-gheh fr'ow!"
"But of course, madam!"

„Wie viele möchten Sie?"
„Vee FEEL-eh MERKH-ten zee?"
"How many do you want?"

„Geben Sie mir drei gute Schnitzel
„GAYB'en ZEE meer dry GOO-teh SHNITS-el
"Give me three good cutlets

und ein halbes Pfund Aufschnitt."
oont ine HAHL-bess p'foont OW'F-shnit."
and half a pound of cold cuts."

„Wünschen Sie sonst noch etwas?"
„VÜN-shen zee sohnst nokh ET-vahss?"
"Would you like something else besides?"

„Geben Sie mir auch ein halbes Dutzend Würstchen."
„GAYB'en zee meer ow'kh ine HAHL-bess DOOTS-end
VÜRST-khen."
"Give me also half a dozen sausages."

Im Gemüseladen kauft sie
Im geh-MÜ-zeh-la-den kowft zee
In the vegetable store she buys

fünf Pfund Kartoffeln
fünf P'foont kar-TOHF-feln
five pounds of potatoes,

und auch Erbsen, Kohl, Kopfsalat,
oont ow'kh ERP-sen, kohl, KOHPF-za-laht,
and also beans, cabbage, lettuce,

Gurken, Spargel und Mohrrüben.
GOOR-ken, SHPAR-ghehl oont MOR-rû-ben.
cucumbers, asparagus, and carrots.

Dann zahlt sie und
Dahn t'sahlt zee oont
Then she pays and

fragt den Verkäufer:
frahkt den fehr-KOY-fer:
asks the shopkeeper:

> **Vergessen Sie nicht!**
> Note the change of meaning according to the prefix:
>
> > *kaufen* — to buy
> > *Käufer* — buyer (customer)
> > *verkaufen* — to sell
> > *Verkäufer* — seller (salesman)

„Haben Sie keine Apfelsinen heute?"
„HAHB'en zee KINE-eh ahp-fel-ZEE-nen HOY-teh?"
"Don't you have any oranges today?"

„Leider nicht," antwortet er.
„LYE-der nikht," AHNT-vor-tet ehr.
"Unfortunately not," he answers.

„Kommen Sie doch morgen früh wieder."
„KOHM'en zee dokh MOR-gen frû VEE-der."
"But come back early tomorrow."

Dann schaut sie auf ihrer Einkaufsliste nach
Dahn sh'ow't zee ow'f EER-er INE-kowfs-list-eh nahkh
Then she looks at her shopping list

und stellt fest,
oont shtellt fest,
and she notices,

> **Feststellen — to notice**
> **Fest**stellen is another separable prefix verb and
> means "to notice," "to ascertain."

daß sie noch ein Dutzend Eier,
dahss zee nokh ine DOOTS-end EYE'er,
that she must still buy a dozen eggs,

ein Viertelpfund Butter, etwas Schweizer Käse
ine FEER-tel-pfoont BOO-ter, ET-vahss SHVYE-ts'er KAY-zeh
a quarter pound of butter, some Swiss cheese,

und einen Liter Milch kaufen muß.
oont INE-en LEE-ter milkh KOWF'en mooss.
and a liter of milk.

> **Inverted word order**
> This is a good example of inverted word order.
> In German the key to the meaning of a long
> sentence is frequently at the end, rather than
> the beginning, as in English.

Dann fällt ihr noch etwas ein:
Dahn felt eer nohkh ET-vahss ine:
Then something else occurs to her:

„Was soll ich zum Nachtisch servieren?"
„Vahss zohl ikh ts'oom NAKH-tish ser-VEER'en?"
"What should I serve for dessert?"

Dann kauft sie einen Apfelkuchen
Dahn KOW'ft zee INE-en AHP-fel-koo-khen
Then she buys an apple cake

und noch etwas Schokoladengebäck.
oont nohkh ET-vahss sho-ko-LA-den-geh-bek.
and also some chocolate pastry.

Sie fragt sich:
Zee frahkt zikh:
She wonders:

143

„Habe ich jetzt alles, was ich brauche?
„HA-beh ikh yetst AH-less, vahss ikh BROW-kheh?
"Do I now have all I need?

Ach ja! — Ich darf nicht vergessen,
Akh ya! — Ikh dahrf nikht fehr-GUESS'en,
Oh yes! — I must not forget,

> **Dürfen — may (or) must**
> The auxiliary *dürfen* conveys the meaning of
> "may" (permission) in the affirmative and
> "must" when used with the negative
>
> May I? — *Darf ich?*
>
> The other forms are:
> er (*sie, es*) — *darf*
> sie (*wir, sie*) — *dürfen*

Bier zu kaufen,
beer ts'oo KOWF'en,
to buy beer too,

denn wir haben nur noch vier Flaschen im Kühlschrank."
den veer HAHB'en noor nohkh feer FLA-shen im KÜL-shrahnk."
since we have only four bottles left in the refrigerator."

INSTANT CONVERSATION:
IN A RESTAURANT

— Herr Ober! Einen Tisch für eine Person bitte.
Hair OH-ber! INE-en tish für INE-eh pair-ZOHN, BIT-teh.
Waiter! A table for one, please.

— Jawohl! Wollen Sie hier Platz nehmen?
Ya-VOHL! VOHL-en zee here plahts NAYM'en?
Yes indeed! Will you sit here?

Da kommt schon die Kellnerin
Da kohmt shohn dee KEHL-neh-rin
Here comes the waitress

mit der Speisekarte.
mit dehr SHPY-zeh-kahrt-eh.
with the menu.

— Danke. Na, was gibt's denn heute?
DAHN-keh. Na, vahss gipt's den HOY-teh?
Thanks. Well, what is there today?

Also als Vorspeise . . .
AHL-zo ahls FOR-shpy-zeh . . .
Let's see, for an appetizer . . .

möchte ich einen Rollmops.
MERKH-teh ikh INE-nen ROLL-mops.
I'd like pickled herring.

— Möchten Sie auch Suppe?
MERRKH-ten zee ow'kh ZOO-peh?
Would you also like soup?

Heute haben wir sehr schmackhafte Erbsensuppe.
HOY-teh HAHB'en veer zehr SHMAHK-hahft-eh EHRP-sen-zoo-peh.
Today we have a very tasty pea soup.

— Nein, danke. Keine Suppe für mich.
Nine, DAHN-keh. KINE-eh ZOO-peh für mikh.
No, thank you. No soup for me.

Sagen Sie, was können Sie noch empfehlen?
ZA-ghen zee, vahss KERN'en zee nohkh emp-FAIL'en?
Tell me, what else can you recommend?

— Ich empfehle Ihnen unseren Sauerbraten
Ikh emp-FAIL-eh EE-nen OON-zeh-ren ZOW-er-brah-ten
I recommend our pot roast

mit Knödeln und Gurkensalat.
mit KNERD'eln oont GOOR-ken-za-laht.
with dumplings and cucumber salad.

— Wie ist das Wiener Schnitzel?
Vee isst dahss VEE-ner SCHNITS-el?
How is the Viennese veal cutlet?

— Hervorragend!
Hehr-FOR-ra-gent!
Outstanding!

— Gut. Das werde ich ausprobieren.
Goot. Dahss VEHR-deh ikh OW'S-pro-beer'en.
Good. I'll try it.

— Und etwas zu trinken?
Oont ET-vahss ts'oo TRINK'en?
And something to drink?

— Bringen Sie mir zuerst ein Glas Steinhäger
BRING'en zee meer ts'oo-EHRST ine glahs SHTINE-hay-ger
Bring me first a glass of Steinhäger (gin)

und eine halbe Flasche Rheinwein für später.
oont INE-eh HAHL-beh FLAH-sheh RINE-vine für SHPAY-ter.
and a half bottle of Rhein wine for later.

> **Für das Essen und Trinken**
> When a food, drink or other commodity is measured, as here, it is not in the genitive, but stays in the nominative.

a bottle of beer — *eine Flasche Bier*
a cup of coffee — *eine Tasse Kaffee.*

Die Kellnerin stellt die Vorspeise
Dee KELL-ner-in shtelt dee FOR-shpy-zeh
The waitress places the appetizer

auf den Tisch und sagt: „Guten Appetit!"
ow'f den tish oont zahkt: „GOO-ten ah-peh-TEET!"
on the table and says: "Good appetite!"

> *Guten Appetit!* is in the accusative case be-
> cause the waitress is wishing it to a customer.
> Other typical expressions are *Gute Reise!* —
> "Have a good trip!", *Glückliches Wiederkom-*
> *men!* — "A happy return!", *Gute Bes-*
> *serung!* — "A good recovery!" as well as
> *Guten Morgen, Guten Tag,* and *Gute Nacht,*
> which you learned in the first steps.

— Und was wünscht der Herr zum Nachtisch?
Oont vahss vûnsht dehr hehr ts'oom NAHKH-tish?
And what will the gentleman have for dessert?

Der Pflaumenkuchen ist
Dehr PFL'OW-men-koo-khen isst
The plum cake is

eine Spezialität unseres Haues.
INE-eh spets-ya-lee-TAIT OON-zer-ress HOW-zess.
a speciality of our house.

— Schön. Ich versuche ihn.
Shern. Ikh fer-ZOOKH-eh een.
Fine. I'll try it.

— Darf ich jetzt den Kaffee bringen?
Darf ikh yetst den KAHF-feh BRING'en?
May I bring the coffee now?

— Ja, ohne Sahne bitte.
Ya, OH-neh ZAH-neh BIT-teh.
Yes, without cream, please.

147

Und ein Glas Kognak.
Oont ine glahss KOHN-yak.
And a glass of Cognac.

_____

— Fräulein, bitte!
FROY-line, BIT-teh!
Miss, please!

Wieviel bin ich schuldig?
vee-FEEL bin ikh SHOOL-dig?
How much do I owe you?

> **Schuldig**
> *Schuldig* means "owing," so this expression is
> literally "How much am I owing?" It is interest-
> ing to note that *schuldig* also means "guilty."

— Hier ist die Rechnung, mein Herr.
Here isst dee REKH-noong, mine hehr.
Here is the bill, sir.

— Ist das Trinkgeld eingeschlossen?
Isst dahss TRINK-ghelt INE-gheh-shlohss'en?
Is the tip included?

— Ja, zehn Prozent.
Ya, ts'ayn pro-ts'ENT.
Yes, ten percent.

Danke sehr. Ich bringe sofort Ihr Wechselgeld.
DAHN-keh zehr. Ikh BRING-eh zo-FORT eer VEX-el-gelt.
Thank you very much. I'll bring your change right away.

— Schon recht. Behalten Sie den Rest.
Shohn rekht. Beh-HAHLT'en zee den rest.
Never mind. Keep the rest.

— Vielen Dank, mein Herr.
FEE-len dahnk, mine hehr.
Many thanks, sir.

Kommen Sie bald wieder!
KOHM-en zee bahlt VEE-der!
Come back soon!

TEST YOUR GERMAN

Match the following words. Score 5 points for each correct answer. See answers on following page.

1. Gemüse	A. bread
2. Fleisch	B. sausages
3. Butter	C. cold cuts
4. Milch	D. cucumber salad
5. Brot	E. plums
6. Eier	F. pickled herring
7. Apfelsinen	G. peas
8. Obst	H. meat
9. Käse	I. vegetables
10. Nachtisch	J. milk
11. Suppe	K. eggs
12. Kartoffeln	L. oranges
13. Aufschnitt	M. fruits
14. Erbsen	N. dessert
15. Würstchen	O. soup
16. Rollmops	P. potatoes
17. Gurkensalat	Q. cheese

18. Äpfel   R. cake

19. Pflaumen   S. apples

20. Kuchen   T. butter

Answers: 1-I; 2-H; 3-T; 4-J; 5-A; 6-K; 7-L; 8-M; 9-Q; 10-N; 11-O; 12-P; 13-C; 14-G; 15-B; 16-F; 17-D; 18-S; 19-E; 20-R.

SCORE _____%

step 14

WHEN TO USE THE "FAMILIAR" PRONOUN AND VERB FORMS

Es gibt Situationen,
Ess ghipt zee-too-ah-TS'YON-en,
There are situations

wo man das familiäre „du"
vo mahn dahss fah-mil-YEH-reh „doo"
where one uses the familiar "you"

anstatt des höflichen „Sie" gebraucht.
ahn-SHTAHT dess HERF-likh-en „zee" gheh-BROW'KHT.
instead of the polite "you."

The use of "du"

Sie, the word you have learned for "you" is the formal form, which, with its corresponding verb form is the same for singular and plural. Now we present the informal word for "you" — *du*, used when speaking to one person with whom you are on familiar terms.

This informal *du* is used between members of a family, close friends, young people talking to each other and generally in informal situations, such as those you will observe in this Step. The present tense of the verb form used with *du* is easy to recognize because it ends in *-st*. The object form of *du* is *dich*, the dative form is *dir* and the possessive is *dein*.

In der Familie.
In dehr fa-MEE-lee-yeh.
In the family.

DIE MUTTER:
Dee MOO-ter:
THE MOTHER:
Hör mal!
Her mahl!
Now, listen!

> **The imperative for "du"**
> The imperative for *du* is generally the corresponding verb form for *du* without the -*st* and without *du:*
>
> *Du trinkst.* — You are drinking.
> *Trink!* — Drink!
> *Du sagst.* — You are saying.
> *Sag!* — Say!
> *Du gehst.* — You are going.
> *Geh!* — Go!

Du mußt alles aufessen!
Doo moost AH-less OW'f-ess'en!
You must eat it all up!

DIE TOCHTER:
Dee TOHKH-ter:
THE DAUGHTER:
Aber Mutti, ich habe gar keinen Hunger!
AH-ber MOO-tee, ikh HA-beh gar KINE-en HOONG-er!
But mother, I am not hungry at all! (*Mutti* is the familiar for mother.)

DIE MUTTER:
Trink doch etwas Milch!
Trink dohkh ET-vahss milkh!
Drink some milk then!

DIE TOCHTER:
Ich habe aber auch keinen Durst.
Ikh HA-beh AH-ber ow'kh KINE-en doorst.
But I am not thirsty either.

> "To be hungry " (*hungrig*) or "thirsty" (*durstig*) can also be expressed by *Hunger haben* or *Durst haben* — literally "to have hunger" or "to have thirst."

152

DIE MUTTER:
Wenn du kein Frühstück ißt,
Ven doo kine FRÛ-shtûk isst,
If you don't eat any breakfast,

dann kannst du Samstag nicht ins Kino gehen.
dahn kahnst doo SAHM-stahg nikht inss KEE-no gay'n.
then you can't go to the movies Saturday.

DIE TOCHTER:
Warum willst du, daß ich so viel esse?
Va-ROOM vilst doo, dahss ikh zo feel ESS-eh?
Why do you want me to eat so much?

Use of the comma
The comma is used before subordinate clauses.
The girl is saying "Why do you want, that I eat so much."

The verb form for "du"
In the present tense the verb form for *du* uses the same base as the form for *er, sie, es* except that it always ends in *-st:*

> *er hat*
> *du hast*

> *er kommt*
> *du kommst*

> *er will*
> *du willst*

> *er sieht*
> *du siehst*

The *Du*-Form, as it is called in German, corresponds to the pronoun "thou" in English which used to be current but is now archaic.

Ich will nicht so dick werden.
Ikh vill nikht zo dick VEHRD'en.
I do not want to become so fat.

Werden — to become
Werden — "to become" is irregular. The key
forms are: *ich werde, er wird, wir werden.*

Die Du-Form ist natürlich zwischen Freunden.
Dee doo-form isst na-TÜR-likh TS'VISH'en FROYN-den.
The familiar "you" is natural between friends.

OTTO:

Morgen, Paul! Wie geht's?
MORE-gen, P'OWL! vee GAY'ts?
Morning, Paul! How is it going?

Wie geht's?
Occasionally the *-e* is dropped in the word *es,*
and *Wie geht es?* becomes *Wie geht's?* with an
apostrophe s.

PAUL:

Mir geht es gut. Und dir?
Meer gayt ess goot. Oont deer?
I am doing all right. And you?

OTTO:

Nicht schlecht.
Nikht schlekht.
Not bad.

Heute gehe ich zu Ludwig.
HOY-teh GAY-eh ikh ts'oo LOOD-vig.
Today I am going to Ludwig's.

"Zu" and "bei" with names
Zu ("to") or *bei* ("by") can be used directly
with a proper name to mean "to someone's (or)
at someone's house."

Heute ist sein Geburtstag.
HOY-teh isst zine geh-BOORTS-tahk.
Today is his birthday.

PAUL:
Wann gehst du denn hin?
Vahn gayst doo dort-HIN?
When are you going there then?

OTTO:
Um halb neun. Kommst du mit?
Oom hahlp noyn. Kohmst doo mit?
At half past eight. Are you coming along?

PAUL:
Nein. Ich bin nicht eingeladen.
Nine. Ikh bin nikht INE-geh-lahd'en.
No. I am not invited.

OTTO:
Aber das spielt doch keine Rolle!
AH-ber dahss shpeelt dokh KINE-eh ROLL-eh!
But that really doesn't matter!

Die Übersetzung
The special idiom Otto uses here literally
means: "That doesn't play any role."

Es ist eine Überraschung.
Ess isst INE-eh Ů-behr-ra-shoong.
It's a surprise.

Komm doch mit mir.
Kohm dokh mit meer.
Come with me then.

PAUL:
Ich kann nicht.
Ikh kahn nikht.
I cannot.

Martha wartet auf mich.
MAR-ta VAHR-tet ow'f mikh.
Martha is waiting for me.

OTTO:

Um so besser. Bring sie mit.

Oom zo BESS-er. Bring zee mit.

So much the better. Bring her along.

Und bring eine Flasche Wein mit.

Oont BRING-eh INE-eh FLA-sheh vine mitt.

And bring a bottle of wine with (you).

PAUL:

Aber natürlich!

AH-ber na-TÜR-likh!

But naturally!

OTTO:

Vergiß nicht zu kommen!

Fair-GHISS nikht ts'oo KOHM'en!

Don't forget to come!

Verliebte gebrauchen auch die Du-Form.

Fair-LEEB-teh geh-BROW-khen owkh dee DOO-form.

Lovers also use the ''you'' (familiar) form.

SIE:

Liebst du mich?

Leepst doo mikh?

Do you love me?

ER:

Ja, mein Schatz,

Ya, mine shahts,

Yes, my treasure,

ich liebe dich sehr.

ikh LEE-beh dikh zehr.

I love you very much.

SIE:

Für immer?

Für IMM-er?

Forever?

ER:
Wer weiß? Wer kann das sagen?
Vehr vice? Vehr kahn dahss ZAGH'en?
Who knows? Who can say that?

SIE:
Warum sagst du — „Wer weiß?"
Va-ROOM zahkst doo — „Vehr vice?"
Why do you say — "Who knows?"

Du bist ekelhaft!
Doo bist EH-kel-haft!
You are horrible!

Ich hasse dich!
Ikh HAHSS-eh dikh!
I hate you!

Man sagt „du," wenn man mit einem Kind spricht.
Mahn zahkt doo, ven mahn mit INE-em kint shprikht.
One says "you" (familiar) when one is speaking with a child.

— Komm doch mal her, Kleine!
Kohm dohkh mahl hehr, KLINE-eh!
Come over here, little one!

Wie heißt du denn?
Vee hy'st doo den?
What's your name?

Conversational extras
In conversational German several short words are very often used either to intensify the meaning or to lend a certain amount of informality or emphasis to the conversation. The basic meanings of these "linking words" are as follows:

denn — then, for, because
schon — already, yet
noch — still, yet, besides, further, as yet
wohl — indeed, well
nun — now, then
da — there, here
nur — only, but, scarcely

157

doch — still, yet, nevertheless, then
mal — (see step 9)

When you converse in German with people, listen for these words and note how they are used so you can acquire their use yourself — a proof of fluency and ease in German conversation.

— Ich heiße Magda.
Ikh Hy-seh MAHG-da.
My name is Magda.

— Ist das dein Brüderchen?
Isst dahss dine BRÛ-der-khen?
Is this your little brother?

The diminutive
The diminutive of nouns is formed by adding -*chen* or -*lein* to the noun. These endings make the nouns either smaller or more endearing.

Brother — *Bruder*
Little brother — *Brüderchen*

Dog — *Hund*
Little dog — *Hündchen*

House — *Haus*
Little House — *Häuschen*

Bird — *Vogel*
Little bird — *Vöglein*

Words of all genders become neuter in the diminutive.

— Ja. Er ist noch sehr klein.
Ya. Ehr isst nohkh zehr kline.
Yes. He is still very small.

Er kann noch nicht sprechen.
Ehr kahn nokh nikht SHPREKH'en.
He cannot talk yet.

— Aber du sprichst schon sehr gut, nicht wahr?
AH-ber doo shprikhst shohn zehr goot, nikht vahr?
But you talk very well already, don't you?

— Ja! Vati sagt, daß ich zuviel rede.
Ya! FA-tee zahkt dahss ikh ts'oofeel RAY-deh.
Yes! Daddy says that I talk too much.

— Hier ist ein Stück Schokolade für dich.
Here isst ine shtůk sho-ko-LA-deh fůr dikh.
Here is a piece of chocolate for you.

Und eines für dein Brüderchen.
Oont INE-ess fůr dine BRŮ-der-khen.
And one for your little brother.

Setzt euch dorthin, ihr beide,
ZETS oykh dort-HIN, eer BY-deh,
Sit down over there,

> **"Ihr," the plural form of "du"**
> When the gentleman speaks to both children he
> uses the plural of *du*, which is *ihr*. Its present
> tense form ends in -*t*, the same as that for *er*,
> *sie, es:*
>
> > *ihr sagt*
> > *ihr sprecht*
> > *ihr schreibt*
>
> The imperative forms of the verb:
>
> > *Sagt!*
> > *Sprecht!*
> > *Schreibt!*
>
> The reflexive pronoun for *ihr* is *euch. Setzt
> euch* is literally "Set yourselves."
>
> *Euch* is also the direct object pronoun, while
> the indirect object pronoun is *ihr.*

vor den Brunnen.
for den BROO-nen.
in front of the fountain.

Ich will euch beide fotografieren.
Ikh vill oykh BY-deh fo-toh-gra-FEER'en.
I want to take a picture of both of you.

159

Die Du-Form ist auch richtig für Tiere.
Dee DOO-form isst ow'kh RIKHT-ikh für TEE-reh.
The "you" (familiar) form is also correct for animals.

> **When speaking to animals**
> As we recommend using the *du*-form when speaking to animals one might ask whether animals would notice if you use the right form — *du* for the singular and *ihr* when speaking to more than one. Although animals don't care about grammar this summarizes the entire concept of the familiar form — that it is "informal," and that you are on familiar or informal terms with whomever you are speaking to. Besides, if you used the formal "*Sie*" to talk or give orders to a pet or a horse, the onlookers, if not the animal, would certainly give you a curious look.

— Wolf! Du sollst nicht auf dem Sofa sitzen!
Volf! Doo zohlst nikht ow'f dem ZO-fa ZITS'en!
Wolf! You aren't allowed to sit on the sofa!

Und laß die Katze in Ruhe!
Oont LAHSS dee KAHT-seh in ROO-heh!
And leave the cat alone!

Ruhig! Raus mit dir!
ROO-hikh! Row'ss mit deer!
Quiet! Out with you!

Du bist ein böser Hund.
Doo bist ine BER-zer hoont.
You are a bad dog.

> **Eine Ausnahme — (an exception)**
> *Du bist* is an exception to the rule that the present tense of the *du* — form is always based on the *er, sie, es* — form by substituting -*st* for the ending.

INSTANT CONVERSATION: AT A SIDEWALK CAFÉ

EINE FRAU:
Ich bin müde und durstig.
Ikh bin MÜ-deh oont DUR-stikh.
I am tired and thirsty.

Sollen wir etwas trinken?
ZOHL'en veer ET-vahss TRINK'en?
Should we have something to drink?

EIN MANN:
Eine großartige Idee!
INE-eh gross-AR-tee-geh ee-DAY!
A great idea!

Gehen wir in dieses Lokal.
GAY'en veer in DEE-zess lo-KAHL.
Let's go in this café.

Hier ist ein Tisch frei.
Here isst ine tish fry.
Here is a table free.

Ein guter Platz.
Ine GOO-ter plahts.
A good spot.

Man kann alle Leute vorbeigehen sehen.
Mahn kahn AH-leh LOY-teh for-BY-gay'en ZAY'en.
One can see everybody go by.

DIE FRAU:
Ja sicher! Du willst nur wieder den
Ya ZIKH-er! Doo villst noor VEE-der den
Yes, of course! You only want to watch

161

hübschen Mädchen nachsehen!
HÜB-shen MAYT-yen NAHKH-zay'en!
the pretty girls!

DER MANN:

Na komm!
Na kohm!
Come on now!

Du weißt doch, daß ich nur Augen für dich habe.
Doo vice'st dohkh, dahss ikh noor OW-ghen für dikh HA-beh.
You know that I have eyes only for you.

Herr Ober!
Hehr OH-ber!
Waiter!

KELLNER:

Womit kann ich den Herrschaften dienen?
Vo-MIT kahn ikh den HEHR-shahft-en DEEN'en?
What can I do for the gentlemen?

> **An echo of the past**
> *Herrschaften,* a formal word for "gentlemen,"
> or "lady and gentleman," also means "the
> power" as well as the "master and mistress" or
> "lords" of a house, an instance of excessive
> politeness inherited from an earlier day.

DER MANN:

Was soll ich für dich bestellen?
Vahss zohl ikh für dikh beh-SHTEL'en?
What shall I order for you?

DIE FRAU:

Ich weiß selbst nicht.
Ikh vice zelpst nikht.
I don't know myself.

Vielleicht ein Bier?
Feel-LY'KHT ine beer?
Perhaps a beer?

DER MANN:
Bringen Sie eine kleine Flasche Bier
BRIN'en zee INE-eh KLINE-eh FLA-sheh beer
Bring a small bottle of beer

für die Dame —
für dee DA-meh —
for the lady —

und ein Glas Kognak für mich.
oont ine glahs KOHN-yak für mikh.
and a glass of cognac for me.

FRAU:
Ach, Liebling,
Ahkh, LEEP-ling,
Oh, my dear,

kannst du unsere Bestellung ändern?
kahnst doo OON-zeh-reh beh-SHTEL-loong EN-dern?
can you change our order?

Ich trinke lieber ein Glas Wein.
Ikh TRINK-eh LEE-behr ine glahss vine.
I'd rather drink a glass of wine.

MANN:
So etwas! Die Frauen wissen nie,
Zo ET-vahss! Dee FR'OW-en VISS'en nee,
Here we go! Ladies never know

was sie wollen!
vahss zee VOHL'en!
what they want!

Kellner! Moselwein anstatt Bier bitte!
KELL-ner! MO-zel-vine ahn-SHTAHT beer BIT-teh!
Waiter! Moselle wine instead of the beer, please!

FRAU:
Du bist hoffentlich nicht böse auf mich?
Doo bisst HO-fennt-likh nikht BER-zeh ow'f mikh?
You aren't, I hope, angry with me?

MANN:

Wer kann dir denn böse sein?

Vehr kahn deer den BER-zeh zine?

Who can really be angry with you?

FRAU:

Wirklich? Oh, da sind schon unsere Getränke.

VEERK-likh? Oh, dah zint shohn OON-zeh-reh gheh-TREN-keh.

Really? Oh, here are our drinks.

Zum Wohl, mein Schatz.

TS'oom vohl, MINE shahts.

To (your) health, my treasure.

MANN:

Dein Wohl, mein Herz!

Dine vohl, mine HEHRTZ!

Your health, my heart!

TEST YOUR GERMAN

Translate these phrases into German, using the familiar form. Score 10 points for each correct translation. See answers below.

1. Are you hungry? (use *hungrig*) _____

2. You must drink something! _____

3. At what time are you coming? _____

4. Bring her along! _____

5. Who is going with you? _____

6. Sit down, both of you! _____

7. Here is something for you and for your little brother. _____

8. I love you! _____

9. I hate you! _____

10. You never know what you want. _____

SCORE ____%

step 15 DAYS, MONTHS, DATES, SEASONS, THE WEATHER, HOLIDAYS

Die sieben Tage der Woche sind:
Dee ZEE-ben TA-geh dehr VO-kheh zint:
The seven days of the week are:

Montag, Dienstag, Mittwoch,
MOHN-tahk, DEENS-tahk, MITT-vokh,
Monday, Tuesday, Wednesday,

Donnerstag, Freitag, Samstag (Sonnabend)
DOHN-ners-tahk, FRY-tahk, ZAHMS-tahk (ZOHN-ah-bent)
Thursday, Friday, Saturday,

An alternate word
Sonnabend is an alternate word for "Saturday,"
principally used in northern Germany.

und Sonntag.
oont ZOHN-tahk.
and Sunday.

Die zwölf Monate des Jahres heißen:
Dee ts'verlf MO-NA-teh dess YA-ress HI'sen:
The twelve months of the year are called:

Januar, Februar, März,
YAHN-wahr, FAYB-ru-wahr, mairts,
January, February, March,

April, Mai, Juni, Juli,
ah-PREEL, my, YOO-nee, YOO-lee,
April, May, June, July,

August, September, Oktober,
ow-GOOST, sep-TEM-ber, ok-TOH-ber,
August, September, October,

November, Dezember.
no-VEM-ber, day-T'SEM-ber.
November, December.

Januar ist der erste Monat des Jahres.
YAHN-wahr isst dehr EHR-steh MO-naht dess YA-ress.
January is the first month of the year.

Der erste Januar ist der Neujahrstag.
Dehr EHR-steh YAHN-wahr isst dehr NOY-yars-tahk.
The first of January is New Year's Day.

Wir sagen zu unseren Freunden:
Veer ZAHG'en ts'oo OON-zeh-ren FROYN-den:
We say to our friends:

„Prosit Neujahr!"
„PRO-zit NOY-yar!"
"Happy New Year!"

Prosit!
Prosit is a word often used in toasts — equivalent to "Congratulations!" "Your health!" etc.

Weihnachtsabend fällt
Vye-nakhts-AH-bent felt
Christmas Eve falls

Fallen — to fall (Umlaut)
Fallen takes an umlaut for the *er, sie, es*-form:
ich falle, er fällt, wir fallen.

auf den vierundzwanzigsten Dezember.
ow'f den feer-oont-TS'VAHN-ts'ik-sten day-TS'EM-ber.
on the 24th of December.

The accusative for dates
When something is said to fall on a certain day the date becomes accusative. In German correspondence the date on the top of the letter is also written in the accusative. "Jan. 2nd." —
den 2. Januar.

Die Leute wünschen sich:
Dee LOY-teh VÜNSH'en zikh:
The people wish each other:

Sich — (each other)
The *sich* used here is a dative form of the third person pronoun meaning "one another" or "each other."

„Fröhliche Weihnachten!"
„FRER-likh-eh VY-nakh-ten!"
"Happy Christmas!"

In Deutschland und in Österreich
In DOYTCH-lahnt oont in ER-stehr-rykh
In Germany and in Austria

machen die meisten Leute im August Urlaub.
MA-khen dee MY-sten LOY-teh im ow-GOOST OOR-l'ow'p.
most people take their vacation in August.

In ihrem Urlaub fahren die Deutschen
In EER-em OOR-l'ow'p FAR'en dee DOYTCH-en
For their vacation Germans like to

Fahren (with umlaut)
Fahren uses the umlaut only for *er, sie, es:*
er fährt.

gern ins Ausland.
gehrn ins OW'S-lahnt.
travel abroad.

Wenn jemand auf Reisen geht,
Ven YEH-mahnt ow'f RI-zen gate,
When someone goes on a trip,

wünschen wir ihm:
VŮNSH'en veer eem:
we wish him:

„Gute Reise!"
„GOO-teh RI-zeh!"
"(a) good trip!"

Das Jahr ist in vier Jahreszeiten eingeteilt:
Dahss yahr isst in feer YA-ress-TS'ITE-en INE-geh-ty'lt:
The year is divided in four seasons:

Achtung! word order
Eingeteilt — "divided" — is the past participle
of the verb *einteilen* — "to divide." Past participles always come at the end of a sentence as
you will see in Step 18 when we examine the
past and the past tense.

Frühling, Sommer, Herbst und Winter.
FRÜ-ling, ZO-mer, hehrpst oont VIN-ter.
spring, summer, autumn, and winter.

Similar words
You will note that two of the German seasons
are almost the same in English but their pronunciation is different. Many Basic German words
are almost the same as their English counter-
parts but are difficult to recognize in conversation because of their inflected endings and
those of their preceding adjectives. This is why
it is so important to recognize the articles and
adjectives used in the different cases.

Im Winter ist es kalt,
Im VIN-ter isst ess kahlt,
In winter it is cold,

und im Sommer ist es heiß.
oont imm ZO-mer isst ess hice.
and in summer it is hot.

Im Frühling ist das Wetter meistens gut.
Im FRÜ-ling isst dahss VET-ter MY-stens goot.
In spring the weather is generally good.

Im Herbst fallen die Blätter
Im hehrpst FAHL-len dee BLET-ter
In autumn the leaves fall

von den Bäumen.
fonn den BOY-men.
from the trees.

The umlaut for the plural
The singular forms of *Blätter* and *Bäume* are *Blatt* and *Baum*. Their plurals are formed not only by the addition of a plural ending but also by an umlaut. When two vowels come together as in *Bäume* the umlaut is placed over the first vowel.

Im Herbst findet das Oktoberfest
Im hairpst FIN-det dahss
In autumn the October Festival takes place

in München statt,
in MÜNT-yen shtaht,
in Munich,

To take place
Stattfinden — "to take place" (Literally — "to find place") is a separable prefix verb.

mit viel Bier und lustigem Gesang.
mit feel beer oont LOOS-tee-ghem geh-ZAHNG.
with plenty of beer and jovial singing.

Ein anderes lustiges Fest
Ine AHN-deh-ress LOOS-tig-ess fest
Another lively festival

ist der Karneval, besonders im Rheinland
isst dehr Kar-ne-VAHL, beh-ZOHN-ders im RINE-lahnt
is Carnival, especially in the Rhineland,

und auch in Bayern, wo er Fasching heißt.
oont ow'kh in BA-yern vo ehr FA-shing hice.
and also in Bavaria where it is called "Fasching."

Zu jeder Jahreszeit ist in Deutschland
Ts'oo YEH-der YA-ress-ts'ite isst in DOYTCH-lahnt
In every season in Germany there is

viel Interessantes zu sehen.
feel in-teh-reh-SAHN-tess ts'oo ZAY'en.
much of interest to see.

Da gibt es Musikfestspiele,
Da ghipt ess moo-ZEEK-fest-shpeel-eh,
There are music festivals,

Freilichtspiele, Messen und Volksfeste.
FRY-likht-shpeel-eh, MESS-en oont FOLKS-fess-teh.
open air plays, fairs and pageants.

Aber am interessantesten von allem
AH-ber ahm in-teh-reh-SAHN-tess-ten fohn AH-lem
But the most interesting of all

ist das Land selbst,
isst dahss LAHNT zelpst,
is the land itself,

mit seinen hohen Bergen,
mit ZINE-en HO-hen BEHR-ghen,
with its high mountains,

lieblichen Tälern, alten Städten
LEEP-lee-khen TAY-lern, AHL-ten SHTAY-ten
lovely valleys, old cities

und romantischen Burgen.
oont ro-MAHN-tish-en BOORG-en.
and romantic castles.

INSTANT CONVERSATION:
TALKING ABOUT THE WEATHER

Jeder spricht über das Wetter.
YEH-der shprikht ÜH-ber dahss VET-ter.
Everyone talks about the weather.

Im Frühling, wenn die Sonne scheint
Im FRÜ-ling, ven dee ZOH-neh shine't
In spring, when the sun shines

> **When — (Die Übersetzung)**
> The English "when" may be translated by three
> separate concepts:
>
> when? — *wann?*
> when (something happened) — *als*
> when (containing an element of "if" —"when
> the sun shines," etc.) — *wenn.*
>
> This latter example is the regular word for "if"
> in German and this close similarity causes con-
> fusion for Germans learning English as well as
> for English-speaking people learning German.

und der Himmel blau ist,
oont dehr HIM-mel bl'ow isst,
and the sky is blue,

sagt man:
zahkt mahn:
one says:

„Was für ein herrlicher Tag!"
„Vahss für ine HEHR-lick-er tahkh!"
"What a fine day!"

Und wenn der Abend klar ist
Oont ven dehr AH-bent klahr isst
And when the evening is clear

172

und wir den Mond und die Sterne sehen,
oont veer den mohnt oont dee SHTAIR-neh ZAY'en,
and we see the moon and the stars,

sagen wir:
ZAHG'en veer:
we say:

„Was für ein schöner Abend!"
„Vahss fûr ine SHER-ner AH-bent!"
"What a beautiful evening!"

Im Sommer, wenn es sehr heiß ist,
Im ZO-mer, ven ess zehr hice isst,
In summer when it is very hot,

klagen wir:
KLAHG'en veer:
we complain:

„Was für eine Hitze!"
„Vahss fûr EYE-neh HIT-zeh!"
"How hot it is!"

Wenn es stark regnet,
Ven ess shtark RAYK-net,
When it rains hard,

sagen wir:
ZAHG'en veer:
we say:

„Es gießt! —
„Ess gheest! —
"It's pouring! —

Vergiß nicht deinen Regenschirm!"
Fair-GISS nikht DINE-en RAY-ghen-shirm!"
Don't forget your umbrella!"

Und im Winter,
Oont im VIN-ter,
And in winter,

173

wenn es schneit und friert,
ven ess shnite oont freert,
when it snows and freezes,

sagen wir:
ZAHG'en veer:
we say:

„Es ist bitter kalt draußen.
„Ess isst BIT-ter kahlt DR'OW-sen.
"It's bitter cold outside.

Das Fahren auf der Autobahn
Dahss FAR-en ow'f dehr OW-toh-bahn
Travelling on the expressway

ist sicher sehr gefährlich heute,
isst ZIKH-er zair geh-FAIR-likh HOY-teh,
is surely very dangerous today,

des Eises und des Schnees wegen.
dess EYE-zess oont dess shnayss VAY-ghen.
because of the ice and snow.

Es ist besser, zu Hause zu bleiben,
Ess isst BES-ser, ts'oo HOW-zeh ts'oo BLY'ben,
It's better to stay home,

bis es aufhört zu schneien."
biss ess OW'F-hurt ts'oo SHNY'en."
until it stops snowing."

Zu with the infinitive
When an infinitive is used within a sentence
with a verb, adverb or adjective it is preceded
by *zu* except for the special verbs which are
used directly with an infinitive such as *müssen,*
sollen, wollen, dürfen and *mögen.*

TEST YOUR GERMAN

Translate into English. Score 10 points for each correct translation. See answers below.

1. Die meisten Leute gehen im Sommer auf Urlaub.

2. Ich reise gern ins Ausland.

3. Wenn jemand auf Reisen geht, sagen wir ,,Gute Reise!''

4. In Deutschland gibt es hohe Berge und liebliche Täler.

5. Was für ein herrlicher Tag!

6. Was für ein schöner Abend!

7. Es ist sehr heiß, nicht wahr?

8. Es gießt! Vergiß nicht deinen Regenschirm!

9. Es ist bitter kalt draußen.

10. Schneit es schon?

SCORE _____%

step 16

HOW TO USE REFLEXIVE VERBS

Herr Schuster steht früh auf.
Hair SHOOS-ter shtay't frü ow'f.
Mr. Schuster gets up early.

Er wäscht sich das Gesicht,
Ehr vesht zikh dahss geh-ZIKHT,
He washes his face,

putzt sich die Zähne und rasiert sich.
poots't zikh dee TSAY-neh oont ra-ZEERT zikh.
brushes his teeth, and shaves.

Reflexive verbs and pronouns
Wäscht sicht, putzt sich and *rasiert sich* (*sich waschen, sich putzen, sich rasieren*) are examples of reflexive verbs. Reflexive verbs are so called because the subject of the verb acts on itself such as "to wash oneself," "to dress oneself," "to comb one's hair" and "to sit (oneself) down" — *Setzen Sie sich!* ("Set yourself down!") is an expression you will frequently hear. The reflexive pronouns are used as follows: *ich setze mich, du setzt dich, er setzt sich, wir setzen uns, ihr setzt euch, Sie (sie) setzen sich.*

Dann nimmt er ein Bad und zieht sich an.
Dahn nimt ehr ine baht oont ts'eet zikh ahn.
Then he takes a bath and gets dressed.

Anziehen (sep. prefix)
"To get dressed" — *sich anziehen* — is a separable prefix verb.

Die Kinder stehen etwas später auf.
Dee KIN-der SHTAY'en ET-vahss SHPAY-ter ow'f.
The children get up a little later.

Sie waschen sich, kämmen sich die Haare
Zee VAHSH'en zikh, KAME-en zikh dee HA-reh
They wash themselves, comb their hair

und ziehen sich schnell an.
oont TS'EE-hen zikh shnel ahn.
and get dressed quickly.

Dann setzen sie sich an den Tisch,
Dahn ZETS'en zee zikh ahn den tish,
Then, they sit down at the table

Achtung!
Tisch is in the accusative case because of the action implied to the table when one sits down at it.

um zu frühstücken.
oom ts'oo FRÜ-shtůk'en.
to eat breakfast.

Zum Frühstück
Ts'oom FRÜ-shtůk
For breakfast

essen sie Brötchen mit Butter und Marmelade
ESS'en zee BRERT-khen mit BOOT-ter oont MAR-meh-la-deh
they eat rolls with butter and marmalade

Essen — to eat
Essen is somewhat irregluar. Its key forms are *ich esse, er ißt, wir essen.*

und trinken Milchkaffee.
oont TRINK'en milkh-ka-FEH.
and drink coffee with milk.

Herr Schuster muß sich beeilen,
Hair SHOO-ster moos zikh beh-ILE'en,
Mr. Schuster must hurry

177

um pünktlich im Büro zu sein.
oom PUNKT-likh im bü-RO ts'oo zine.
to be at the office on time.

Die Kinder machen sich fertig für die Schule.
Dee KIN-der MAHKH'en zikh FEHR-tikh für dee SHOO-leh.
The children get themselves ready for school.

Frau Schuster sagt zu dem Jüngsten:
Fr'ow SHOO-ster zahkt ts'oo dem YÜNG-sten:
Mrs. Schuster says to the youngest:

„Mach' schnell, es wird spät."
„Mahkh shnel, ess veert shpayt."
"Hurry up, it is becoming late."

„Aber ich beeile mich doch," sagt er.
„AH-ber ikh beh-ILE-eh mikh dohkh," zahkt ehr.
"But I am already hurrying," he says.

„Ich bin schon fast fertig."
„Ikh bin shohn fahst FEHR-tikh."
"Soon I'll be almost ready."

Dann verabschieden sich alle von der Mutter
Dahn fehr-AHP-shee-den zikh AHL-leh fohn dehr MOO-ter
Then they all say good-bye to the mother

> **Die Übersetzung**
> *Sich verabschieden* can be translated as "to take leave of" or "to say goodbye to."

und gehen.
oont GAY'en.
and go.

Frau Schuster sieht sich im Spiegel an
Fr'ow SHOOS-ter zeet zikh im SHPEE-gel ahn
Mrs. Schuster looks at herself in the mirror

> **Sich ansehen — (sep. prefix)**
> *Sich ansehen* — "to look at oneself" — is a separable prefix verb. The separable prefix is separated here from the verb by the reflexive

pronoun as well as by the phrase "in the mirror" — *im Spiegel.*

und sagt sich: „Ich sehe müde aus,
oont zahkt zikh: „Ikh ZEH-heh MÜ-deh ow'ss,
and says to herself: "I look tired,

ich brauche noch etwas Schlaf —
ikh BROW-kheh nohkh ET-vahss sh'lahf —
I still need some sleep —

ich muß mich noch eine halbe Stunde hinlegen."
ikh mooss mikh nohkh INE-eh HAHL-beh SHTOON-deh
HIN-lay'ghen."
I must lie down for about a half hour."

Not always separable
Sich hinlegen, translated here as "lie down,"
literally means "to lay oneself down" — a
rather apt rendition. Remember that the separable prefix does not separate from the infinitive,
as shown here.

INSTANT CONVERSATION:
GOING TO A BUSINESS MEETING

— Wir müssen uns beeilen.
Veer MŮSS'en oonts beh-ILE'en.
We have to hurry up.

Wir wollen nicht zu spät zu der Konferenz kommen.
Veer VOHL'en nikht ts'oo shpayt ts'oo dehr kohn-fer-ENTS
KOHM'en.
We don't want to arrive late for the conference.

— Machen Sie sich keine Sorgen darüber;
MAHK'en zee zikh KINE-eh ZOR-ghen da-RŮ-ber;
Don't worry about it;

wir haben noch eine halbe Stunde Zeit.
veer HAHB'en nokh INE-eh HAHL-beh SHTOON-deh ts'ite.
we still have another half hour's time.

Schließlich wollen wir ja nicht zu früh kommen.
SHLEES-likh VOHL'en veer nikht ts'oo frů KOHM'en.
After all we certainly don't want to be early.

Wir wollen doch nicht übereifrig erscheinen.
Veer VOHL'en dohkh nikht Ů-be eye-frik ehr-shin'en.
We don't want to appear over anxious.

Übrigens — haben Sie alle Unterlagen dabei?
ŮB-ree-ghens — HAHB'en zee AHL-leh OONT-ehr-la-ghen da-BY?
Incidentally — Have you all the correspondence (and reports) at hand?

— Natürlich, hier sind die Unterlagen
Na-TUR-likh, here zint dee OONT-ehr-la-ghen
Of course, here are the correspondence (reports)

für den Vertrag.
fûr den fehr-TRAHK.
for the contract.

— Und der Vertrag selbst?
Oont dehr fehr-TRAHK selpst?
And what about the contract itself?

— Um Gottes Willen! Wo ist er?
Oom GOHT-tess VILL'en! Vo isst ehr?
For God's sake! Where is it?

— Beruhigen Sie sich,
Beh-ROO-eeg'gen zee zikh,
Calm yourself,

Reflexive verbs and the emotions
Other reflexive verbs include those relating to
emotional states, such as "to get excited" —
sich aufregen; "to calm down" — *sich beruhi-*
gen; "to hurry up" — *sich beeilen* and even
other mental activities such as "to remember" — *sich erinnern,* although, oddly, "to forget" — *vergessen* is not reflexive.

Sie haben ihn in ihrer eigenen Aktentasche.
Zee HAHB'en een in eer-er I-ghen-en AHK-ten-tahsh-eh.
you have it in your own briefcase.

— Oh ja —jetzt erinnere ich mich.
Oh ya — yetzt eh-RIN-ner-eh ikh mikh.
Oh yes — now I remember.

Warten Sie hier, ich hole uns ein Taxi.
VART'en zee here, ikh HO-leh oonts ine TAHK-see.
Wait here, I'll get us a taxi.

— Nicht nötig; sehen Sie,
Nikht NER-tikh; ZAY'en zee,
Not necessary; look,

da steht schon eines vor dem Eingang.
da shtay't shohn INE-ess for dem INE-gang.
there is one standing right by the entrance.

181

— Gott sei Dank!
Goht zy dahnk!
Thank God!

Also gehen wir jetzt! Aber schnell!
AHL-zo GAY'n veer yetzt AH-ber shnel!
So let's go now! But quickly!

— Aber regen Sie sich bitte nicht mehr auf!
AH-ber RAY-ghen zee zik BIT-teh nikht mehr ow'f!
But don't get excited again, please!

Und vor allen Dingen,
Oont for AH-len DING'en,
And above all,

werden Sie nicht nervös
VEHRD'en zee nikht ner-VERS
don't become nervous

während der Konferenz!
VEHR-ent dehr kohn-fehr-ENTS!
during the meeting!

The genitive after adverbs
Die Konferenz becomes *der Konferenz* because it is in the genitive case. This is because certain adverbs automatically take the genitive. These include *während* — "during," *wegen* — "on account of," and *anstatt* or *statt* — "instead of."

TEST YOUR GERMAN

Translate these sentences into German using reflexive verbs. Use the *Sie*-form instead of the *du*-form for numbers 5 through 10. Score 10 points for each correct translation. See answers below.

1. She is getting dressed. _____

2. Please, sit down at the table. _____

3. I must hurry. _____

4. The children are getting themselves ready for school. _____

5. Hurry up, it is getting late. (use
   du-form) _____

6. Comb your hair! (use *Sie* for
   6–10) _____

7. Calm yourself! _____

8. Do you remember? _____

9. Don't get excited! _____

10. Don't become nervous! _____

Answers: 1. Sie zieht sich an. 2. Bitte setzen Sie sich an den Tisch! 3. Ich muß mich beeilen. 4. Die Kinder machen sich fertig für Schule. 5. Mach schnell, es wird spät. 6. Kämmen Sie sich die Haare! 7. Beruhigen Sie sich! 8. Erinnern Sie sich? 9.Regen Sie sich nicht auf! 10. Werden Sie nicht nervös!

SCORE _____%

Remember, in German, an order is always followed by an exclamation mark.

step 17 HOW TO FORM THE FUTURE TENSE

Die Zukunft des Verbes
Dee TS'OO-koonft dess VEHR-bess
The future (tense) of the verb

ist nicht schwer zu bilden.
isst nikht shvehr ts'oo BILD'en.
is not difficult to construct.

Man benutzt *werden*
Mahn beh-NOOT'st VEHRD'en
One uses "to become"

zusamen mit dem Infinitiv
ts'oo-ZAHM-men mitt dem IN-fee-nee-teef
together with the infinitive

des nachfolgenden Verbes.
dess NAKH-fohl-gend'en VEHR-bess.
of the following verb.

Werden which you saw in Step 16 used as "to become" is used with its different forms in the present to form the future tense. The verb with which *werden* is used stays in the infinitive. Here is the future of "to go":

I will go — *Ich werde gehen*
You (familiar) will go — *du wirst gehen*
He, (she, it) will go — *er (sie, es) wird gehen*
we will go — *wir werden gehen*
you (familiar plural) will go — *ihr werdet gehen*
you (formal plural) (or "they") will go — *Sie (sie) werden gehen*

The table we have followed to show how the future is formed is the one we will use for new tenses in the following Steps, that is six verb forms, including *du* and *ihr*. The negative future "will not" or "won't" is formed by using *nicht* before the infinitive, as in, *Ich werde nicht gehen.*

Ich werde + Infinitiv

Morgen werde ich früh aufstehen.
MOR-ghen VEHR-deh ikh frů OW'F-shtay'en.
Tomorrow morning I will get up early.

Ich werde zum Arzt gehen.
Ikh VERH-deh ts'oom arts't GAY'en.
I will go to the doctor's.

Ich werde ihn um etwas gegen meinen Husten bitten.
Ikh VEHR-deh een oom ET-vahss GAY-ghen MY-nen HOO-sten BITT'en.
I will ask him for something for my cough.

Ich werde Sie vom Arzt aus anrufen.
Ikh VEHR-deh zee fohm ahrts't owss AHN-roof'en.
I will call you from the doctor's.

Dann werde ich Ihnen sagen,
Dahn VEHR-deh ikh EE-nen ZAHG'en,
I'll tell you then,

wann ich zurückkomme.
vahn ikh ts'oo-RŮK-ko-meh.
when I'll be back.

Was ist los? — (What's the matter?)
The regular word for the doctor is *der Arzt*, but when you speak to him you call him *Herr Doktor*, a title widely used in Germany for other professions as well. When consulting a doctor you will find the following phrases useful:

I have a headache. — *Ich habe Kopfschmerzen.*
I have a sore throat. — *Ich habe Halsschmerzen.*

> I feel dizzy. — *Mir ist schwindlig.*
> I have a stomach ache. — *Ich habe*
> *Magenschmerzen.*
> I have a pain here. — *Ich habe hier*
> *Schmerzen.*
> The prescription — *das Rezept.*
> A drugstore — *eine Apotheke.*

Possible things a doctor may say to you:

> You must stay in bed. — *Sie müssen im Bett*
> *bleiben.*
> Take this three times a day. — *Nehmen Sie*
> *das dreimal am Tag.*
> Come back in two days. — *Kommen Sie in*
> *zwei Tagen wieder.*
> Do you feel better? — *Geht es Ihnen besser?*

You will find specific parts of the body listed in the dictionary at the end of this book.

Er (sie, es) wird + Infinitiv

— Wann wird Kurt aus England ankommen?
Vahn veert Koort ow'ss EHNG-lahnt AHN-kohm'en?
When will Kurt arrive from England?

— Sein Flugzeug soll heute nachmittag um zwei Uhr landen.
Zine FLOOK-ts'oyk zoll HOY-teh NAKH-mit-tahkh oom ts'vy oor
LAHND'en.
His plane is supposed to land this afternoon at two o'clock.

— Aber sein Flugzeug hat Verspätung.
AH-ber zine FLOOK-ts'oig haht Vehr-SHPAY-toong.
But his plane is delayed.

Look for the final verb
Note how adverbial phrases are put in between the word that introduces the future and the following infinitive.

— Ich will mit ihm sprechen.
Ikh vill mit eem SHPREKH'en.
I want to speak with him.

Achtung!
Remember that *"will"* (from *wollen*) means
"want" or "wish" and not the English "will."

— Ich glaube nicht, daß er in die Stadt kommen wird.
Ikh GL'OW-beh nikht, dahss ehr in dee shtaht KOHM'en veert.
I don't think that he will come into town.

Er wird am Flughafen bleiben,
Ehr veert ahm FLOOK-ha-fen BLYB'en,
He'll stay at the airport

Inverted Order
In inverted order forms of *werden* follow the infinitive. This is true of the other auxiliary verbs such as *müssen, wollen,* etc. as you can see below.

weil er einen Anschlußflug nehmen muß.
vile ehr INE-en AHN-shlooss-flook NAYM'en mooss.
because he must take a connecting flight.

— Und wohin wird er dann fliegen?
Oont vo-HIN veert ehr dahn FLEEG'en?
And where will he fly then?

— Nach Österreich,
Nakh ERST-ehr-rykh,
To Austria,

wo er unsere Filiale besichtigen wird.
vo ehr OON-zeh-reh feel-YAHL-eh beh-ZIKH-teeg'en veert.
where he will inspect our branch offices.

Dann, wenn er Zeit hat,
Dahn, ven ehr ts'ite haht,
Then, if he has time,

will er die Leipziger Messe besuchen.
vill ehr dee LIPE-ts'eeg-er MESS-seh beh-ZOOKH'en.
he wants to visit the Leipzig fair.

— Ich fürchte, dann werde ich
Ihn FÜRKH-teh, dahn VEHR-deh ikh
I am afraid that then I won't

ihn leider nicht sehen können.
een LY-der nikht ZAY'en KERN'en.
be able to see him, unfortunately.

— Doch! Hören Sie—Sie können mit mir
Dokh! HER-ren Zee — Zee KERN'en mit meer
On the contrary! Listen — You can come with me

zum Flughafen kommen.
ts'oom FLOOK-ha-fen KOHM'en.
to the airport.

Es wird sicher eine Gelegenheit geben,
Ess veert ZIKH-er INE-eh geh-LAY-gen-hite GAYB'en,
There will surely be an opportunity

mit ihm zu sprechen.
mit eem ts'oo SHPREKH'en.
to speak with him.

Du wirst + infinitiv:

— Wirst du mich morgen anrufen?
Veerst doo mikh MOR-gen AHN-roof'en?
Will you call me tomorrow?

— Das wird leider kaum möglich sein,
Dahss veert LYE-der kow'm MERG-likh zine,
Unfortunately that will hardly be possible,

weil ich sehr früh wegfahren muß.
vile ihkh zehr frů wek-FAR'en mooss.
as I have to leave very early.

— Wann wirst du zurückkommen?
Vahn veerst doo ts'oo-RŮK-kohm'en?
When will you come back?

— Ich bin um sechs Uhr abends zurück.
Ihkh bin oom zeks oor ah-bents ts'oo-RŮK.
I'll be back at six o'clock in the evening.

The present to express the future
As we have seen in the beginning of Step 17, the future tense of a verb is formed by *werden* in combination with the infinitive of the verb you are using. But the future is often expressed, especially in everyday conversation, by the present tense of the verb when used with a word indicating a point in the future. English does almost the same thing with the present progressive:

Next summer I'm going to Berlin.
Nächsten Sommer fahre ich nach Berlin.

As German has no progressive mood the present is often used to indicate the future.

Ich rufe dich sofort an.
Ihkh ROO-feh dik zo-FORT ahn.
I'll call you right away.

Wirst du zu Hause sein?
Veerst doo ts'oo HOW-zeh zine?
Will you be at home?

More separable prefixes
Several more separable prefix verbs have just been introduced in this conversation — **an**ru-*fen*, **weg**fahren, and **zurück**kommen.

Wir (sie, sie) werden + infinitiv

Ein junger Mann:
Ine yoong-er mahn:
A young man:

— Glauben Sie, daß die Menschen eines Tages
GL'OWB'en zee, dahss dee MEN-shen INE-ness TA-guess
Do you believe that men one day

Vergnügungsreisen zum Mond machen werden?
fehr-GNÜ-goongs-ry-zen ts'oom mohnt MA'khen VEHRD'en?
will make pleasure trips to the moon?

189

The genitive
Eines Tages, which is in the genitive case, is translated as "one day." The German literally reads "of one day."

Ein alter Mann:
Ine AHL-ter mahn:
An old man:

— Ohne Zweifel — Die Astronauten werden bald
OH-neh TS'VYE-fel — dee ahs-tro-NOW-ten VEHRD'en bahlt
Without doubt — The astronauts will soon

oft und regelmäßig zum Mond fliegen,
oft oont RAY-gel-MAY-sikh ts'oom mohnt FLEEG'en,
frequently and regularly fly to the moon,

und gewöhnliche Touristen werden sicherlich bald folgen.
oont geh-VERN-likh-eh too-RIS-ten VEHRD'en ZIKH-ehr-likh bahlt FOLGH'en.
and ordinary tourists will surely follow soon.

— Glauben Sie, daß wir auch zu den Planeten reisen werden?
GL'OWB'en zee, dahss veer ow'kh ts'oo dehn plahn-NAY-ten RY-zen VEHRD'en?
Do you think that we will fly to the planets, too?

— Bestimmt, sobald Mondflüge zur Regel werden,
Beh-SHTIMT, zo-BAHLT MOHNT-flů-geh ts'oor RAY-gel VEHRD'en,
Of course, as soon as the moon flights become the rule,

werden auch die anderen Flüge möglich.
VEHRD'en ow'kh dee AHN-deh-ren FLŮ-geh MERG-likh.
the other flights will also become possible.

— Dann werden die Astronauten weitere Entfernungen
Dahn VEHRD'en dee ah-stro-NOW-ten VY-teh-reh ent-FEHR-noon-gen
Then the astronauts will be able to reach

erreichen können.
ehr-RYKH'en KERN'en.
farther distances.

Aber ich bezweifle, daß sie
AH-ber ikh beh-TS'VY-fleh, dahss zee
But I doubt that in the near future they will

die Sterne so bald erreichen werden.
dee SHTER-neh zo bahlt ehr-RYKH-en VEHRD'en.
reach the stars so soon.

— Vielleicht wird es eines Tages geschehen,
Feel-LYKHT veert ess INE-ness TA-gess geh-SHAY'en,
Maybe it will happen some day,

und Sie werden es sehen können,
oont zee VEHRD'en ess ZAY'en KERN'en,
and you will be able to see it,

aber ich werde es sicher nicht miterleben.
AH-ber ikh VEHR-deh ess ZIKH-er nikht mehr MIT-ehr-layb'en.
but I undoubtedly will not personally witness it.

Leben
Miterleben is an interesting example of how a verb can change its meaning through a prefix. Leben means "to live." The prefix -er makes it erleben — "to experience," while mit prefacing both of them gives the meaning of "to personally witness" or "to experience it with others."

INSTANT CONVERSATION:
PLANNING A TRIP TO GERMANY

MAGDA:

Im nächsten Monat werden Sie beide
Im NAYKH-sten MOH-naht VEHRD'en zee BY-deh
Next month you will both

nach Deutschland fahren, nicht wahr?
nakh DOYTCH-lahnt FAR'en, nikht vahr?
go to Germany, won't you?

LIESL:

Ja, aber wir werden nicht zusammen fliegen.
Ya, AH-ber veer VEHRD'en nikht ts'oo-ZAHM-men FLEEG'en.
Yes, but we won't be flying together.

Herbert wird zuerst nach Frankfurt fliegen,
HEHR-behrt veert ts'oo-EHRST nahkh FRAHNK-foort FLEEG'en,
Herbert will fly to Frankfurt first,

und ich werde ihm eine Woche später folgen.
oont ikh VEHRD'eh eem INE-eh VOKH-eh SHPAY-ter FOHLG'en.
and I will follow him a week later.

MAGDA:

Warum reisen Sie nicht zusammen?
Va-ROOM RYE'sen zee nikht ts'oo-ZA-men?
Why aren't you traveling together?

LIESL:

Weil er in Frankfurt viele Geschäftsbesuche erledigen will,
Vile ehr in FRAHNK-foort FEE-leh geh-SHEFTS-beh-zoo-kheh ehr-
                                                    LAY-deeg'en vill,
Because he wants to make many business calls in Frankfurt,

und ich langweile mich nicht gerne.
oont ikh LAHNG-vy-leh mikh nikht GERN-neh.
and I don't like being bored.

Gerne
Gern is an adverb which, combined with a verb means "to like" or "to dislike" according to whether it is used affirmatively or negatively is sometimes written with an optional final *-e*.

Lang + Weile
Langweilen "to be bored" is a combination of *lang* — "long" and *Weile* — "while," rather a good description of boredom.

MAGDA:
Das kann ich verstehen.
Dahss kahn ikh fehr-SHTAY'en.
That I can understand.

LIESL:
Wir wollen uns anschließend in Köln treffen
Veer VOHL'en oons AHN-shlees-send in kerln TREF'en
We want to meet in Cologne after that

und eine Rheinfahrt unternehmen.
oont INE-eh RINE-fart oon-ter-NAYM'en.
and take a trip on the Rhine.

MAGDA:
Vergessen Sie nicht,
Fehr-GESS-en zee nikht,
Don't forget to

ein paar gute Rheinweine zu probieren.
ine pahr GOO-teh RHINE-vine-eh ts'oo pro-BEER'en.
taste some of the good Rhine wines.

LIESL:
Ganz bestimmt nicht —
Gahnts beh-SHTIMMT nikht —
Definitely not —

193

Herbert hat schon seine Weinliste bereit!
HEHR-behrt haht shone ZINE-eh VINE-list-eh beh-RITE!
Herbert already has his wine list ready!

Dann werden wir in die Alpen fahren.
Dahn VEHRD'en veer in dee AHL-pen FAR'en.
Then we will go to the Alps.

MAGDA:
Das klingt gut — ich hoffe, Sie werden
Dahss klinkt goot — ikh HO-feh, zee VEHRD'en
That sounds good — I hope you will

dann auch die berühmten Königsschlösser
dahn ow'kh dee beh-RŮM-ten KERN-iks-shlers-sehr
then also visit the famous royal castles

in Bayern besuchen.
in BY-ern beh-ZOOKH'en.
in Bavaria.

LIESL:
Sie meinen die Schlösser des
Zee MINE-en dee SHLERS-sehr dess
You mean the castles of

> **"To mean" or "to say"**
> *Meinen* means "to mean" or "to say" depending on the context.

verrückten Königs, Ludwig von Bayern?
fehr-RŮK-ten KERN-iks, LOOD-vig fohn BY-ern?
the mad king, Ludwig of Bavaria?

MAGDA:
Ja — übrigens, mein Neffe arbeitet
Ya — Ů-bree-ghens, mine NEHF-feh AHR-by-tet
Yes — By the way, my nephew is working

im Schloß Neuschwanstein
im shlohss noy-SHVAHN-shtine
in the Neuschwanstein castle

194

als Fremdenführer.
ahls FREM-den-fů-rer.
as a tourist guide.

Er wird Ihnen sicher gerne
Ehr veert EE-nen ZIKH-er GEHR-neh
He definitely will be happy to

die Gegend zeigen.
dee GAY-ghent TSYG'en.
show you the surroundings.

LIESL:
Danke, würden Sie mir
DAHN-keh, VŮRD'en zee meer
Thanks, would you like to

seinen Namen geben?
ZINE-nen NA-men GAYB'en?
give me his name?

MAGDA:
Sicher — und welche anderen Städte
ZIKH-er — oont VEL-kheh AHN-deh-ren SHTAY-teh
Surely, and which other cities

wollen Sie besuchen?
VOHL'en zee beh-ZOOKH'en?
do you want to visit?

LIESL:
München natürlich, und Wien,
MŮN-khen nah-TŮR-likh, oont veen,
Munich, of course, and Vienna,

wo wir in die Staatsoper gehen wollen.
vo veer in dee SHTAHTS-oh-per GAY'en VOHL'en.
where we want to go to the State Opera.

Wir wollen auch nach Berlin fahren;
Veer VOHL'en ow'kh nahkh behr-LEEN FAR'en;
We also want to go to Berlin;

195

Herbert will die Berliner Mauer fotografieren —
HEHR-behrt vill dee behr-LEEN-er M'OW-er fo-toh-gra-FEER-en —
Herbert wants to take pictures of the Berlin Wall —

und, wenn er kann, Ost-Berlin besuchen.
oont, ven ehr kahn, OST-behr-LEEN beh-ZOOKH'en.
and if he can, to visit East Berlin.

MAGDA:
Während Sie in Deutschland sind,
VAY-rent zee in DOYTCH-lahnt zint,
While you are in Germany,

müssen Sie unbedingt auch ein paar
MÜSS-en zee OON-beh-dinkt ow'kh ine pahr
you definitely have to

alte Städte besuchen, so wie
AHL-teh SHTAY-teh beh-ZOOKH'en, zo vee
visit some old towns, such as

Rothenburg und Nördlingen.
RO-ten-boork oont NERRD-ling-en.
Rothenburg and Nördlingen.

Dann werden Sie
Dahn VEHRD'en zee
Then you will get

einen unvergeßlichen Eindruck
INE-en oon-fehr-GESS-lick-hen INE-drook
an unforgettable impression

vom alten Deutschland bekommen.
fohm AHL-ten DOYTSH-lahnt beh-KOHM'en.
of old Germany.

LIESL:
Ein guter Vorschlag!
Ine GOO-ter FOR-shlahk!
An excellent suggestion!

Danke vielmals!
DAHN-keh FEEL-mahls!
Thanks very much!

TEST YOUR GERMAN

Translate the first 5 sentences into German and the second five sentences into English. Score 10 points for each correct answer. See answers below.

1. When will she be here? _____

2. We will go to the doctor's. _____

3. I will call you at 6 o'clock. _____

4. I'll see you later. _____

5. When will the plane land? _____

6. Ich werde ihn nicht sehen können. _____

7. Wirst du mich morgen nachmittag anrufen? _____

8. Vielleicht wird es eines Tages geschehen. _____

9. Ich werde ihr eine Woche später folgen. _____

10. Wir werden uns in Köln treffen. _____

SCORE _____%

197

HOW TO USE THE
PAST TENSE
WITH HABEN

Wenn man durch eine deutsche Stadt geht,
Venn mahn doorkh INE-eh DOYT-cheh shtaht gay't,
When walking through a German town,

kann man viele Schilder mit Aufschriften sehen,
kahn mahn FEEL-eh SHIL-der mit OWF-schrift-ten ZAY'en,
one can see many signs with notices,

die das Partizip Perfekt benutzen,
dee dahss par-tee-TS'EEP PER-fekt beh-NOOTS'en,
that use the Past Participle,

wie zum Beispiel die folgenden:
vee ts'oom BY-shpeel dee FOL-gend'en:
as for example the following ones:

SONNTAGS GESCHLOSSEN!
ZONN-tahks gheh-SHLOSS'en!
CLOSED ON SUNDAYS!

AUSVERKAUFT!
OWSS-fehr-kow'ft!
SOLD OUT!

EINTRITT VERBOTEN!
INE-tritt fehr-BOHT'en!
ENTRANCE FORBIDDEN!

RAUCHEN VERBOTEN!
R'OWKH'en fehr-BOHT'en!
SMOKING FORBIDDEN!

MINDERJÄHRIGE NICHT ZUGELASSEN!
Min-der-YAY-ree-geh nikht TS'OO-geh-lahss'en!
MINORS NOT ADMITTED!

The past participle

The past participle corresponds to the English past participle of any verb such as "closed," "opened," "sold," "forbidden," "taken," "given," "seen," etc. Most verbs add ge- before the verb and end in -t or -en. Some verbs do not add a prefix.

INFINITIVE PAST PARTICIPLE

sprechen	gesprochen	spoken
sagen	gesagt	said
schreiben	geschrieben	written
haben	gehabt	had
verlieren	verloren	lost
geben	gegeben	given
sehen	gesehen	seen
finden	gefunden	found
wissen	gewußt	known
hören	gehört	heard
essen	gegessen	eaten
trinken	getrunken	drunk
wünschen	gewünscht	wished
machen	gemacht	made, done
tun	getan	done
verbieten	verboten	forbidden
schließen	geschlossen	closed
öffnen	geöffnet	opened
wohnen	gewohnt	lived
verstehen	verstanden	understood
kaufen	gekauft	bought

Man benutzt dieses Partizip,
Mahn beh-NOOT'ST DEE-zess par-tee-TS'EEP,
One uses this participle,

um die Vergangenheit zu bilden.
oom dee fehr-GAHNG-en-hite ts'oo BILD'en.
to form the past tense.

The past tense and how to form it

To form the past tense simply combine the present tense of haben with the past participle. Most verbs use haben to form the past tense

199

but some use *sein* instead, as you will see in step 19.

ich habe gesehen — I have seen, I saw
du hast gesehen — you (fam. sing.) have seen, saw
er (sie, es) hat gesehen — he (she, it) has seen, saw
wir haben gesehen — we have seen, saw
ihr habt gesehen — you (fam. pl.) have seen, saw
Sie (sie) haben gesehen — You (they) have seen, saw

Beispiele für die Vergangenheit
BY-shpee-leh für dee fehr-GANG'en-hite
Examples of the past tense

ich — Sie

— Verzeihung! Haben Sie zufällig
Fehr-TS'Y-oong! HAHB'en zee TS'OO-fell-ikh
Excuse me! Have you by chance

hier einen Fotoapparat gefunden?
here INE-en FO-toh-ah-pa-raht geh-FOOND'en?
found a camera here?

Ich glaube, ich habe meinen hier liegengelassen.
Ikh GL'OW-beh, ikh HA-beh MINE-en here-LEE-ghen-
                                   geh-LAHSS'en.
I believe I left mine lying here.

Gestern habe ich hier eine Rolle Farbfilm gekauft.
GHESS-tern HA-beh ikh here INE-eh ROLE-leh FARP-film
                                   geh-KOW'FT.
Yesterday I bought a role of color film here.

— Nein, ich habe leider keinen gesehen.
Nine, ikh HA-beh LY-der KINE-en geh-ZAY'en.
No, I haven't seen one, unfortunately.

Was für einen Apparat haben Sie verloren?
VAHSS für INE-en ah-pa-RAHT HAHB'en zee fehr-LOR'en?
What kind of camera have you lost?

— Ich habe meine Leica verloren.
Ikh HA-beh MINE-eh LY-ka fehr-LOR'en.
I have lost my Leica.

— Einen Moment, bitte!
INE-en mo-MENT, BIT-teh!
One moment, please!

Kurt, haben Sie nicht gestern von einem
Koort, HAHB'en zee nikht GUESS-tern fohn INE-em
Kurt, didn't you talk

Fotoapparat gesprochen?
FO-toh-ah-pa-raht geh-SHPROHKH'en?
about a camera yesterday?

Was haben Sie damit gemacht?
Vahss HAHB'en zee DA-mitt geh-MAHKHT?
What have you done with it?

— Ich habe ihn unter den Ladentisch gelegt.
Ikh HA-beh een OON-ter dehn LA-den-tish geh-LAYKT.
I put it under the counter.

Hier ist er. Ist das Ihrer?
Here isst ehr. Isst dahss EER-er?
Here it is. Is this yours?

Wir —

— Was haben Sie schon von unserer Stadt gesehen?
Vahss HAHB'en zee shohn fohn OON-zeh-rer Shtat geh-ZAY'en?
What have you already seen of our town?

As you explore around town or in stores you will note the following important signs or instructions, in addition to the signs using the past participle given on page 198.

ACHTUNG GEFAHR — ATTENTION, DANGER
AUSKUNFT — INFORMATION
DAMEN — LADIES
HERREN — GENTLEMEN
BESETZT — OCCUPIED
EINGANG — ENTRANCE

AUSGANG — EXIT
VORSICHT — CAUTION
DREHEN — TURN
ZIEHEN — PULL
DRÜCKEN — PUSH
AUFHALTEN — STOP
KEIN EINTRITT — NO ADMITTANCE

— Wir haben schon viele Kirchen gesehen
Veer HAHB'en shohn FEEL-eh KEER-khen geh-ZAY'en
We have already seen many churches

und haben die Altstadt und
oont HAHB'en dee AHLT-shtat oont
and have visited the old part of town and

das Schloß besichtigt.
dahss shlohss beh-ZIKH-tikt.
the castle.

— Und was haben Sie abends gemacht?
Oont vahss HAHB'en zee AH-bents geh-MAHKT?
And what have you been doing at night?

A choice of translation
The past tense we are now studying can be
translated by all three English meanings:

Was haben Sie kürzlich gemacht? — "What
have you done recently?" "What have you
been doing recently?" "What did you do
recently?"

— Nicht sehr viel . . .
Nikht zehr feel . . .
Not very much . . .

Wir haben uns ein Konzert angehört und ein Theaterstück gesehen.
**Veer HAHB'en oonts ine kohn-TSERT AHN-geh-hert oont ine
tay-AH-ter-shtŭk geh-ZAY'en.**
We have heard a concert and seen a play.

Dann haben wir einen Spaziergang
Dahn HAHB'en veer INE-en shpa-TS'EER-gahng
Then we took a walk

auf der Promenade am See gemacht
owf dehr pro-meh-NA-deh ahm zay geh-MAHKHT
along the promenade by the lake,

> **But it's still water**
> The meaning of *See* changes according to gender:
>
> *der See* — the lake
> *die See* — the sea

und haben ein sehr schönes Feuerwerk gesehen.
oont HAHB'en ine zair SHER-ness FOY-er-vairk geh-ZAY'en.
and saw some very beautiful fireworks.

> **Fireworks**
> *Das Feuerwerk* is another example of a word that is singular in German and plural in English.

— Und haben Sie auch schon eins von
Oont HAHB'en zee ow'kh shohn ine'ts fohn
And have you already visited one

unseren neuen Nachtlokalen besucht?
OON-zeh-ren NOY-en NAHKT-lo-ka-len beh-ZOOKHT?
of our new night clubs?

— Nein, wir haben bisher noch keins entdeckt.
Nine, veer HAHB'en biss-HEHR nokh KINE'ts ent-DEKT.
No, we haven't discovered any so far.

— Aber Sie dürfen keinesfalls wegfahren,
AH-ber zee DÜRF'en KINE-ess-fahls VEK-far'en,
But under no circumstances must you leave

ohne den Rialto Club gesehen zu haben!
OH-neh dehn ree-AHL-toh kloop geh-ZAY'en ts'oo HAHB'en!
without having seen the Rialto Club!

Ich werde Sie persönlich dort hinführen.
Ikh VEHR-deh zee per-ZERN-likh dort HIN-fûr'en.
I will take you there personally.

Er — sie — es

— Hat jemand angerufen?
Haht yay-mahnt AHN-geh-roof'en?
Has anyone called?

— Ja, Frau Siebert hat telefoniert.
Yah, fr'ow ZEE-behrt haht teh-leh-fo-NEERT.
Yes, Mrs. Siebert telephoned.

— Was hat sie gesagt?
Vahss haht zee geh-ZAHKT?
What did she say?

Hat sie irgendeine Nachricht hinterlassen?
Haht zee EER-ghent ine-eh NAHKH-rikht hin-ter-LAHSS'en?
Did she leave any message?

— Ja, sie hat mir ihre Nummer gegeben.
Ya, zee haht meer EER-eh NOOM-mer ghe-GAYB'en.
Yes, she has given me her number.

Ich habe sie auf diesem Zettel aufgeschrieben.
Ikh HA-beh zee owf DEE-zem TSET-tel owf-ghe-shreeb'en.
I wrote it down on this piece of paper.

Du — Ihr

— Sagt mal, Kinder, habt ihr heute gut
Sahgt mahl, KIN-der, hahbt eer HOY-teh goot
Tell me then, children, have you paid

aufgepaßt in der Schule?
OW'F-geh-pahst in dehr SHOO-leh?
attention today in school?

Hans, hast du heute mit den anderen
Hahns, hahst doo HOY-teh mitt dehn AHN-dehr'en
Hans, have you played football today

Jungen Fußball gespielt?
YOONG-en FOOSS-bahl geh-SHPEELT?
with the other boys?

Watch for the last word
As the past participle usually comes at the end
of a German sentence the word order varies
considerably from English and sometimes you
have to wait for the end of a sentence to find
the meaning. This is a peculiarity of German
which takes care of all subordinate phrases and
then caps the sentence with its principal
meaning.

Monika, hast du deine Brote
MO-nee-ka, hahst doo DINE-eh BROH-teh
Monika, have you eaten

alle aufgegessen?
AHL-leh OW'F-geh-gess'en?
all of your sandwiches?

— Ja, Mutti, ich habe alles aufgegessen.
Ya, MOO-tee, ikh HA-beh AHL-less OW'F-geh-gess'en.
Yes, mother, I have eaten them all up.

— Sie lügt, Mutti, sie hat die Tauben
Zee lükt, MOO-tee, zee haht dee T'OW-ben
She is lying, mother, she fed the pigeons

damit gefüttert.
da-MIT geh-FÜT-tert.
with them.

— Hans, du Lügner, du hast ja gar nichts
Hahns, doo LÜG-ner, doo hahst ya ga nikhts
Hans, you liar, you didn't see

gesehen, denn du hast die ganze Zeit
geh-ZAY'en, denn doo hahst dee GAHN-ts'eh ts'ite
anything, because you

Fußball gespielt.
FOOSS-bahl geh-SHPEELT.
played football the whole time.

205

— Kinder, ich sehe, ihr habt
KIN-der, ikh ZAY-eh, eer hahpt
Children, I see that

euch wieder gestritten.
oykh VEE-der geh-SHTRITT'en.
you've been quarreling again.

INSTANT CONVERSATION:
WHAT HAPPENED AT THE OFFICE

— Guten Morgen, Herr Generaldirektor!
GOO-ten MOR-ghen, hair gay-nay-RAHL-dee-rek-tohr!
Good morning, (Mr.) General Manager!

Use of titles
Titles are more generally used (and appreciated) in German conversation than in English.

Haben Sie einen guten Urlaub verbracht?
HAHB'en zee INE-en GOO-ten OOR-l'owp fehr-BRAHKHT?
Did you spend a good vacation?

— Ganz angenehm, danke.
Gahnts AHN-geh-nehm, DAHN-keh.
Quite pleasant, thanks.

Und was gibt's hier Neues?
Oont vahss gipts here NOY-ess?
And what is new here?

— Herr Wagner hat sechs Wagen
Hehr Vahg-ner haht zeks VA-gen
Mr. Wagner has sold six cars

verkauft während Ihrer Abwesenheit.
fair-KOW'FT VAY-rent EER-er AHP-veh-zen-hite.
during your absence.

— Ausgezeichnet! Und was haben die anderen
Ow'ss-geh-TS'YKH-net! Oont vahss HAHB'en dee AHN-der'en
Excellent! And what have the other

Verkäufer gemacht?
Fehr-KOY-fehr geh-MAHKT?
salesmen done?

— Sie haben vier von den neuen Sportmodellen,
Zee HAHB'en feer fohn den NOY-en SHPORT-mo-dehl-len,
They have sold four of our new sports models,

zwei Lastwagen and zehn
ts'vye LAHST-vaghen oont ts'ayn
two trucks and ten

Motorräder verkauft.
Mo-TOHR-ray-dehr fehr-KOW'FT.
motor bikes.

— Sehr gut! Und haben die Verkäufer
Zehr goot! oont HAHB'en dee fehr-KOY-fehr
Very good! And have the salesmen

alle ihre Provision erhalten?
AHL-leh EE-reh pro-veez-YOHN ehr-HAHLT-en?
all received their commission?

— Jawohl, Herr Direktor.
Ya-VOHL, hehr dee-REK-tohr.
Certainly, Sir.

— Großartig! Ich sehe, daß Sie keine Zeit
GROHSS-ar-tikh! Ikh ZAY-eh, dahss zee KINE-eh ts'ite
Splendid! I see that you have not

vertan haben.
fehr-TAHN HAHB'en.
wasted any time.

— Allerdings! Ich habe jeden Abend bis sieben
AHL-ler-dinks! Ikh HA-beh YAY-den AH-bent biss ZEE-ben
That's for certain! I have worked every evening

Uhr gearbeitet, um alles zu erledigen.
oor geh-AHR-bite-et, oom AHL-less ts'oo ehr-LAY-deeg'en.
until seven o'clock, in order to get everything done.

— Und hat Ilse Ihnen dabei geholfen?
Oont haht ILL-zeh EE-nen da-BY geh-HOL-fen?
And has Ilse been helping you with it?

— Leider nicht, sie hat drei Tage nicht
LY-dehr nikht, zee haht dry TA-geh nikht
Unfortunately not, she has not

gearbeitet wegen einer Erkältung.
geh-AR-bite-tet VAY-ghen ine-er ehr-KAYL-toong.
worked for three days because of a cold.

> **Vergessen Sie nicht**
> *Wegen* — "on account of" or "because of" is
> another preposition that always takes the
> genitive.

— Und was hat die neue Empfangsdame gemacht?
Oont vahs haht dee NOY-eh emp-FAHNKS-da-meh geh-MAHKT?
And what has the new receptionist been doing?

— Sie hat sehr wenig gearbeitet.
Zee haht zehr VAY-nikh geh-AR-bite-et.
She has done very little work.

— Sie hat die meiste Zeit am Telefon verbracht.
Zee haht dee MY-steh ts'ite ahm teh-leh-FON fehr-BRAHKHT.
She has spent most of the time on the telephone.

— So! Übrigens, hat irgend jemand für mich
Zo! UH-bree-ghens, haht IR-ghent YAY-mahnt für mikh
Is that so! By the way, has anyone

> **Irgend and its combinations**
> The prefix *irgend* — "any" or "some" — com-
> bines in a variety of other words:
> *irgend jemand* — somebody or anybody
> *irgendeiner* — someone or anyone
> *irgend etwas* — something or anything
> *irgendeinmal* — anytime or sometime
> *irgendwie* — somehow or anyhow
> *irgendwo* — somewhere or anywhere

angerufen?
AHN-geh-roof'en?
called me?

— Ich habe alles aufgeschrieben.
Ikh HA-beh AHL-less OW'F-geh-shreeb'en.
I have written everything down.

Ein Fräulein von Wunderlich hat
Ine FROY-line fohn VOON-dehr-likh haht
A Miss von Wunderlich has

ein paarmal angerufen.
ine PAHR-mahl AHN-geh-roof'en.
called a couple of times.

Aber sie hat keine Telefonnummer
AH-behr zee haht KINE-eh TEH-leh-fohn-noom-mehr
But she has left no

hinterlassen.
hin-ter-LAHSS'en.
telephone number.

— Ah ja! Ich glaube, ich weiß, wer das ist.
Ah ya! ikh GL'OW-beh ikh vice vehr dahss isst.
Oh yes! I think I know who that is.

Wo haben Sie meine Anrufe hingelegt?
Vo HA-ben zee mine-eh AHN-roof-eh HIN-geh-laykt?
Where have you put my calls?

— In Ihre Schreibtischschublade.
In EE-reh SHRYP-tish-shoop-la-deh.
In your desk drawer.

Hier sind die Schlüssel.
Here zint dee SHLÜS-sel.
Here are the keys.

— Danke! Sie haben prima gearbeitet!
Dahn-keh! zee HAHB'en PREE-ma geh-AHR-bite-et!
Thanks! You've done a great job!

Dabei fällt mir ein . . .
DA-by failt meer ine . . .
That reminds me . . .

ich will Ihnen die Gehaltserhöhung geben,
ikh vill EE-nen dee geh-HAHLTS-ehr-her-oong GAYB'en,
I want to give you that salary increase,

von der wir schon gesprochen haben.
fohn dehr veer shohn geh-SHPROKH'en HAHB'en.
which we have already discussed.

— Wirklich? . . . Vielen Dank, Herr Generaldirektor!
VEERK-likh? . . . FEEL-len dahnk, hair gay-nay-RAHL-dee-rek-tor!
Really? . . . Many thanks, (Mr.) General Manager!

TEST YOUR GERMAN

Match these signs, Score 5 points for each correct match. See answers on following page.

1. Sonntags geschlossen	A. Smoking forbidden
2. Ausverkauft	B. No entrance
3. Besetzt	C. Closed on Sundays
4. Vorsicht	D. Information
5. Eintritt verboten	E. Caution
6. Rauchen verboten	F. Exit
7. Eingang	G. Occupied
8. Achtung Gefahr	H. Sold out
9. Auskunft	I. Entrance
10. Ausgang	J. Attention — Danger

Translate these sentences in the past tense into German. Score 5 points for each correct translation. See answers on following page.

11. Have you found a camera? _____

12. I left it (mas.) here. _____

13. No, I haven't seen one. _____

14. What did you do? _____

15. What did you see yesterday? _____

16. We took a walk. _____

17. Who called? _____

18. What did he say? _____

19. We heard a concert. _____

20. We saw a play. _____

Answers: 1-C; 2-H; 3-G; 4-E; 5-B; 6-A; 7-I; 8-J; 9-D; 10-F
11. Haben Sie einen Fotoapparat gefunden? 12. Ich habe ihn hier liegengelassen. 13. Nein, ich habe keinen gesehen. 14. Was haben Sie gemacht? 15. Was haben Sie gestern gesehen? 16. Wir haben einen Spaziergang gemacht. 17. Wer hat angerufen? 18. Was hat er gesagt?
19. Wir haben ein Konzert gehört. 20. Wir haben ein Theaterstück
gesehen.

SCORE ____%

step 19

HOW TO FORM THE PAST TENSE WITH *SEIN*

Die Zeitwörter der Bewegung
Dee TS'ITE-verr-ter dehr beh-VAY-goong
The verbs of movement

benutzen das Hilfzeitwort *sein*
beh-NOOTS'en dahss HILFS-ts'ite-vohrt *sein*
use the auxiliary verb "to be"

für die Vergangenheit.
für dee fehr-GAHNG-en-hite.
for the past tense.

Zum Beispiel:
Ts'oom BY-shpeel:
For example:

— Sind Sie vorher schon einmal hier
   Zint zee FOR-hehr shohn INE-mahl here
   Have you already

   in Deutschland gewesen?
   in DOYTCH-lahnt geh-VAYZ'en?
   been here in Germany before?

Verbs that form the past tense with "sein."
In Step 18 we saw how *haben* is used to form the past while now in step 19 we see verbs that form the past by combining their past participle with the present tense of *sein*. *Haben, sein,* and *werden* are auxiliary verbs — that is, in addition to their basic meanings they are also used to change the tense of other verbs. Most of the verbs that use *sein* for the past and other compound tenses are verbs that denote action "to" or "from" a place or staying at a place. The verb *sein* itself uses *sein* as its own auxiliary.

— Ja, ich bin vor fünf Jahren
Ya, ikh bin fohr fünf YA-ren
Yes, I was here once

einmal hier gewesen.
INE-mahl here geh-VAYZ'en
five years ago.

— Wie sind Sie diesmal gereist?
Vee zint zee DEES-mahl geh-RY'st?
How did you travel this time?

— Diesmal bin ich mit dem Flugzeug gekommen.
DEES-mahl bin ikh mitt dehm FLOOK-ts'oyk geh-KOHM'en.
This time I came by plane.

Das letzte Mal bin ich mit dem Schiff gefahren.
Dahss LEHTS-teh mahl bin ikh mitt dehm Shiff geh-FAR'en.
Last time I travelled by boat.

Erzählen sie mir ein bißchen über Ihren Flug.
Ehr-TS'AYL'en zee meer ine BISS-yen Ü-ber EER-en flook.
Tell me a bit about your flight.

Ist alles gut gegangen?
Isst AHL-less goot geh-GAHNG'en?
Did everything go well?

— Es ist sehr gut gegangen —
Ess isst zehr goot geh-GAHNG'en —
It went very well —

schnell und bequem.
shnel oont bek-VAYM.
fast and comfortable.

— Wann sind Sie von Amerika abgeflogen?
Vahn zint zee fohn ah-MAY-ree-ka AHP-geh-flohg'en?
When did you take off from America?

— Wir sind um zehn Uhr abends abgeflogen
Veer zint oom ts'ayn oor AH-bents AHP-geh-flohg'en
We left at ten o'clock at night

und sind um zehn Uhr morgens
oont zint oom ts'ayn oor MOR-ghens
and arrived at ten o'clock in the morning

in Frankfurt angekommen.
in FRAHNK-foort AHN-geh-kohm'en.
in Frankfurt.

— Ist Ihre Frau auch mitgekommen,
Isst EER-eh fr'ow owkh MIT-geh-kohm'en,
Did your wife come also,

oder ist sie in Amerika geblieben?
OH-der isst zee in ah-MAY-ree-ka geh-BLEEB'en?
or did she stay in America?

Other less-evident verbs of motion

At the beginning of this Step you read that verbs of motion form the past tense with *sein* instead of *haben*. This means that verbs meaning "to travel," "to go," "to come," "to arrive," implying physical motion to or from a place, are in this category. You may ask why *bleiben* ("to remain") is in this category, as it seems to imply a lack of motion. It is in this group because it is still connected with coming or going. Two other important verbs connected, in a general sense, with coming or going are also conjugated with *sein* "to be born" and "to die." "Beethoven was born in Bonn and died in Vienna." *Beethoven ist in Bonn geboren und ist in Wien gestorben.* The auxiliary verb *werden* — "to become" also combines with *sein* to form the past.

— Sie ist mitgekommen, aber sie
Zee isst MIT-geh-kohm'en, AH-ber zee
She came along, but she

hat ein bißchen Angst gehabt, weil
haht ine BISS-yen ahngst geh-HAHBT, vile
was a bit worried since

sie noch nie vorher geflogen ist.
zee nokh nee FOR-her geh-FLOGH'en isst.
she has never flown before.

Aber nach einer Weile ist es
AH-ber nakh INE-er VILE-eh isst ess
But after a while she

ihr besser gegangen, und schließlich
eer BESS-er geh-GAHNG'en, oont SHLEESS-likh
felt better, and finally

ist sie begeistert gewesen.
isst zee beh-GICE-tert geh-VAYS'en.
she became enthusiastic.

Verben für sportliche Betätigungen
FEHR-ben fur SHPORT-lick-heh-TAY-tih-goong-en
Verbs for sports activities

gebrauchen auch *sein*
geh-BROWKH'en ow'kh *sein*
also use *"to be"*

für die Vergangenheit:
für dee fehr-GAHNG-en-hite:
for the past tense:

Verbs pertaining to sports
Verbs pertaining to sports such as "to run" —
laufen, "to jump" — *springen,* "to swim" —
schwimmen, "to ski" — *Ski laufen,* "to
skate" — *Schlittschuh laufen,* form their past
with *sein* because they indicate action to and
from a given point. *Spielen* — "to play" (a
game or a musical instrument) uses *haben.*

— Was haben Sie
Vahss HAHB'en zee
What have you been doing (or *done*)

hier in Garmisch gemacht?
here in GAR-mish geh-MAHKT?
here in Garmisch?

217

No progressive mood
The same past tense is used to translate either
"What have you done?" or "What have you
been doing?" as the progressive mood is not
used in German as in English.

— Oh, wir sind viel spazierengegangen
Oh, veer zint veel shpa-TS'EER'en geh-GAHNG'en
Oh, we have gone for lots of walks,

und sind schwimmen gegangen
oont zint SHVIM-men geh-GAHNG'en
and have gone swimming

im geheizten Schwimmbad des Hotels.
imm geh-HITES-ten SHVIM-baht dess ho-TELS.
in the heated pool of the hotel.

Aber leider sind wir auch
AH-ber LY-der zint veer ow'kh
But unfortunately we also

Skilaufen gegangen.
SHEE-LOW'F-en geh-GAHNG'en.
went skiing.

— Aber warum „leider"?
AH-ber va-ROOM LY-der?
But why "unfortunately"?

— Weil Else zu schnell den Berg
Vile el-zeh ts'oo shnel dehn behrg
Because Else skied too fast

hinabgefahren ist
hin-AHP-geh-far'en isst
down the mountain,

The importance of prefixes
In the verb **hinab**gefahren we have two adverbial prefixes attached to *fahren* — "to travel."
Abfahren means "to leave" or "to take off,"
while **hinab**gefahren gives the concept of taking
off in a downward direction, the exact verb to

describe Else's action. As you read more German you will notice that you can grasp the meaning of longer verbs by breaking them up into their component parts. Some of the more important separable prefixes include:

ab — away from, down from
zu — to
auf — up, on
unter — under
über — over
gegen — against

Occasionally these prepositions are prefixed by *hin* (corresponding in meaning to the old English "thither" or "thence"). When *hin* is combined with the above separable prefixes it intensifies the meaning or direction:

hinüber — over (to) there, across
hinab — down (to) there, downwards
hinzu — to there, toward
hinauf — up (to) there, upward
hinunter — down (to) there, downwards

und dabei gefallen ist
oont da-BY geh-FAHL'en isst
and in doing so she fell,

und sich leider das Bein gebrochen hat.
oont zikh LYE-der dahss bine geh-BROHK-en haht.
and unfortunately she broke her leg.

— Ach, das tut mir aber leid!
Akh, dahss toot meer AH-ber lite!
Oh, I am so sorry!

So ein Pech!
Zo ine pekh!
Such bad luck!

— Sie ist noch im Krankenhaus,
Zee isst nokh im KRAHNK-en-house,
She is still in the hospital,

aber wird heute oder morgen entlassen.
AH-ber veerd HOY-teh OH-der MOR-ghen ent-LAHSS'en.
but is being released today or tomorrow.

The Passive
The present tense of *werden* combined with the past participle forms the present passive. Observe the following:

They are seen everywhere together. —
Sie werden überall zusammen gesehen.

(See the following pages for additional examples of the passive.)

Das Passiv
Dahss Pahs-SEEF
The passive

Man bildet das Passiv mit *werden*
Mahn BILL-det dahss pahs-SEEF mit *WERDEN*
The passive voice is formed with "to become"

und dem Partizip Perfekt,
oont dehm par-tee-TS'EEP pehr-FEKT,
and the past participle,

z.B.:
ts'oom by-shpeel:
for example:

z.B.
Zum Beispiel (for example) is abbreviated to *z.B.*, a combination you will constantly encounter when reading German newspapers or books.

Deutsch wird in Deutschland,
Doytch veert in DOYTCH-lahnt,
German is spoken in Germany,

Names of Countries
The names of countries are mostly neuter and, to denote "to" or "in," the definite article is not used. Some names of countries:

Deutschland	Germany
Frankreich	France

Österreich	Austria
England	England
Polen	Poland
Italien	Italy
Ungarn	Hungary
Amerika	America
Rußland	Russia
Kanada	Canada
Australien	Australia
Spanien	Spain
Griechenland	Greece

"Switzerland," "Czechoslovakia," and "Turkey" keep the article (die Schweiz, die Tschechoslowakei, die Türkei) as do compound names: "The United States" — die Vereinigten Staaten, "The Soviet Union" — die Sowjet Union. The two parts of Germany also retain the definitive article. "West Germany" — die Bundesrepublik Deutschland, and "East Germany" — die Deutsche Demokratische Republik.

Österreich und in
ERST-air-rykh oont in
Austria, and in

der Schweiz gesprochen.
dehr Shvy'ts geh-SHPROKH'en.
Switzerland.

Es wird auch in einigen Teilen
Ess veert ow'kh in INE-ee-gen TY-len
It is also used in some parts

Mitteleuropas benützt, sowie auch
MIT-tell-oy-RO-pahss beh-NÜTST so-VEE ow'kh
of Central Europe, as well

an anderen Orten, wo deutschsprachige
an AHN-deh-ren OHR-ten, voh DOYTCH-SHPRA-kee-geh
in other places where German-speaking

Menschen wohnen.
MEN-shen VOHN'en.
people live.

Außerdem wird Deutsch in den meisten Ländern studiert,
OWSS-er-dem veert Doytch in dehn MY-sten LEHN-dern
                                    shtoo-DEERT,
Moreover, German is studied in most countries,

wegen seiner Bedeutung
VAY-gen ZINE-er beh-DOY-toong
because of its significance

für die Wissenschaften, wie z.B. die Psychologie,
für dee VISS-sen-shahff-ten, vee ts'm BY-shpeel dee
                                    psû-kho-lo-GEE,
in the sciences, for example psychology,

Medizin, Physik, Mathematik,
May-dee-TS'EEN, fû-ZEEK, ma-tay-may-TEEK,
medicine, physics, mathematics,

sowie Raketenbau und Raumforschung.
zo-VEE ra-KAY-ten-b'ow oont ROWM-for-shoong.
as well as rocket construction and space exploration.

Die deutsche Sprache wird auch oft
Dee DOYTCH-eh SHPRA-kheh veert ow'kh oft
The German language is also often needed

für das Studium der Musik,
für dahss SHTOO-dee-oom dehr moo-ZEEK,
for the study of music,

der Kunstgeschichte und Philosophie benötigt.
dehr KOONST-geh-shikh-teh oont fee-lo-zo-FEE beh-NER-tikt.
art history and philosophy.

INSTANT CONVERSATION: WHAT HAPPENED AT THE PARTY

— Haben Sie sich gut unterhalten
HAHB'en zee zikh goot oon-ter-HAHLT'en
Did you have a good time

> **As you will hear them**
> In the ensuing conversation verbs that form the past tense with *haben* are mixed with those that form the past with *sein* so you can become accustomed to hearing them in the same conversation.

gestern abend?
GUEST-ern AH-bent?
last night?

— Na, es geht . . . ich bin mit
Na, ess gayt . . . ikh bin mit
Well, more or less . . . I went out

Marion ausgegangen.
Marion OWSS-geh-gahng'en.
with Marion.

— Sie scheinen nicht sehr begeistert,
Zee SHY'nen nikht zair beh-GYST-ert,
You don't sound very enthusiastic,

was ist geschehen?
vahss isst geh-SHAY'en?
what happened?

> **Was geschieht?**
> *Geschehen* — "to happen" — is conjugated with *sein*. To ask "What *is* happening?" you say, *Was geschieht?*

223

— Ach, sie hat sich über mich geärgert.
Akh, zee haht zikh ů-ber mikh geh-EHR-gert.
Well, she became angry with me.

— Wieso? Erzählen Sie, was passiert ist!
Vee-ZO? Ehr-TS'AYL'en zee, vahss pahs-SEERT isst!
How come? Tell me what went on!

— Wir sind Klaus besuchen gegangen.
Veer zint klow's beh-ZOO-khen geh-GAHNG'en.
We went to visit Klaus.

Peter hat auf seiner Gitarre gespielt,
PAY-ter haht ow'f ZINE-er ghee-TA-reh geh-SHPEELT,
Peter played (on) his guitar,

und Lisbet hat gesungen.
oont LEES-bet haht geh-ZOONG'en.
and Lisbet sang.

Dann haben wir Tonbänder angehört.
Dahn HAHB'en veer TOHN-ben-der AHN-geh-hurt.
Then we listened to some tapes.

Alles ist wirklich sehr nett gewesen . . .
AHL-less isst VEERK-likh zehr net geh-VAYZ'en . . .
Everything was really quite nice . . .

Dann ist Helga plötzlich angekommen.
Dahn isst HEL-ga PLERTS-likh ahn-geh-KOHM'en.
Then Helga suddenly arrived.

Sie hat sehr mit mir geflirtet,
Zee haht zehr mit meer geh-FLIR-tet,
She flirted with me quite a bit,

und ich habe ein paarmal mit ihr getanzt.
oont ikh HA-beh ine PAR-mahl mit eer geh-TAHNTS'T.
and I danced with her a couple of times.

Da ist Marion eifersüchtig geworden.
Da isst Marion EYE-fehr-zůkh-tikh geh-VORD'en.
Then Marion became jealous.

— Kein Wunder! Und was ist dann geschehen?
Kine VOON-der! Oont vahss isst dahn geh-SHAY'en?
No wonder! And what happened then?

— Sie hat darauf bestanden,
Zee haht da-R'OW'F beh-SHTAHND'en,
She insisted on

sofort nach Hause zu gehen.
zo-FORT nahkh HOUZE-eh ts'oo GAY'en.
going home at once.

Ich habe sofort ein Taxi bestellen müssen,
Ikh HA-beh zo-FORT ine TAHK-see beh-SHTEL'en MÜSS'en,
I had to order a taxi immediately

um sie nach Hause zu bringen.
oom zee nakh HOW-zeh ts'oo BRING'en.
to take her home.

Sie ist einfach ausgestiegen
Zee isst INE-fakh ow's-geh-SHTEE-ghen
She simply got out

und hat sich nicht einmal bedankt
oont haht zikh nikht INE-mahl beh-DAHNKT
and didn't even say thank you

oder mir gute Nacht gesagt.
OH-der meer GOO-teh nahkt geh-ZAHKGT.
or good night to me.

— Und haben Sie sie heute angerufen?
Oont HAHB'en zee zee HOY-teh AHN-geh-roof'en?
And have you called her today?

— Ja, ich habe sie angerufen,
Ya, ikh HA-beh zee AHN-geh-roof'en,
Yes, I called her,

aber sie hat sofort aufgehängt. . . .
AH-ber zee haht zo-FORT OW'F-geh-hengt. . . .
but she hung up immediately. . . .

Sie hat mir nicht einmal Zeit
Zee haht meer nikht INE-mahl ts'ite
She did not even leave me any time

für eine Erklärung gelassen.
für INE-eh air-KLAIR-oong geh-LAHSS'en.
for an explanation.

Was kann man machen?
Vahss kahn mahn MAK'khen?
What can one do?

Sie ist immer ein eifersüchtiger Mensch gewesen!
Zee isst IM-er ine IFE-er-zükh-tee-ger mensh geh-VAYZ'en!
She always was a jealous person!

— Falls Sie es noch nicht getan haben,
fahls zee ess nokh nikht geh-TAHN HAHB'en,
In case you haven't done so yet,

warum schicken Sie ihr nicht ein paar Blumen?
va-ROOM SHIK'en zee eer nikht ine par BLOO-men?
why not send her some flowers?

Das wird vielleicht
Dahss veert feel-LY'KHT
That will perhaps

alles wieder gutmachen.
AHL-less VEE-der goot-MA'khen.
make everything all right again.

TEST YOUR GERMAN

Fill in past participles as indicated and the corresponding form of *sein*, *haben* or *werden*. Score 10 points for each correct answer. See answers on following page.

1. Have you been here before?
   _____ Sie schon hier _____ ?
      (*sein*)   (*sein*)

2. How did you travel?
   Wie _____ Sie _____ ?
         (*sein*)   (*reisen*)

3. I went by ship.
   Ich _____ mit dem Schiff _____ .
          (*sein*)   (*fahren*)

4. We arrived in Bremen at 2 o'clock.
   Wir _____ um zwei Uhr in Bremen
          (*sein*)
   _____ .
   (*ankommen*)

5. Did your wife stay in America?
   _____ Ihre Frau in Amerika _____ ?
      (*sein*)   (*bleiben*)

6. English is spoken in America.
   In Amerika _____ Englisch _____ .
             (*werden*)   (*sprechen*)

7. I saw her last night.
   Ich _____ sie gestern abend _____ .
          (*haben*)   (*sehen*)

8. We went out together.
   Wir _____ zusammen _____ .
          (*sein*)   (*ausgehen*)

9. Why did she become angry?

   Warum _____ sie ärgerlich _____ ?

   (*sein*) (*werden*)

10. What happened?

    Was _____ _____ ?

    (*sein*) (*geschehen*)

Answers: 1. Sind — gewesen. 2. sind — gereist. 3. bin — gefahren. 4. sind — angekommen. 5. Ist — geblieben? 6. wird — gesprochen. 7. habe — gesehen. 8. sind — ausgegangen. 9. ist — geworden. 10. ist — geschehen.

SCORE _____%

step 20 THE IMPERFECT TENSE — A TENSE TO USE WHEN TELLING A STORY

Nach Ausdrücken wie
Nahkh OW'SS-drǔ-ken vee
After expressions such as

als, einmal, im vorigen Jahre, ehemals,
ahls, INE-mahl, imm FOHR-ee-ghen YA-reh, EH-eh-mahls,
when, once, in the past year, formerly,

es war einmal und so weiter,
ess vahr INE-mahl oont zo VY-ter,
once there was, and so on,

> **Usw. — and so forth**
> *Und so weiter* is frequently abbreviated in print
> to *usw.* And remember that *z.B.* (*zum Beispiel*)
> means "for example."

benutzt man das Imperfekt.
beh-NOOTS'T mahn dahss IMM-per-FEKT.
one uses the imperfect (tense).

Als ich jung war,
Ahlts ikh yoong vahr,
When I was young

lebten wir in Wien.
LAYPT'en veer in Veen.
we lived in Vienna.

Einmal hatte ich einen Hund,
INE-mahl HA-teh ikh INE-en hoont,
Once I had a dog,

der Lohengrin hieß.
dehr LO-en-grin heess.
who was called Lohengrin.

Früher verbrachten wir unsere
frǚ-her fehr-BRAHKHT'en veer OON-zeh-reh
Formerly we used to spend our

Sommerferien in Italien oder in Griechenland.
**ZOHM-mehr-fay-ree-en in ee-TAHL-yen OH-der in
GREEKH-en-lahnt.**
summer vacations in Italy or in Greece.

Und für Märchen:
Oont fǚr MAIR-khen:
And for fairy tales:

Es war einmal eine schöne Prinzessin.
Ess vahr INE-mahl INE-eh SHER-neh prin-TS'ESS-in.
Once upon a time there was a beautiful princess.

Eines Tages kam ein schöner Prinz zum Schloß. . . .
INE-ess TA-ghes kahm ine SHERN-er prints ts'oom schlohss. . . .
One day a handsome young prince came to the palace. . . .

The imperfect tense

The imperfect tense is generally equivalent in
use to the past tense in English, that is, with
words like "had," "saw," "was," "told,"
"heard," "gave," "lived" etc. In addition the
imperfect translates both the English concept of
"used to" — such as "used to have," "used to
be," as well as the progressive past "was having," "was being" etc. This tense is formed for
most verbs by adding certain endings to the
stems or by changing the stem. Here is the imperfect of *sein* — ("to be") and *haben* — ("to
have"):

ich war	*ich hatte*
du warst	*du hattest*
er (sie, es) war	*er (sie, es) hatte*
wir waren	*wir hatten*

ihr wart   ihr hattet
Sie (sie) waren   Sie (sie) hatten

Most verbs form the imperfect like *leben* —
"to live"

ich lebte
du lebtest
er (sie, es) lebte
wir lebten
ihr lebtet
Sie (sie) lebten

Verbs that form the past in this way are called
"weak" verbs and are the same ones that have
a past participle with *ge-* at the beginning and *-t*
at the end.

"Strong" and "weak" verbs
Verbs that do not form the past by adding *-te* to
the stem are called "strong" verbs (possibly
because they are strong enough to change their
behavior pattern). *Kommen* — "to come" is
one of these:

ich kam
du kamst
er (sie, es) kam
wir kamen
ihr kamt
Sie (sie) kamen

You will notice that the forms for *ich* and *er* are
the same as well as those for *wir* and *Sie*.

Although "weak" verbs greatly outnumber the
"strong" ones the "strong" verbs tend to be
used frequently in everyday conversation, so
that you should learn them individually.

Here is the imperfect of some of the more important "strong" verbs you have already had:

beginnen   *ich begann* (I began)
bitten   *ich bat* (I asked)
essen   *ich aß* (I ate)

231

fahren	ich fuhr (I drove)
geben	ich gab (I gave)
gehen	ich ging (I went)
lesen	ich las (I read)
heißen	ich hieß (I was called)
nehmen	ich nahm (I took)
schreiben	ich schrieb (I wrote)
sehen	ich sah (I saw)
sprechen	ich sprach (I spoke)
werden	ich wurde (I became)

Other verbs while forming the past with -te have slight spelling changes:

kennen	ich kannte (I was aquainted with)
denken	ich dachte (I thought)
wissen	ich wußte (I knew)
bringen	ich brachte (I brought)
senden	ich sandte (I sent)

Hier ist ein typisches Beispiel einer Geschichte
Here isst ine TŬ-pish-ess BY-shpeel INE-er geh-SHIKH-teh
Here is a typical example of a story

im Imperfekt:
im IM-peh-fekt:
in the imperfect tense:

Ich erinnere mich an eine lustige Geschichte,
Ikh ehr-INN-eh-reh mikh ahn INE-eh LOOSS-tee-geh
                                    geh-SHIKH-teh,
I remember a funny story,

Vergessen Sie nicht!
To remember something is *sich erinnern an* with
an governing the accusative case.

die mein Großvater uns über
dee mine GROHSS-fa-ter oons ŬH-ber
which my grandfather used to tell us about

Friedrich den Großen erzählte.
FREE-drikh dehn GROHSS-en ehr-TS'EHL-teh.
Frederic the Great.

Der König hatte viele
Dehr KER-nikh HA-teh FEE-leh
The king had many

ausländische Soldaten in seiner Armee.
OWSS-len-dish-eh zoll-DA-ten in ZINE-er ar-MAY.
foreign soldiers in his army.

Manche von diesen sprachen kein Deutsch.
MAHN-kheh fohn DEE-zen SPRA'khen kine Doytch.
some of them didn't speak any German.

Einmal sollte der König zu einer
INE-mahl ZOLL-teh dehr KER-nikh ts'oo INE-er
Once the king was supposed to come to an

Regimentsinspektion kommen.
Ray-ghee-MENTS-in-spek-ts'yohn KOHM'en.
inspection of his regiment.

Ein böhmischer Soldat,
Ine BER-mish-er zoll-DAHT,
A Bohemian soldier,

der kein Deutsch sprach,
dehr kine Doytch shprahkh,
who spoke no German,

fürchtete die Fragen des Königs,
FÜRKH-teh-teh dee FRA-gen dess KER-niks,
was afraid of the king's questions,

weil es ihm klar war,
vile ess eem klahr vahr,
because it was clear to him,

daß er sie nicht beantworten konnte.
dahss ehr zee nihkt beh-AHNT-vort'en KOHN-teh.
that he couldn't answer them.

Imperfect of the auxiliary verbs
The verbs that combine directly with the infinitive of a second verb form the imperfect with a final *-te* or *-ten* although four of them have

minor changes. The imperfect of *dürfen,
können, mögen, müssen, sollen, wollen,* are: *ich
durfte, ich konnte, ich mochte, ich mußte, ich
sollte, ich wollte.*

Seine Kameraden beruhigten ihn:
ZINE-eh ka-meh-RAH-den beh-ROO-hy'ten een:
His comrades assured him:

„Keine Sorge, Seine Majestät fragt
„Kine-eh ZOHR-geh, ZINE-eh ma-yes-TAYT frahkt
"Don't worry, His Majesty always asks

immer dieselben Fragen in
IM-mer dee-ZELL-ben FRA-gen in
the same questions in

derselben Reihenfolge:
dehr-ZELL-ben RY-en-fohl-geh:
the same order:

Nämlich, ‚Wie alt bist du?'
NEHM-likh, ‚Vee ahlt bisst doo?'
Namely, 'How old are you?'

‚Wie lange bist du in meiner Armee?'
‚Vee LAHNG-eh bisst doo in MINE-er ar-MAY?'
'For how long have you been in my army?'

The present instead of the perfect
When we ask how long something has been
going on, and is still going on, we use the present tense in German where we would use the
perfect tense in English:

How long have you been waiting here
already?
— *Wie lange warten Sie hier schon?*

und ‚Was gefällt dir besser, das Essen
oont ‚Vahss geh-FELLT deer BESS-er, dahss ESS-en
and 'What do you like better, the food

oder die Uniform?'
OH-der dee Oo-nee-FORM?'
or the uniform?'

Auf die erste Frage sollst du antworten:
Ow'f dee EHR-steh FRA-gheh zollst doo AHNT-vort'en:
To the first question you must answer:

,Zweiundzwanzig Jahre'.
,TS'VYE-oont-ts'vahn-ts'ikh YA-reh'.
'Twenty-two years'.

Auf die zweite: ,Zwei Jahre.'
Ow'f dee TS'VYE-teh: ,Tsvye YA-reh.'
To the second: 'Two years.'

Und auf die dritte: ,Beide, Majestät.' "
Oont ow'f dee DRIT-teh: ,BY-deh, ma-yes-TAYT.' "
And to the third: 'Both, Majesty.' "

Aber als der König kam
AH-ber ahlts dehr KER-nikh kahm
But when the king came

und schließlich den jungen Rekruten ansprach,
oont SHLEESS-likh dehn YOONG-en ray-KROO-ten AHN-shprahkh,
and finally addressed the young recruit,

änderte er die Reihenfolge seiner Fragen
END-er-teh ehr dee RY-en-fol-geh ZINE-er FRA-gen
he changed the order of his questions

und fragte zuerst:
oont FRAHK-teh ts'oo-EHRST:
and asked first:

„Wie lange bist du in meiner Armee?"
„Vee LAHNG-eh bisst doo in MINE-er ar-MAY?"
"For how long have you been in my army?"

The du-form
Note that Frederick the Great in speaking to his
soldiers addresses them by the familiar or informal form, implying, certainly here, a sense of

235

superiority on his part since the soldiers address him as *Majestät* — "Majesty."

It is also noteworthy that in present, more democratic times, officers use the polite *Sie* to soldiers of their command.

Worauf der Böhme antwortete:
Voh-R'OWF dehr BER-meh AHNT-vor-teh-teh:
To which the Bohemian replied:

„Zweiundzwanzig Jahre, Majestät!"
„TS'VYE-oont-ts'vahn-ts'ikh YA-reh, ma-yes-TAYT!"
"Twenty-two years, Majesty!"

„Wie ist das möglich," rief der König.
„Vee isst dahss MERK-likh," reef dehr KER-nikh.
"How is that possible," the king exclaimed.

„Wie alt bist du denn?"
„Vee ahlt bisst doo den?"
"How old are you then?"

„Zwei Jahre," antwortete der Soldat,
„Tsvye YA-reh," AHNT-vor-teh-teh dehr zoll-DAHT,
"Two years," the soldier replied,

wie auswendig gelernt.
vee OWSS-vehn-dikh geh-LEHRNT.
as learned by heart.

„Donnerwetter," rief der König,
„DOHNN-ner-vet-ter," reef dehr KER-nikh,
"Thunderation," the king exclaimed,

„wer von uns beiden ist verrückt,
„vehr fohn oons BY-den isst fair-RŮKT,
"which one of us is crazy,

du oder ich?"
doo OH-der ikh?"
you or I?"

„Beide, Majestät," antwortete
„BY-deh, ma-yes-TAYT," AHNT-vor-teh-teh
"Both, Majesty," replied

der Soldat.
dehr zoll-DAHT.
the soldier.

The basic verb forms

The above anecdote illustrates how the imperfect is used to tell a story or to describe a scene which took place in the past. In everyday conversation the perfect tense which we examined in Steps 18 and 19 (which can mean either "went" or "have gone" — "saw" or "have seen") is used to describe specific actions which took place in the recent past, while the imperfect is used for describing a situation in the more remote past, for telling stories and for describing something that happened frequently or "used to" happen.

Now that you have learned how to use the imperfect you can appreciate the basic classification of German verbs which is the infinitive, the imperfect and the past participle. For example:

leben	*lebte*	*gelebt*
sein	*war*	*gewesen*
kommen	*kam*	*gekommen*
essen	*aß*	*gegessen*
geben	*gab*	*gegeben*
gehen	*ging*	*gegangen*
sprechen	*sprach*	*gesprochen*
werden	*wurde*	*geworden*
sagen	*sagte*	*gesagt*
lesen	*las*	*gelesen*
machen	*machte*	*gemacht*

Actually, German uses the same basic plan as English verbs, another instance of the similarity of the two languages.

INSTANT CONVERSATION: A FAMILY REUNION — RECALLING THE PAST

ER:
Ehr:
HE:

Heute abend sind wir bei meinen
HOY-teh AH-bent zint veer by MINE-en
This evening we are

Großeltern zum Essen eingeladen.
GROHSS-el-tern ts'oom ESS-en INE-gheh-LAHD'en.
invited for dinner at my grandparents' house.

Sie werden viel über mich sprechen.
Zee VEHR-den feel Ů-ber mikh SHPREKH'en.
They will be talking a lot about me.

Sie werden dir sicher erzählen,
Zee VEHR-den deer ZIKH-er ehr-TS'AYL'en
They will surely tell you

wie ich war und was ich immer alles tat,
vee ikh vahr oont vahss ikh IM-mer AHL-less taht,
how I was and everything that I always used to do

als ich klein war.
ahlts ikh kline vahr.
when I was small.

Später
SHPAY-ter
Later

DIE GROßMUTTER:
Dee GROHSS-moot-ter:
THE GRANDMOTHER:

Wissen Sie, Richard hat immer seine
VISS'en zee, RIKH-art haht IM-mer ZINE-eh
You know, Richard always used to

238

Sommerferien bei uns in Lindau verbracht.
ZOHM-mer-fay-ree-yen by oons in LIN-d'ow fehr-BRAHKHT.
spend all of his summer vacations with us in Lindau.

Er war ein bildhübscher kleiner Junge,
Ehr vahr ine BILLT-hûp-sher KLINE-er YOONG-geh,
He was as pretty as a picture as a little boy,

und er war sehr intelligent.
oont ehr vahr sehr in-tel-lee-GHENT.
and he was very intelligent.

Aber er machte uns so viel Sorgen . . .
AH-ber ehr MAHKH-teh oons zo feel ZOR-gen . . .
But he used to give us so many worries . . .

DER GROßVATER:
Dehr GROHSS-fa-ter:
THE GRANDFATHER:

Er ging immer fort, ohne uns zu sagen,
Ehr ging IM-mer fort, OH-neh oons ts'oo ZAHG'en,
He always used to leave without telling us

wohin er ging.
vo-HIN ehr ging.
where he went.

Oft lief er sehr spät am Abend davon
Oft leef ehr zehr shpayt ahm AH-bent da-FOHN
Often he ran off quite late at night

und traf sich mit den Dorfkindern am See.
oont trahf zikh mit dehn DORF-kinn-dern ahm zay.
to meet with the village children by the lake.

Wir wußten niemals genau, wo er war.
Veer VOOST'en NEE-mahls geh-NOW, vo ehr vahr.
We never knew just where he was.

Und wir waren immer besorgt.
Oont veer VAR'en IM-mer beh-ZORKT.
And we were always worried.

Er erfand immer wilde Spiele,
Ehr ehr-FAHNT IM-mehr VILL-deh SHPEE-leh,
He always invented wild games,

und er organisierte eine richtige Bande.
oont ehr or-ga-nee-ZEER-teh INE-eh RIKH-tee-gheh BAHN-deh.
and he organized a regular gang.

Sie bewarfen sich mit Steinen
Zee beh-VARF'en zikh mit SHTINE-nen
They would throw stones at each other

und kämpften wüste Schlachten.
oont KEMPF'ten VÜSS-teh SHLAHKH-ten.
and would fight violent battles.

Die Nachbarn regten sich oft auf
Dee NAHKH-barn RAYK-ten zikh oft owf
The neighbors often used to get upset

und kamen, um sich zu beklagen.
oont KAHM'en, oom zikh ts'oo beh-KLAHG'en.
and would come over to complain.

Ins Kino ging er am liebsten,
Inns KEE-no ging ehr am LEEPST'en,
He liked best to go to the movies,

wenn es Wildwest-Filme gab.
venn ess vilt-VEST-fill-meh gahp.
when they played Westerns.

Er sagte immer, daß er eines Tages
Ehr ZAHK-teh IM-mehr, dahss ehr INE-ness TA-ghess
He always said that one day

nach Amerika gehen wollte,
nahkh Ah-MAY-ree-ka GAY'en vohl-teh,
he wanted to go to America,

um die Cowboys und die Rothäute zu sehen.
oom dee COW-boys oont dee ROHT-hoy-teh ts'oo ZAY'en.
to see the cowboys and the redskins.

240

DIE GROßMUTTER:

Aber zu uns war er immer sehr
AH-ber ts'oo oons vahr ehr IM-mer zehr
But with us he always was very

lieb und aufmerksam.
leep oont OWF-mehrk-zahm.
affectionate and attentive.

Als er dann in die
Ahlts ehr dahn in dee
And then when he left for the

Vereinigten Staaten fuhr, dachten wir,
fehr-INE-nihk-ten SHTA-ten foor, DAHKH-ten veer,
United States we thought,

daß er nur auf Besuch dorthin fuhr
dahss ehr noor owf beh-ZOOKH DORT-hin foor
that he only was going there for a visit

und daß er vorhatte, bald
oont dahss ehr FOR-haht-teh, bahlt
and that he was planning soon

zurückzukommen.
ts'oo-RŮK-ts'oo-kohm'en.
to return.

Wir wußten natürlich nicht,
Veer VOOSS-ten na-TŮR-likh nikht,
Naturally, we didn't know,

daß er vorhatte, ein amerikanisches
dahs ehr FOR-ha-teh, ine ah-may-ree-KA-nish-ess
that he planned to marry

Mädchen zu heiraten.
MAYT-yen ts'oo HY-raht'en.
an American girl.

German Step by Step

DER GROßVATER:

... und noch dazu eine so
... oont nokh da-TS'OO INE-eh zo
... and on top of it such

reizende junge Amerikanerin.
RYE-tsen-deh YOONG-eh ah-may-ree-KA-neh-rin.
a charming young American.

Wir wollten dich schon seit langer
Veer VOHLT'en dikh shohn zite LAHNG-er
We wanted to get to know you

A question of etiquette

The grandmother uses the familiar form here to her granddaughter-in-law, even though this is the first time they have met. While this would be perfectly natural for an older person, the younger person should properly continue to use *Sie* until a closer and more familiar relationship has been established.

Zeit kennenlernen.
ts'ite KEN'en LEHRN'en.
for so long.

Kennenlernen — to get to know

"To get to know (someone)" is expressed by *kennenlernen*, literally "to learn to know," a rather apt descriptive expression.

DIE GROßMUTTER:

Kommt, Kinder!
Kohmt, KIN-der!
Come, children!

Das Abendessen ist serviert.
Dahss AH-bent-ESS'en isst zehr-VEERT.
Dinner is served.

Heute gibt es Schweinshaxen
HOY-teh gipt ess SHVINES-hahx-en
Today we're having pigs' knuckles

mit Sauerkraut und Knödeln.
mit S'OW-er-k'rowt oont KNER-deln.
with sauerkraut and dumplings.

Das war Richards Lieblingsspeise,
Dahss vahr RIKH-arts LEEP-links-shpy-zeh,
That was Richard's favorite dish

als er noch ein kleiner Junge war.
ahlts ehr nokh ine KLY-ner YOONG-eh vahr.
when he was still a little boy.

> Später
> **SHPAY-ter**
> Later

SIE:
Zee:
SHE:

Also, heute habe ich aber wirklich
AHL-zo, HOY-teh HA-beh ikh AH-ber VEERK-likh
Well, today I really learned

viel über dich erfahren!
feel Ü-ber dikh ehr-FAR'en!
quite a lot about you!

Lauter Dinge, die ich noch nicht wußte!
L'OW-ter DING-geh, dee ikh nohkh nikht voos-teh!
All sorts of things I didn't know until now!

ER:
Hab' ich's dir nicht gesagt?
Hahb ikh's deer nikht geh-zahgt?
Didn't I tell you so?

> **Dropping the "e"**
> Note how the final *e* on *habe* and the *e* of *es*
> are both abbreviated in rapid and informal
> speech by an apostrophe, as is often done in
> English with vowel sounds (I'm, I'd, isn't, he'd,
> etc.)

Und ich war wirklich nicht so schlimm,
Oont ikh vahr VEERK-likh nikht zo shlim,
And I really wasn't quite as bad

wie sie behaupten.
vee zee beh-HOWPT'en.
as they were saying.

TEST YOUR GERMAN

Translate these sentences into German, using the imperfect tense. Score 10 points for each correct translation. See answers below.

1. When he was young he lived in Bavaria. (**Bayern**) _____

2. Once we had a cat who was called Siegfried. _____

3. I used to spend my summer vacations in France. _____

4. He asked her something. _____

5. She didn't want to answer. _____

6. They didn't tell us where they were going. _____

7. He often went to the movies. _____

8. They were planning to go to America. _____

9. We never knew where he was. _____

10. Grandfather always used to tell us stories. _____

Answers: 1. Als er jung war, lebte er in Bayern. 2. Einmal hatten wir eine Katze, die Siegfried hieß. 3. Ich verbrachte meine Sommerferien in Frankreich. 4. Er fragte sie etwas. 5. Sie wollte nicht antworten. 6. Sie sagten uns nicht, wohin sie gingen. 7. Er ging oft ins Kino. 8. Sie hatten vor, nach Amerika zu fahren. 9. Wir wußten nie, wo er war. 10. Großvater erzählte uns immer Geschichten.

SCORE _____%

245

step 21

HOW TO USE THE PAST PERFECT — THE PAST *BEFORE* THE PAST

Um ein Ereignis zu beschreiben,
Oom ine ehr-IKE-niss ts'oo beh-SHRIBE'en,
In order to describe an event

das in der Vergangenheit passiert ist,
dahsfs in dehr fehr-GAHNG-en-hite pahs-sEERT isst,
which happened in the past,

gebraucht man das Imperfekt
geh-BR'OWKHT mahn dahss IM-per-fekt
one uses the Imperfect tense

von *haben* oder *sein.*
fohn *haben* OH-der *sein.*
of "haben" and "sein"

The past before the past

When we describe an action which took place *before* another action we use the past perfect. *die Vorvergangenheit.* This corresponds to the English past perfect as in "had been," "had come," "had had," "had finished," etc. All you have to do to form the past perfect in German is to use the past participle of the verb combined with the imperfect tense of *haben* or *sein.* For a review take another look at Steps 18 and 19 to help you remember which verbs take *haben* and which take *sein.*

Als ich gestern abend zu Ihnen kam,
Ahlts ikh GEH-stern AH-bent ts'oo EE-nen kahm,
When I came to see you last night,

sagte man mir, daß Sie mit jemand
ZAHK-teh mahn meer, dahss zee mit YAY-mahnt
I was told that you had gone out

anders ausgegangen waren.
AHN-ders OWS-geh-gahng'en VAHr'en.
with someone else.

Als wir am Bahnhof ankamen,
Ahlts veer ahm BAHN-hohf AHN-kahm'en,
When we arrived at the station,

war der Zug schon abgefahren.
var dehr ts'ook shohn AHP-geh-far'en.
the train had already left.

Ich hatte gerade einen Brief an sie geschrieben,
Ikh HA-teh geh-RA-deh INE'en breef ahn zee geh-SHREEB'en,
I had just written her a letter,

als sie anrief.
ahlts zee AHN-reef.
when she called.

Und nun Beispiele der Vorvergangenheit,
Oont noon BY-shpee-leh dehr FOR-vehr-gahng-en-hite,
And now some examples of the Past Perfect

wo *sein* und *haben* vermischt sind.
vo zine oont HAHB'en fehr-MISHT zint.
where "to be" and "to have" are mixed together.

Wir hatten gerade Abendbrot gegessen,
Veer HAHT-en geh-RA-deh AH-bent-broht geh-GHESS'en,
We had just finished eating supper,

Das Essen
Both *Abendbrot* — "evening bread" and
Abendessen — "evening meal" are used for
"supper" or "dinner." In like manner *Mittagessen* (midday meal) means "lunch."

247

aber wir saßen noch am Tisch,
AH-ber veer ZAHSS'en nokh ahm tish,
but we were still sitting at the table,

als wir vor unserem Haus
ahlts veer for OON-zehr-em hou'ss
when we heard, in front of our house

einen lauten Krach hörten.
INE-en L'OW-ten krakh HERT'en.
a loud crash.

Wir rannten hinaus und sahen, daß ein Auto
Veer RAHNT'en hin-OW'SS oont ZAH'en, dahss ine OW-toh
We ran outside and saw that a car

unseren Wagen angefahren hatte,
OON-zehr-en Va-gen ahn-geh-FAR'en HAHT-eh,
had hit against our car,

den wir vor dem Haus geparkt hatten.
den veer for dem howss geh-parkt HAHT'en.
that we had parked in front of the house.

Ein gerade vorübergehender Nachbar,
Ine geh-RA-deh for-Ü-ber-geh-en-der NAHKH-bar,
A neighbor just going by,

der den Unfall gesehen hatte,
dehr den OON-fahl geh-ZAY'en HAHT-eh,
who had seen the accident,

The Present Participle
Although the progressive tense is not used in German a present participle of the verb exists, ending in -*end*, which corresponds to the "-ing" ending in English as in the words "speaking" and flying."

In German this present participle is used only as an adjective as in the following:

She was lying sleeping on the sofa.
Sie lag schlafend auf dem Sofa.

Danger! Children playing.
Vorsicht! Spielende Kinder.

The Flying Dutchman.
Der Fliegende Holländer.

German is simple (sometimes)
Fußgänger — literally "footgoer" is simpler than the English "pedestrian." German, less under Latin influence than English, has many such words that one can easily understand by breaking them into their component parts.

gab uns eine Beschreibung des Unfalls.
gahp oonts INE-eh beh-SHRY-boong dess OON-fahls.
gave us a description of the accident.

Ein Fahrer hatte versucht
Ine FAR-er HAHT-eh fehr-ZOOKT
A driver had tried

vor unserem Auto zu parken,
for OON-zehr-em OW-toh ts'oo PARK'en,
to park in front of our car,

da die Parklücke aber zu klein war,
da dee PARK-lůk-eh AH-ber ts'oo kline var,
but the parking lot was too small,

war er dabei in unser Auto hineingefahren.
var ehr da-BY in OON-zehr OW-toh hin-INE-geh-far'en.
(and because of this) he had run into our car.

Als er sah, was er angerichtet hatte,
Ahlts ehr za, vahss ehr AHN-geh-rikh-tet HAHT-teh,
When he saw what he had caused,

fuhr er in großer Eile davon.
foor ehr in GROSS-er ILE-eh da-FOHN.
he drove off in a great hurry.

Wurde ist nützlich, um sich
VOOR-deh isst NŮTS-likh, oom zikh
Wurde ("became") is useful for asking

249

German Step by Step

nach historischen Tatsachen zu erkundigen:
nakh hiss-TOR-ish-en TAHT-zah-khen ts'oo er-KOON-deeg'en:
information about historical matters:

> **The past of the passive**
> *Wurde* is the imperfect of *werden* — "to be-
> come" and is used together with the past parti-
> ciple of another verb to form the passive and is
> translated as "was" or *wurden* — "were."

— Wann wurde dieses Schloß gebaut?
Vahn VOOR-deh DEE-zess shlohss geh-B'OWT?
When was this castle built?

— Wie wurde es zerstört?
Vee VOOR-deh ess ts'ehr-shtert?
How was it destroyed?

— Wann wurden die Türme errichtet?
Vahn VOOR-den dee TÜR-meh er-RIKH-tet?
When were the towers erected?

— Von wem wurde dieses Bild gemalt?
Fohn vem VOOR-deh DEE-zess bilt geh-MAHLT?
By whom was this picture painted?

Wie die Vorvergangenheit
Vee dee FOR-fehr-gahng-en-hite
As the past perfect

eine Handlung beschreibt, die schon
INE-eh HAHND-loong beh-SHRYPT, dee shohn
describes an action which is already

beendet ist in der Vergangenheit,
beh-EN-det isst in dehr fehr-GAHNG-en-hite,
finished in the past,

so beschreibt die zweite Zukunft
zo beh-SHRYPT dee ts'vite-eh TS'OO-koonft
so the future perfect describes

250

The future perfect
Die zweite Zukunft, literally "the second future" is equivalent to the English *future perfect*, such as "will have finished," "will have gone," "will have received," etc. The past perfect is sometimes referred to as "the second past" — *die zweite Vergangenheit* as well as *die Vorvergangenheit*, literally "before the past."

Handlungen in der Zukunft, die (vermutlich)
HAHND-loong-en in dehr TS'OO-koonft, dee (fehr-MOOT-likh)
actions in the future which (supposedly)

schon beendet sind.
shohn beh-EN-det zint.
are already finished.

z.B.:
Ts'oom BY-shpeel:
For example:

— Was wird in hundert Jahren passiert sein?
Vahss veert in HOON-dert YA-ren pa-SEERT zine?
What will have happened in a hundred years?

— Wir werden sicher Stationen auf
Veer VEHRD'en ZIKH-er shtahts-YO-nen owf
We will surely have established

den anderen Planeten gebaut haben.
den AHN-der-en plahn-AY-ten geh-b'owt HAHB'en.
stations on the other planets.

Die Wissenschaftler werden
Dee VISS-en-shahft-ler VEHRD'en
The scientists will have

neue Nahrungsquellen gefunden haben.
NOY-eh NA-roongs-K'VEL-len geh-FOOND'en HAHB'en.
found new sources of food.

Die Fortschritte in der Medizin werden
Dee fort-SHRIT-eh in dehr may-dee-TS'EEN VEHRD'en
The progress in medicine will have

251

die menschliche Lebensspanne
dee MEN-shlikh-eh LAY-bens-shpahn-eh
lengthened man's

verlängert haben.
fehr-LENG-ert HAB'en.
span of life.

Und der Computer wird die
Oont dehr kom-POOT-er veert dee
And the computer will have

Lehrmethoden verändert haben.
LEHR-may-toh-den fer-END-ert HAHB'en.
changed teaching methods.

— Wer weiß, vielleicht wird man auch
Vehr vice, fee-LYKH'T veert mahn ow'kh
Who knows, perhaps they will also

Wege gefunden haben, die Steuern zu senken?
VAY-geh geh-FOOND'en HAHB'en, dee SHTOY-ern ts'oo ZENK'en?
have found ways to reduce taxes?

TEST YOUR GERMAN

Translate the first five sentences into German and the next five into English. Score 10 points for each correct translation. See answers below.

1. When I came they had already gone out. _____

2. We thought that someone had run into our car. _____

3. A pedestrian had seen the accident. _____

4. The driver had tried to park his car. _____

5. When he saw what he had done he drove off. _____

6. Wann wurde dieses Haus gebaut? _____

7. Wann wurde dieses Bild gemalt? _____

8. Wie wurde dieses Gebäude zerstört? _____

9. Was wird im Jahre 2000 passiert sein? _____

10. Wird der Computer unser Leben verändert haben? _____

Answers: 1. Als ich kam, waren sie schon ausgegangen. 2. Wir dachten, daß jemand unseren Wagen angefahren hatte. 3. Ein Fußgänger hatte den Unfall gesehen. 4. Der Fahrer hatte versucht, seinen Wagen zu parken. 5. Als er sah, was er getan hatte, fuhr er davon. 6. When was this house built? 7. When was this picture painted? 8. How was this building destroyed? 9. What will have happened by the year 2000? 10. Will the computer have changed our lives?

SCORE _____%

253

Wenn wir etwas wiederholen,
Ven verr ET-vahss veed-er-HOLE'en,
When we repeat something

was jemand sagt
vahss YAY-mahnt zahkt
that someone else says

oder gesagt hat,
OH-der geh-ZAHKT haht,
or has said,

gebrauchen wir den Konjunktiv.
geh-BR'OWKH'en veer den KON-yoonk-teef.
we use the subjunctive.

THE SUBJUNCTIVE FOR REPORTED SPEECH
The subjunctive is a special form of the verb principally used when reporting what someone says, asks, or otherwise indicates. The form of the present subjunctive resembles that of the present indicative except that the *er, sie, es* form does not end in -*t*, but has the same form as *ich*. He asks whether she is coming. — *Er fragt, ob sie komme.*

He says that she speaks German very well.
Er sagt, daß sie sehr gut Deutsch spreche.

He writes that he is working hard.
Er schreibt, daß er schwer arbeite.

In considering the regular verb *leben* you can see how little change there is in the present subjunctive for most verbs.

ich lebe
du lebest
er, (sie, es) lebe
wir leben
ihr lebet
Sie, (sie) leben

The verbs *sein, wissen, dürfen, können, mögen, müssen, sollen,* and *wollen* do not have the same base in the present subjunctive as in the present indicative but, in fact, stick closer to their infinitive and form the first form of the subjunctive in the following pattern: *ich sei, ich wisse, ich dürfe, ich könne, ich möge, ich müsse, ich solle, ich wolle.*

Nowadays, in modern spoken German, it is generally permissible to use the indicative in reported speech when you use *daß* in front of the reported verb.

He writes that he is working hard.
Er schreibt, daß er schwer arbeitet. (But remember to use the *daß.*)

Wenn die Behauptung in der Gegenwart ist,
Ven dee be-HOW'PT-oong in der GAY-ghen-wahrt isst,
If the statement is in the present,

benutzen wir den Konjunktiv der Gegenwart.
beh-NOOT-ts'en veer den KON-yoonk'teef der GAY-ghen-wahrt.
we use the present subjunctive.

Sie sagt, sie sei verheiratet.
Zee zahkt. zee zye fehr-HY-ra-tet.
She says she is married.

Er sagt, seine Frau sei krank.
Ehr zahgt, ZINE-eh fr'ow zye krahnk.
He says his wife is sick.

Inverted word order for the subjunctive
When *daß* is used in reporting something that someone says the word order is inverted and the subjunctive comes at the end. When *daß* is

dropped as in the above sentence — "She says she is married." — the word order is the same as in English. But don't forget the comma, which is always used in German to introduce a relative clause, reported speech or subordinal clauses starting with *daß, wenn, wann, wo, wer, wie,* etc.

Sie behaupten, sie seien sehr beschäftigt.
Zee beh-HOW'PT'en, zee zy'en zehr beh-SHEF-tikht.
They claim they are very busy.

Wenn die Behauptung
Ven dee beh-HOW'PT-oong
If the statement

in der Vergangenheit ist,
in dehr fehr-GAHNG-en-hite isst,
is in the past,

so muß der Konjunktiv auch
zo mooss dehr KON-yoonk-teef ow'kh
then the subjunctive also

in der Vergangenheit sein.
in dehr fair-GAHNG-en-hite zine.
must be in the past.

Sie sagte, daß sie es wüßte.
Zee ZAHK-teh, dahss zee ess VŮSS-teh.
She said she knew it.

Sie erklärten, daß sie nicht gehen wollten.
Zee er-KLEHRT'en, dahss zee nikht GAY'en VOHLT'en.
They explained that they didn't want to go.

Sagten Sie ihnen nicht, daß Sie enttäuscht wären?
ZAHK-ten zee EE-hen nikht, dahss zee ent-TOYSHT VEHR-en?
Didn't you tell them that you were disappointed?

The past subjunctive
Verbs expressing what someone said, used in the last three sentences, are in the past or imperfect subjunctive, a form that is used not only

for reporting what someone said in the past but especially useful, as you will see in Step 23, for forming suppositions. The imperfect subjunctive for regular verbs has the same form as the imperfect, which you learned in Step 20. But for the irregular verbs, that is verbs that have stem changes, the subjunctive is generally based on the imperfect with the addition of an umlaut over the vowel and the addition of a final -e to the form for *ich* and *er*, as follows:

> *ich wäre*
> *du wärst*
> *er (sie, er) wäre*
> *wir wären*
> *ihr wärt*
> *Sie (sie) wären*

When the final -e already exists, as in *ich hatte* ("I had"), the subjunctive becomes:

> *ich hätte*
> *du hättest*
> *er hätte*
> *wir hätten*
> *Ihr hättet*
> *Sie hätten*

Wenn man in der Vergangenheit
Ven mahn in dehr fehr-GAHNG-en-hite
When one speaks in the past

von einer zukünftigen Handlung spricht,
fohn INE-er TS'OO-künf-tig-en HAHND-loong shprikht,
about a future action,

dann muß man *werden* benutzen.
dahn mooss mahn VEHRD'en beh-NOOT-ts'en.
then one must use *werden*.

The future referred to in the past
The imperfect subjunctive of *werden* is equivalent to the English "would," used in repeating something someone has said in the past to express a future plan.

257

He told me he would do it.
Er sagte mir, er würde es machen.

I thought that I would go to the movies.
Ich dachte, daß ich ins Kino gehen würde.

Er sagte, daß er um 8 Uhr hierher kommen würde.
Er zahk-teh, dahss ehr oom akht oor HERE-hehr KOHM-en VǛR-deh.
He said that he would come here at 8 o'clock.

Sie haben mir versprochen, Sie würden es heute beendigen.
**Zee HAHB'en meer fehr-SHPROKH'en, zee VǛRD'en ess HOY-teh
be-END-ee-ghen.**
You promised me you would finish it today.

Ich habe ihnen gesagt, daß
Ikh hahb'eh EE-nen geh-ZAHKT, dahss
I have told them that

ich die Einladung annehmen würde.
ikh dee INE-la-doong AHN-nay-men VǛR-deh.
I would accept the invitation.

INSTANT CONVERSATION:
LEAVING A TELEPHONE MESSAGE

— Hallo! Ich möchte mit Fräulein Röhm sprechen.
HA-lo! Ikh MERKH-teh mit FROY-line Rerm SHPREKH'en.
Hello! I would like to speak to Miss Röhm.

The past subjunctive of mögen and werden
Ich möchte is the imperfect subjunctive form of
mögen which in the present means "I like." You
will remember that we have used *ich möchte* in
previous steps as it is more polite to say "I
would like" or "might I" than "I want" or "I
wish." This use of *ich möchte* or *möchten
Sie* — "would you like" — is a special form of
politeness. But remember that "would" as reported speech is expressed by the imperfect
subjunctive of *werden*, which goes:
ich würde
du würdest
er (sie, es) würde
wir würden
ihr würdet
Sie (sie) würden

— Sie ist leider nicht hier.
Zee isst LY-der nikht here.
Sorry, she is not here.

— Hat sie Ihnen gesagt, wohin sie gehen würde?
Haht zee EE-nen geh-ZAHKT, wo-HIN zee GAY'en VÜR-deh?
Did she tell you where she was going? (would go)

Sie sagte, sie würde mich um sieben Uhr
Zee ZAHK-teh zee VÜR-deh mikh oom ZEE-ben oor
She said she would meet me at seven

im Ratskeller treffen.
im RAHTS-kel-ler TREFF'en.
at the Ratskeller.

—Sie sagte, sie würde zuerst einkaufen gehen,
Zee ZAHK-teh, zee VǓR-deh ts'oo-ERST INE-kow'f'en GAY'en,
She said she would go shopping first,

dann in die Bibliothek,
dahn in dee bee-blee-yo-TAYK,
then to the library

und daß sie danach vorhätte,
oont dahss zee da-NAKH FOR-het-teh,
and that after that she planned

einen Freund zu treffen.
INE-en froynt ts'oo TREFF'en.
to meet a friend.

—Hat sie Ihnen gesagt, wann
Haht zee EE-nen geh-ZAHKT, vahn
Did she tell you when

sie zurück sein würde?
zee ts'oo-RǓK zine VǓR-deh?
she would be back?

—Nein, sie sagte nur,
Nine, zee ZAHK-teh noor
No, she said only

sie würde etwas später kommen.
zee VǓR-deh ET-vahss SHPAYT-er KOHM'en.
she would arrive a little later.

Möchten Sie vielleicht
MERKH-ten zee feel-LYKHT
Perhaps you would like

noch einmal anrufen?
nokh INE-mahl AHN-roof'en?
to call again?

— Ja, aber wenn Sie von ihr hören,
Ya, AH-ber ven zee fohn eer HER-ren,
Yes, but if you hear from her

sagen Sie ihr bitte,
zAHG-en zee eer BIT-teh,
tell her please,

Herr Jürgens habe angerufen —
Hehr YÜR-ghens HA-beh AHN-gheh-roof'en —
Mr. Jurgens called —

und daß er sie
oont dahss ehr zee
and that he is waiting for her

hier im Ratskeller erwarte.
here im RAHTS-kel-ler er-VAR-teh.
here at the Ratskeller.

What was previously said and what is said now
You will notice that in this conversation the tenses shift from the past subjunctive, in discussing what Miss Röhm has previously said, to the present subjunctive as her friend leaves a message to be given to her; namely, that he is still waiting, now, at the Ratskeller.

TEST YOUR GERMAN

In sentences 1 through 6 fill in the subjunctive form of the verb indicated in the examples of "reported speech." Translate sentences 7 through 10 into German. Score 10 points for each correct answer. See answers below.

1. She says that he is tired.
   Sie sagt, daß er müde _____ .

2. He says she is American.
   Er sagt, sie _____ Amerikanerin.

3. They say that they are going somewhat later.
   Sie sagen, daß sie etwas später _____ .

4. Did he say that he would return?
   Sagte er, daß er zurückkommen _____ ?

5. He promised me that he would give it back.
   Er hat mir versprochen, daß er es zurückgeben _____ .

6. Did she say whether she had an appointment?
   Hat sie gesagt, ob sie eine Verabredung _____ ?

7. Did she say where she was going? _____

8. She said that she would meet me here. _____

9. Would you like to call later? _____

10. Please tell her that I called. _____

Answers: 1. sei; 2. sei; 3. gehen; 4. würde; 5. würde; 6. hätte; 7. Hat sie gesagt, wohin sie gehen würde? 8. Sie sagte, sie würde mich hier treffen. 9. Möchten Sie später anrufen? 10. Sagen Sie ihr bitte, daß ich angerufen habe.

SCORE _____%

262

step 23 CONDITIONS AND SUPPOSITIONS

Sätze wie: „Wenn es morgen regnet,
ZET-seh vee: „Ven ess MOR-ghen RAYG-net,
Sentences like: "If it rains tomorrow,

werden wir nicht ans Meer fahren."
VEHRD'en veer nikht ahns mayr FAR'en."
we won't go to the seashore."

oder, „Wenn er kommt, werde ich
OH-der, „Ven ehr kohmt, VEHR-deh ikh
or "When he comes I will

ihm die Nachricht geben."
eem dee NAHKH-rikht GAYB'en."
give him the message."

sind einfache Annahmen, die
zint INE-fa-kheh AHN-na-men, dee
are simple suppositions which

nur die Zukunft gebrauchen.
noor dee TS'OO-koonft gheh-BROW'KH'en.
only require the future tense.

In vielen Fällen jedoch ist die Annahme
In FEE-len FELL-en yeh-DOKH isst dee AHN-na-meh
In many cases, however, the supposition is

viel unbestimmter, wie z.B.:
feel OON-beh-shtimm-ter, vee ts'oom BY-shpeel:
much more uncertain, as for example:

„Wenn Sie an meiner Stelle wären,
„Ven zee ahn MINE-er SHTELL-eh VEHR'en,
"If you were in my place,

was würden Sie tun?"
vahss VÜRD'en zee toon?"
what would you do?''

„Wenn ich Sie wäre, würde ich nicht kündigen."
„Ven ikh zee VAY-reh, VÜR-deh ikh nikht KÜN-deeg'en."
''If I were you, I would not resign.''

Solche Annahmen nennen wir „unwirklich."
SOHL-kheh AHN-na-men NEN-nen veer „oon-VEERK-likh."
We call such conditions ''unreal.''

> **"Unreal" conditions**
> Suppositions which suppose something which is not true are expressed with the imperfect subjunctive — the forms of which you learned in Step 22 — in one clause while the German equivalent of "would" — *würde* — or other modal auxiliaries form the other part of the supposition.
>
> The sentence: "I would go if I had time." — *Ich würde gehen, wenn ich Zeit hätte*, shows a supposition — that you are "not" going, but that you would if you could. "Would" corresponds to *würde*, "might" to *möchte*, "could" to *könnte*, "ought to" to *sollte*, and "might be allowed to" to *dürfte*.

Annahmen:
AHN-na-men:
Suppositions:

— Was würden Sie tun, wenn Sie einen
Vahss VÜRD'en zee toon, ven see INE-en
What would you do if you heard a

Einbrecher in Ihre Wohnung kommen hörten?
INE-brehkher in EE-reh VO-noong KOHM'en HERT'en?
burglar come into your apartment?

— Ich würde meine Pistole holen
Ikh VÜR-deh MINE-eh piss-TOH-leh HOLE'en
I would get my pistol

und den Einbrecher gefangennehmen.
oont dehn INE-brekher gheh-FAHNG'en-NAYM'en.
and capture the burglar.

— Aber wie würden Sie sich helfen,
AH-ber vee VÜR-den zee zikh HELF'en,
But how would you help yourself

wenn Sie keine Pistole fänden?
ven zee KINE-neh piss-TOH-leh FEND'en?
if you did not find a pistol?

— Dann würde ich natürlich sofort
Dahn VÜR-deh ikh nah-TÜR-likh zo-FORT
Then I would of course immediately

die Polizei rufen.
dee po-lee-TS'Y ROOF'en.
call the police.

— Aber was würden Sie tun, wenn
AH-ber vahss VÜRD'en zee toon, ven
But what would you do if the

die Polizei nicht antwortete?
dee Po-lee-TS'Y nikht AHNT-vor-teh-teh?
police did not answer?

— Warum sollte ich die Polizei nicht erreichen können?
**va-ROOM ZOLL-teh ikh dee po-lee-TS'Y nikht ehr-RYKH'en
KERN'en?**
Why wouldn't I be able to reach the police?

— Wenn der Einbrecher die Telefondrähte zerschneiden
Ven dehr INE-bre'kher dee teh-leh-FOHN-dray-teh ts'ehr-SHNYD'en
If the burglar cut through the telephone wires

würde, könnten Sie gar keine Anrufe machen.
VÜR-deh, KERN-ten zee gahr KINE-eh AHN-roo-feh MA'khen.
you couldn't make any telephone calls.

Was sagen Sie dazu?
Vahss SAHG'en zee DA-ts'oo?
What do you say to that?

— Du lieber Himmel! Es klingt, als ob Sie
Doo LEE-ber HIM-mel! Ess klingt ahlts op zee
For Heaven's sake! It sounds as if

Exclamations
Du lieber Himmel! — literally, "You dear
Heaven!" is a common exclamation. *Mein Gott!*
(My God!) is somewhat stronger.

auf der Seite des Einbrechers wären,
ow'f dehr ZY-teh dess INE-breh'khers VAY'REN,
you were on the burglar's side,

anstatt auf meiner.
ahn-SHTAHT ow'f MINE-er.
instead of on mine.

Instead of
Anstatt and *statt* both mean "instead of" and
are always followed by the genitive of the following noun, pronoun or adjective.

Und so drückt man Dinge aus,
Oont zo drükt mahn DING-eh ow'ss,
And this is how one expresses things

die niemals passiert sind:
dee NEE-mahls pahss-EERT zint:
that never happened:

Wenn Marie-Antoinette
Venn MA-ree-ahn-twa-NET
If Marie-Antoinette

Österreich nicht verlassen hätte,
ERST-ehr-rykh nikht fehr-LAHSS'en HET-teh,
had not left Austria.

dann hätte sie wahrscheinlich
dahn HET-teh zee vahr-SHINE-likh
then she would perhaps

ihren Kopf nicht verloren.
EE-ren kohpf nikht fehr-LOHR'en.
not have lost her head.

Wenn man den Erzherzog Ferdinand nicht erschossen hätte,
**Venn mahn den EHRTS-hehrt-sohg FEHR-din-ahnt nikht
ehr-SHOHSS'en HET-teh,**
If they had not shot the Archduke Ferdinand

hätte dann der erste Weltkreig stattgefunden?
HET-teh dahn dehr ERR-steh VELT-kreek SHTAHT-geh-foond'en?
would the first World War then have taken place?

Suppositions that never happened
The two examples above refer to suppositions
concerned with wondering how things "would
have been" if something else had or had not
happened. To express these remote conditions
we use the pluperfect subjunctive — that is, the
imperfect of *haben* or *sein* with the past participle on both sides of the supposition. The examples given in the text illustrate this because
Marie-Antoinette *did* go to France and *did*
lose her head there, and the assassination of
the Austrian Archduke "did" set off the chain of
events that resulted in World War I (as well as
World War II).

According to the meaning to be conveyed, the
pluperfect can be used on one side of the supposition and the subjunctive imperfect of *werden* on the other side, as in the following:

*Wenn der amerikanische Kongreß während
der Revolution nicht Englisch statt Deutsch als
Landessprache gewählt hätte, dann würden
heute die Amerikaner Deutsch sprechen.* "If the
American Congress, during the Revolution, had
not voted for English instead of German as the
national language, then Americans would be
speaking German today."

By the way, congratulations! You have just pro-
gressed to the most complicated combination of
verb tenses. There is nothing further. You are
now familiar with every verbal concept in
German.

267

INSTANT CONVERSATION: HOW WOULD YOU SPEND 100,000 MARKS?

—Wenn Sie plötzlich einhunderttausend Mark erbten,
Venn zee PLERTS-likh INE-hoon-dert-t'ow-zend mark EHRP-ten,
If you suddenly inherited a hundred thousand marks,

was würden Sie damit tun?
vahss VŮRD'en zee da-MIT toon?
what would you do with it?

—Aber wer auf der Welt würde mir Geld vererben?
AH-ber vehr owf dehr velt VŮRD-eh meer gelt fehr-EHRB'en?
But who in the world would leave me any money?

How to recognize a separable prefix
Erben — "to inherit" when preceded by the prefix ver means "to leave" (for inheritance). The prefix ver is not separable, as are many of the other prefixes you have noted, but stays with the verb in all its forms. As a single basic German verb can form a whole list of different verbs by a change in its prefix, you may wonder how to tell which prefixes are separable and which stay with the verb. Here is an easy rule of thumb: if the stress is on the prefix then the prefix is separable, otherwise it is inseparable. Sometimes the same verb can have two distinct meanings according to how it is stressed. Wiederholen, for example, with stress on the wie means "to go get something again" while wiederholen with stress on the ho means "to repeat." In the first example the prefix is separable and in the second it is inseparable.

—Nun . . . nehmen Sie an, Sie hätten einen Verwandten
Noon . . . NAYM'en zee ahn, zee HAIT'en INE-en fair-VAHNT-en
Well . . . suppose you had a relative

in Südamerika oder Australien, und er würde
in sût-ah-MEHR-ee-ka OH-der ow'ss-TRAHL-yen, oont ehr V̊URD-eh
in South America or Australia, and he would

Ihnen all sein Geld hinterlassen . . .
EE-nen ahl zine gelt hin-ter-LASS'en . . .
leave you all his money . . .

— Zuerst würden wir in ein größeres Haus umziehen.
**Ts'oo-ERST V̊ÛR-den veer in ine GRER-sehr-ess house
OOM-ts'ee'en.**
First we would move to a larger house.

Das würde meine Frau glücklich machen.
Dahss V̊ÛR-deh MINE-eh fr'ow GLÛK-likh MA'khen.
That would make my wife happy.

Dann würde ich mir einen neuen Sportwagen kaufen.
**Dahn V̊ÛRD-eh ikh meer INE-en NOY-en SHPORT-va-ghen
KOWF'en.**
Then I would buy myself a new sports car.

Das würde mir Freude machen.
Dahss V̊ÛRD-eh meer FROY-deh MA'khen.
That would give me pleasure.

Dann würden wir ins Rheinland zu meinen Eltern fahren.
Dahn V̊ÛRD'en veer ins RINE-lahnt ts'oo MINE-en ELT-ern FAR'en.
Then we would take a trip to the Rhineland to my parents.

Ich würde ihnen neue, moderne Maschinen und Geräte
**Ikh V̊ÛRD-eh EE-nen NOY-eh, mo-DERN-neh ma-SHEEN-en oont
gher-AY-teh**
I would buy them new modern machines and equipment

für ihre Weinberge kaufen.
fûr EE-reh VINE-behr-geh KOWF'en.
for their vineyards.

Das würde ihre Arbeit leichter machen.
Dahss V̊ÛRD-eh EE-reh AHR-bite LYE'KH-ter MA'khen.
That would make their work easier.

— Würden Sie weiter in Ihrem Beruf arbeiten?
VÜRD'en zee VITE-er in EER-em beh-ROOF AR-bite'en?
Would you continue to work in your profession?

— Ja, natürlich, denn das Geld würde nicht
Ya, na-TÜR-likh, den dahss gelt VÜRD-eh nikht
Yes, of course, because the money wouldn't

für immer ausreichen.
für im-mer OW'SS-rikh'en.
last forever.

— Aber es wäre doch ein schönes Leben,
AH-ber ess VAY-reh dokh ine SHER-ness LAY-ben,
But it would be a nice life,

solange das Geld ausreichte, nicht wahr?
zo-LAHN-geh dahss gelt OW'S-rikh-teh, nikht var?
while the money lasted, wouldn't it?

— Allerdings! Da fällt mir ein, ich habe in der Tat
AHL-ler-dings! Da failt meer ine, ikh HA-beh in dehr taht
Certainly! That reminds me, I have in fact

einen entfernten Verwandten in Südafrika.
INE-en ent-FEHRN-ten fehr-VAHNT-ten in süd-AHF-ree-ka.
a distant relative in South Africa.

Vielleicht sollte ich ihm einmal schreiben,
Feel-LIKHT ZOLL-teh ikh eem INE-mahl SHRIBE'en,
Perhaps I should write to him sometime,

> **"Should" or "ought to"**
> The imperfect of *sollen* is equivalent to
> "should" or "ought to" in the sense of obliga-
> tion. "You should see that film." — *Sie sollten
> diesen Film sehen.*

um mich zu erkundigen, wie es ihm geht.
oom mikh ts'oo ehr-KOON-dee'ghen vee ess eem gay't.
to find out how he is.

TEST YOUR GERMAN

Fill in the missing verb forms in sentences 1 through 5 and the missing phrases in sentences 6 through 10. Score 10 points for each correct sentence. See answers on following page.

1. If it doesn't rain tomorrow, we will go to the seashore.
   Wenn es morgen nicht regnet, _____ wir ans Meer
   _____.

2. When he comes, I will give him the letter.
   Wenn er kommt, _____ ich ihm den Brief
   _____.

3. If I were you, I wouldn't go.
   Wenn ich Sie _____, _____ ich nicht
   gehen.

4. He would do it if he had time.
   Er _____ es tun, wenn er Zeit _____.

5. If he heard a burglar he would call the police.
   Wenn er einen Einbrecher _____, _____
   er die Polizei rufen.

6. If you were in my place, what would you do?
   Wenn Sie an meiner Stelle wären, _____?

7. If we moved to a new house my wife would be happy.
   Wenn wir in ein neues Haus umzögen, _____.

8. I would buy a sports car if I had the money.
   Ich würde einen Sportwagen kaufen, _____.

9. If the Germans had discovered America, would the Americans speak German today?
   Wenn die Deutschen Amerika endeckt hätten, _____
   _____?

271

10. If I had an uncle in South Africa I would write a letter to him.

_____, würde ich ihm einen Brief schreiben.

Answers: 1. werden — fahren; 2. werde — geben; 3. wäre — würde; 4. würde — hätte; 5. hörte — würde; 6. was würden Sie tun? 7. würde meine Frau glücklich sein. 8. wenn ich das Geld hätte. 9. würden die Amerikaner heute Deutsch sprechen? 10. Wenn ich einen Onkel in Süd-afrika hätte

SCORE _____%

step 24   HOW TO READ GERMAN

Hier sind einige Ratschläge, um Ihnen
Here is some advice to

das Lesen im Deutschen zu vereinfachen.
facilitate your reading in German.

In Geschäftsbriefen
In business correspondence

verwendet man oft
one often uses

den Konjunktiv, um besonders die Höflichkeit
the subjunctive, in order especially to

zu unterstreichen:
stress politeness:

Sehr geehrter Herr!
Dear Sir,

Wir wären Ihnen dankbar, wenn Sie
We would appreciate your

uns sobald wie möglich
sending us as soon as possible

die Ware senden würden, die wir bestellt haben.
the merchandise that we ordered.

Es wäre unbedingt nötig, daß
It would be absolutely necessary that

wir sie vor November erhalten.
we receive it before November.

Falls es unmöglich sein sollte,
In case it should be impossible

die Ware rechtzeitig abzusenden,
to dispatch the merchandise on time,

wären wir Ihnen sehr verbunden,
we would be most obliged

wenn Sie uns mit umgehender Post benachrichtigen würden.
if you could let us know by return mail.

In der Hoffnung, sobald wie möglich von
Hoping to hear from you as soon as possible,

Ihnen zu hören, grüßen wir Sie,
we remain,

Hochachtungsvoll!
Sincerely yours.

Wenn Sie die Zeitung lesen,
When you read the newspaper,

wird Ihnen auffallen, daß die Nachrichten
you will notice that the news items

hauptsächlich das Imperfekt benutzen.
mostly use the imperfect tense.

Sie werden aber auch bemerken,
You will also notice

daß die Sätze meistens länger sind
that the sentences are mostly longer

als englische, und daß erst nach
than English ones, and that the verb comes only after

mehreren Nebensätzen das Verb kommt.
several subordinate clauses.

The key word at the end

As you practice reading German in newspaper and magazine articles try looking at the end of the longer sentences for the key verb which gives the meaning to the whole sentence. After a while you will automatically fall into this German style and these long sentences, which seem complicated, will become easy and natural to you.

Ein typischer Zeitungsbericht:
A typical news article:

Als der Präsident der Vereinigten Staaten
When the President of the United States

am Montag der vergangenen Woche
arrived on Monday of last week

am Bonner Flughafen *ankam,*
at the Bonn airport.

wurde er vom deutschen Bundeskanzler,
he was *greeted* by the German Federal Chancellor,

dem Außenminister und anderen
the Foreign Secretary and other

Mitgliedern der Regierung *begrüßt.*
members of the Government.

Es waren viele Presseleute und Fotografen
There were many people from the press and photographers

anwesend, und eine große Volksmenge war versammelt.
present and a large crowd of people was assembled.

Die Verhandlungen zwischen dem
The discussions between the

Bundeskanzler und dem amerikanischen Präsidenten
Chancellor and the American President

wurden geheimgehalten.
were kept secret.

Jedoch berief der Bundeskanzler am Dienstag
However, the Chancellor called on Tuesday

in Bonn eine Pressekonferenz
a press conference

und erklärte, daß die Unterredung
and he announced that the discussion

höchst erfolgreich *gewesen sei.*
has been (most highly) successful.

Das Imperfekt wird hauptsächlich auch
The imperfect tense is used mostly also

in der Literatur gebraucht,
in literature,

wie z.B. in Romanen, Kurzgeschichten
as in novels, short stories,

and Anekdoten.
and anecdotes.

Als der Kaiser Franz-Joseph von Österreich regierte,
When the Emperor Franz Josef of Austria reigned,

sollte einmal ein Botschafter aus einem kleinen
an ambassador from a small

Balkanland dem kaiserlichen Hof
Balkan country was to be presented to the

vorgestellt werden.
imperial court.

Da er nicht sehr gut Deutsch sprach,
As he did not speak German very well,

gab man ihm einen Dolmetscher.
he was given an interpreter.

Als er dann Seiner Majestät dem Kaiser vorgestellt wurde,
When he was presented to His Majesty, the Emperor,

sprach der Botschafter zuerst nur in seiner Landessprache.
the ambassador spoke at first only in his native language.

Dann blieb er still und überließ
Then he remained silent and left

das Wort dem Dolmetscher.
the word to the interpreter.

Dieser begann dann eine hochtrabende Rede,
The latter thus began a stilted speech

voll von Lob und Bewunderung für die
filled with praise and admiration of the

majestätische Größe des Kaisers.
Emperor's majestic greatness.

Als seine Lobrede zu Ende war,
When his speech of praise was finished,

nahm ihn der Botschafter beiseite und sagte:
the ambassador took him aside and said,

„Ich habe Ihre Übersetzung verstanden, mein Herr,
"I have understood your translation, Sir,

aber es war in keinem Fall, was ich gesagt hatte."
but it was in no case what I had said."

„Sie haben Recht, Exzellenz,"
"You are correct, your Excellency,"

antwortete der Dolmetscher, „das war nicht,
replied the interpreter, "that was not

was Sie gesagt hatten,
what you had said,

aber das war unbedingt,
but that was definitely

was Sie hätten sagen sollen."
what you should have said."

Deutsche Gedichte und Lieder sind mit Recht
German poetry and songs are justly famous

in der ganzen Welt berühmt.
throughout the whole world.

Fast alle Deutschen kennen
Almost all Germans know

die erste Strophe des *Erlkönig*
the first verse of *Elf King*

von Goethe auswendig:
by Goethe by heart

Wer reitet so spät durch Nacht und Wind?
Who rides so late through night and wind?

Es ist der Vater mit seinem Kind.
It is the father with his child.

Er hat den Knaben wohl in dem Arm.
He has the boy well in his arm.

Er faßt ihn sicher, er hält ihn warm.
He holds him sure, he holds him warm.

„Mein Sohn, was birgst du so bang dein Gesicht?"
"My son, why are you making such a frightened face?"

„Siehst, Vater, du den Erlkönig nicht?
"Father, don't you see the King of the Elves?

Den Erlkönig, mit Kron' und Schweif?"
The King of the Elves, with crown and trailing robe?"

„Mein Sohn, es ist ein Nebelstreif." . . .
"My son, it is a cloud of mist." . . .

Eines der berühmtesten deutschen Volkslieder
One of the most famous German folk songs

ist ein Gedicht von Heine. — *Die Lorelei.*
is a poem by Heine — *Die Lorelei.*

Die ersten Zeilen sind
The first lines are familiar

jedem, der Deutsch spricht, bekannt.
to everyone who speaks German.

Ich weiß nicht, was soll es bedeuten,
I know not what it must mean

Daß ich so traurig bin.
That I am so sad.

Ein Märchen aus alten Zeiten,
A story from olden times

Das kommt mir nicht aus dem Sinn. . . .
That will not leave my mind. . . .

In German-speaking countries you will find many instances of the use of the Gothic alphabet in old signs, documents, and books. This is how the first verse of *Die Lorelei,* which you have just read, looks in Gothic letters:

Die Lorelei

Ich weiß nicht, was soll es bedeuten,
Daß ich so traurig bin;
Ein Märchen aus alten Zeiten,
Das kommt mir nicht aus dem Sinn.

The Gothic alphabet is not difficult to read, after a little practice. Here are the 26 letters, in both capitals and small letters:

𝔄 a	A	a		𝔑 n	N	n
𝔅 b	B	b		𝔒 o	O	o
ℭ c	C	c		𝔓 p	P	p
𝔇 d	D	d		𝔔 q	Q	q
𝔈 e	E	e		𝔯 r	R	r
𝔉 f	F	f		𝔖 ſ s	S	s
𝔊 g	G	g		𝔗 t	T	t
𝔥 h	H	h		𝔘 u	U	u
𝔍 i	I	i		𝔙 v	V	v
𝔍 j	J	j		𝔚 w	W	w
𝔎 k	K	k		𝔛 x	X	x
𝔏 l	L	l		𝔜 y	Y	y
𝔐 m	M	m		𝔷 z	Z	z

German Step by Step

Die deutsche Sprache ist so klar und eindeutig,
The German language is so clear and forceful,

daß es möglich ist,
that it is possible

hervorragende Übersetzungen aus der englischen Literatur zu machen.
to make outstanding translations of English literature.

Infolgedessen sind Shakespeares Dramen
As a result of this Shakespeare's plays

genauso beliebt in Deutschland
are just as popular in Germany

wie in den englischsprachigen Ländern.
as they are in the English speaking countries.

Sie sollten einmal versuchen,
You should some time try

einige davon auf deutsch zu lesen,
to read some of them in German,

dann werden Sie sehen, wie leicht
to see how easily

Sie den Sinn erkennen können,
you can understand the meaning,

wie, z.B., als Hamlet sagt:
as, for example, when Hamlet says:

> Sein oder nicht sein,
> Das ist hier die Frage.

oder Julia:
or Juliette:

> O Romeo! warum denn Romeo?
> Verleugne deinen Vater, deinen Namen!
> Willst du das nicht, schwör' dich zu meinem Liebsten,
> Und ich bin länger keine Capulet!

oder Mark Anton:
or Mark Antony

Mitbürger! Freunde! Römer! hört mich an:
Begraben will ich Cäsarn, nicht ihn preisen.
Was Menschen Übles tun, das überlebt sie,
Das Gute wird mit ihnen oft begraben.

Alles, was Sie auf deutsch lesen,
Everything you read in German,

ob es Theaterstücke, Romane,
whether it is plays, novels,

oder Kunst-oder Geschichtsbücher sind,
or art or history books,

wird Ihre Kenntnis der deutschen Sprache
will enlarge your knowledge of the German language,

erweitern und wird Ihnen außerdem viel Freude bereiten.
and will also give you much pleasure.

Aber am wichtigsten ist es natürlich,
But it is, of course, most important

viel zu sprechen und zuzuhören, wenn
to speak a lot and to listen when

andere sprechen, denn um eine Sprache
others are speaking, because, to learn a language

gut zu lernen, muß man bei jeder Gelegenheit üben.
well, one must practice on all occasions.

EIN GUTER RAT —
SOME GOOD ADVICE

While you have learned up to now the essential elements for speaking German, you will encounter, when reading German books, magazines, and newspapers, many words not included in this book. You will be aided, however, in your understanding and use of new words by the fact that there are so many words in English which are similar in German in meaning, and *almost* in spelling.

This is because English belongs to the same group of languages as German, which also include Dutch and the Scandinavian languages. A great percentage of the short words in English have close cognates in German, although the spelling and pronunciation may be somewhat different. Even the longer German words can be understood since they are composed of short ones put together. You will find, therefore, as you learn more and more German, that there are thousands of words that are almost the same as English. All you have to do is get used to their German pronunciation and spelling differences.

When you read new material in German, or when you hear German spoken, you will constantly encounter many words that you may not have studied but that *you already know*. Therefore, if you have a two-way dictionary, use the English/German part frequently for making up your own sentences, but do not use the German/English section, except in rare cases. Let the meaning and construction become evident to you through context and your own initiative — and, above all, read *aloud* at every chance you get. It is suggested that you read German material onto cassettes, or copy spoken material in your own voice, and compare your entries from day to day. As you progress, you will be surprised at how soon you will sound as if you were speaking your own language.

DICTIONARY
ENGLISH — GERMAN

This dictionary contains numerous words not in the preceding text, but which will complete your ability to use current German. It is an interesting linguistic fact that most people use less than 2,000 words in their daily conversation in any language. In this dictionary you have over 2,600 words chosen especially for frequency of use.

N.B.　1. Gender of nouns are indicated by *der, die,* or *das* in parentheses before the German word. When a feminine form of a common noun exists, it is given after the masculine form.

2. Plural forms of nouns are shown by *-e, -n, -en, -er,* etc. after the noun. When the plural is formed by a umlaut change, then the whole form is given. If the noun does not change for the plural, nothing follows.

3. Verbs are given in the infinitive form. Some especially important verbal expressions are given in alphabetical order for easy use.

4. The separable prefix of the verbs which divide or separate are underlined.

5. Irregular past participles of "strong" verbs are indicated, after the infinitive, in parentheses.

6. Adverbs and the simple adjective form are generally interchangeable.

7. When a choice of meaning is approximately equal between two frequently used words or expressions, both are given, separated by a comma. This will help to increase your comprehension of the words you will hear or see in German.

A

a, an *(m)* ein, *(f)* eine, *(n)* ein
able: to be able to können
about *(concerning)* über
    about *(approximately)* etwa;
    ungefähr
above über
absence *(die)* Abwesenheit, -en
absent abwesend
accent *(der)* Akzent, -e
(to) accept annehmen
accident *(der)* Unfall, Unfälle
accidentally zufällig
account *(bank)* *(das)* Konto, -ten
    account *(computation)* *(die)*
    Berechnung, -en
    account *(report)* *(der)*
    Bericht, -e
accurate korrekt
(to) accuse beschuldigen
ache *(der)* Schmerz, -en
across quer über; quer durch
actor *(der)* Schauspieler, -
actress *(die)* Schauspielerin, -nen
(to) add hinzufügen
address *(die)* Adresse, -n
(to) admire bewundern
admission *(der)* Eintritt, -e

(to) advance *(go forward)*
    vorrücken; fortschreiten
adventure *(das)* Abenteuer, -
advertisement *(die)* Anzeige, -n
advice *(der)* Rat
advise raten
affectionate liebevoll
(to be) afraid Furcht haben; Angst
    haben; sich fürchten
Africa *(das)* Afrika
after *(prep. of time)* nach
afternoon *(der)* Nachmittag, -e
again wieder
against gegen
age *(das)* Alter
agency *(die)* Agentur, -en
agent *(der)* Agent, -en
ago vor
agreeable angenehm
(to) agree übereinstimmen
agreed abgemacht
ahead voran, vorne
air *(die)* Luft, Lüfte
air conditioning *(die)* Kilmaan-
    lage, -n
airforce *(die)* Luftwaffe, -n
air mail *(die)* Luftpost
airplane *(das)* Flugzeug, -e

airport (*der*) Flugplatz,
Flugplätze
alcohol (*der*) Alkohol
all alle, alles
   That's all. Das ist alles.
(*to*) **allow** erlauben
all right gut, fein
almost beinahe; fast
alone allein
already schon
also auch
although obwohl
always immer
am: I am ich bin
America (*das*) Amerika
American (*adj.*) amerikanisch
American (*person*) (*der*) Amerikaner, -, (*die*) Amerikanerin,
-nen
among unter; zwischen
amount (*der*) Betrag, Beträge
amusing amüsant
and und
angry böse
animal (*das*) Tier, -e
ankle (*der*) Knöchel, -
anniversary (*der*) Jahrestag, -e
(*to*) **annoy** ärgern
annoying ärgerlich
another ein anderer, eine andere,
ein anderes
answer (*die*) Antwort, -en
   (*to*) **answer** antworten
antiseptic antiseptisch
any (*of*) etwas
any irgendein
anyone (*at all*) irgendeiner
Anyone else? Sonst noch jemand?
anything irgend etwas

Anything else?
Sonst noch etwas?
anywhere irgendwo
apartment (*die*) Wohnung, -en
(*to*) **apologize** sich entschuldigen
appetite (*der*) Appetit
apple (*der*) Apfel, Äpfel
appointment (*die*) Verabredung,
-en
(*to*) **appreciate** schätzen
(*to*) **approve** billigen
April (*der*) April
Arab (*person*) (*der*) Araber, -,
(*die*) Araberin, -nen
Arabic (*adj*) arabisch
architect (*der*) Architekt, -en
architecture (*die*) Architektur, -en
(*you*) **are** (*Sie*) sind
   (*we*) **are** (*wir*) sind
   (*they*) **are** (*sie*) sind
   (*there*) **are** (*es*) gibt
area (*das*) Gebiet, -e
argument (*das*) Argument, -e
arm (*der*) Arm, -e
army (*die*) Armee, -n
arrival (*die*) Ankunft - Ankünfte
around (*surrounding*) rundherum,
-um
   around (*approximately*)
ungefähr
(*to*) **arrange** anordnen
(*to*) **arrest** verhaften
(*to*) **arrive** ankommen
art (*die*) Kunst, Künste
artificial künstlich
artist (*der*) Künstler, -, (*die*)
Künstlerin, -nen
as so, wie; as . . . as so . . . wie
as much as soviel . . .

Asia (*das*) Asien
(*to*) **ask** fragen
asparagus (*der*) Spargel, -
aspirin (*das*) Aspirin
assortment (*die*) Auswahl
at (*location*) in
at (*time*) um
Atlantic (*der*) Atlantik
atomic Atom-
(*to*) **attend** besuchen; **to attend a school** eine Schule besuchen
attention (*die*) Achtung
August (*der*) August
aunt (*die*) Tante, -n
Australia (*das*) Australien
Australian (*person*) (*der*) Australier, -, (*die*) Australierin, -nen
Australian (*adj.*) australisch
Austria (*das*) Österreich
Austrian (*person*) (*der*) Österreicher, -, (*die*) Österreicherin, -nen
Austrian (*adj*) österreichisch
author (*der*) Autor, -en
authoress (*die*) Autorin, -nen
automatic automatisch
automobile (*das*) Auto, -s
autumn (*der*) Herbst, -e
avenue (*die*) Allee, -n
average (*der*) Durchschnitt
(*to*) **avoid** vermeiden
away weg

B

baby (*das*) Baby, -s (*das*) Kindchen, -,
bachelor (*der*) Junggeselle, -n
back (*adverb*) zurück

back (*of body*) (*der*) Rücken, -
backwards rückwärts
bacon (*der*) Speck
bad schlecht
bad luck (*das*) Pech
bag (*der*) Koffer
baggage (*das*) Gepäck; (*die*) Gepäckstücke
bakery (*die*) Bäckerei
ball (*der*) Ball, Bälle
banana (*die*) Banane, -n
band (*music*) (*die*) Kapelle, -n
bandage (*die*) Binde, -n
bank (*die*) Bank, -en
bar (*die*) Bar, -s
barber (*der*) Friseur, -e
basement (*der*) Keller, -
bath (*das*) Bad, Bäder
bathing suit (*der*) Badeanzug, Badeanzüge
bathroom (*das*) Badezimmer, -
battery (*die*) Batterie, -n
battle (*die*) Schlacht, -en
bay (*die*) Bucht, -en
(*to*) **be** sein
beach (*der*) Strand, (*die*) Strände
bean (*die*) Bohne, -n
bear (*der*) der Bär, -en
beard (*der*) Bart, Bärte
beautiful schön
beauty (*die*) Schönheit, -en
beauty shop (*der*) Schönheitssalon, -s
because weil
bed (*das*) Bett, -en
bedroom (*das*) Schlafzimmer, -
beef (*das*) Rindfleisch
been gewesen (*p.p. of sein*)
beer (*das*) Bier, -e

before vor
(to) begin an̲fangen
behind (prep.) hinter
(to) believe glauben
below unten (adv.); unter (adj.)
(to) belong gehören
belt (der) Gürtel, -
Belgium (das) Belgien
Belgian (adj) belgisch
Belgian (person) der Belgier, (die)
Belgierin, -nen
beside neben
best (adj) beste
best (adv) am besten
best (noun) das Beste
best wishes (die) Glückwünsche
bet (die) Wette, -n
better besser
between zwischen
Beware! Vorsicht!
bicycle (das) Fahrrad, Fahrräder
big groß
bill (die) Rechnung, -en
bird (der) Vogel, Vögel
birthday (der) Geburtstag, -e
black schwarz
blanket (die) Decke, -n
blond blond
blood (das) Blut
blouse (die) Bluse, -n
blue blau
boarding house (die) Pension, -en
boat (das) Boot, -e
body (der) Körper, -
bomb (die) Bombe, -n
book (das) Buch, Bücher
bookstore (die) Buchhandlung,
-en
boot (der) Stiefel, -

border (die) Grenze, -n
born geboren
(to) borrow borgen
boss (der) Chef, -s
both beide
(to) bother stören
bottle (die) Flasche, -n
bottom (der) Boden, Böden
bought gekauft (p.p. of kaufen)
bowl (die) Schale, -n; (die)
Schüssel, -n
box (die) Schachtel, -n
boy (der) Junge, -n; (der) Knabe,
-n
bracelet (das) Armband,
Armbänder
brain (das) Gehirn, -e
brake (die) Bremse, -n
brassiere (der) Büstenhalter, -
brave tapfer
bread (das) Brot, -e
(to) break brechen
breakfast (das) Frühstück
breast (die) Brust, Brüste
(to) breathe atmen
breeze (die) Brise, -n
bride (die) Braut, Bräute
bridegroom (der) Bräutigam, -e
bridge (die) Brücke, -n
brief kurz
briefcase (die) Aktentasche, -n
(to) bring bringen; her̲bringen;
mit̲bringen
broken gebrochen, zerbrochen
broom (der) Besen, -
brother (der) Bruder, Brüder
brother-in-law (der) Schwager,
Schwäger
brown braun

brush (*die*) Bürste, -n
(*to*) **build** bauen
building (*das*) Gebäude, -
built gebaut (*p.p. of* bauen)
(*to*) **burn** brennen, verbrennen
bureau (*das*) Büro, -s
bus (*der*) Bus, -se
bus stop (*die*) Bushaltestelle, -n
business (*das*) Geschäft, -e; (*die*)
Beschäftigung, -en
businessman (*der*) Geschäftsmann, Geschäftsleute
busy beschäftigt
but aber
butter (*die*) Butter
button (*der*) Knopf, Knöpfe
(*to*) **buy** kaufen (*gekauft*)
by (*near*) bei, an

C

cab (*das*) Taxi, -s
cabaret (*das*) Kabarett, -e
cabbage (*der*) Kohl
cake (*der*) Kuchen
(*to*) **call** rufen, anrufen
call (*telephone*) (*der*) Anruf,
-e
calm ruhig
camera (*die*) Kamera, -s
can (*able*) können
can you ...? Können Sie ...?
Kannst Du ...?
I can. Ich kann.
I can't. Ich kann nicht.
can (*container*) (*die*) Büchse, -n
can opener (*der*) Büchsenöffner, -
Canada (*das*) Kanada
Canadian person (*der*) Kanadier
(*die*) Kanadierin, -nen

candy (*das*) Bonbon, -s
cap (*die*) Mütze, -n
captain (*sea*) (*der*) Kapitän, -e
captain (*police or army*) (*der*)
Hauptmann, Hauptleute
car (*der*) Wagen, -
carburetor (*der*) Vergaser
capable fähig
careful vorsichtig
be careful! Vorsicht!
careless sorglos, fahrlässig
carrot (*die*) Karotte, -n
(*to*) **carry** tragen
cashier (*der*) Kassierer, -
castle (*die*) Burg, -en, (*das*)
Schloß, Schlösser
cat (*die*) Katze, -n
cathedral (*der*) Dom, -e
catholic katholisch
celebration (*die*) Feier, -n
cellar (*der*) Keller
cemetery (*der*) Friedhof,
Friedhöfe
center (*das*) Zentrum, Zentren
century (*das*) Jahrhundert, -e
certainly sicher(*lich*); bestimmt;
gewiß
chair (*der*) Stuhl, Stühle
(*to*) **change** wechseln (*for money*);
ändern; umsteigen (*for trains*)
charming charmant
chauffeur (*der*) Fahrer, -
cheap billig
check (*money*) (*der*) Scheck, -s
check (*baggage*) der Gepäck-
schein, -e
checkroom (*die*) Garderobe, -n
cheese (*der*) Käse
cherry (*die*) Kirsche, -n

chest (*die*) Brust, Brüste
chicken (*das*) Huhn, Hühner
child (*das*) Kind, -er
China (*das*) China
Chinese (*adj*) chinesisch
Chinese (*person*) (*der*) Chinese,
 -n, (*die*) Chinesin, -nen
chocolate (*die*) Schokolade
chop (*das*) Kotelett, -e, -s
church (*die*) Kirche, -n
cigar (*die*) Zigarre, -n
cigarette (*die*) Zigarette, -n
city (*die*) Stadt, Städte
clean rein
(*to*) clean reinigen; säubern
clear klar
clerk (*der*) Angestellte, -n
clever klug; gescheit; begabt
climate (*das*) Klima, -s
clock (*die*) Uhr, -en
close (*near*) nahe
 (*to*) close schließen
 (*geschlossen*)
closed geschlossen (*p.p. of*
 schließen)
clothes (*die*) Kleider
cloud (*die*) Wolke, -n
coast (*die*) Küste, -n
coat (*der*) Mantel, Mäntel
coffee (*der*) Kaffee
coin (*die*) Münze, -n
cold kalt
cold cuts (*die*) Wurst, Würste;
 (*der*) Aufschnitt
colonel (*der*) Oberst, -en
color (*die*) Farbe, -n
comb (*der*) Kamm, Kämme
(*to*) come kommen

Come here! Kommen Sie
 her!
Come in! Herein!
Come on! Komm mit!
 Komm weiter!
(*to*) come back zurückkommen
comedy (*die*) Komödie, -n
(*to*) comfort trösten
comfortable bequem
(*to*) commence anfangen
commentary (*der*) Kommentar, -e
(*to*) communicate mitteilen;
 benachrichtigen
communist-tic kommunist-isch
companion (*der*) Gefährte, -n,
 (*die*) Gefährtin, -nen
company (*die*) Gesellschaft, -en
(*to*) compare vergleichen
competition (*die*) Konkurrenz
complete vollständig
complicated kompliziert
compliment (*das*) Kompliment, -e
computer (*der*) Komputer, -
concert (*das*) Konzert, -e
confidential vertraulich
confusion (*die*) Verwirrung, -en
congratulation (*der*)
 Glückwunsch, Glückwünsche
(*to*) congratulate
 beglückwünschen
conservative konservativ
(*to*) consider betrachten; erwägen
consul (*der*) Konsul, -n
consulate (*das*) Konsulat, -e
(*to*) continue fortsetzen
contract (*der*) Vertrag, Verträge
convenient bequem, praktisch
conversation (*die*) Unterhaltung,
 -en

289

cook (*der*) Koch, Köche, (*die*)
Köchin, -nen
(*to*) **cook** kochen
cool kühl
copy (*die*) Kopie, -n
corkscrew (*der*) Korkenzieher, -
corn (*der*) Mais
corner (*die*) Ecke, -n
corporation (*die*) Gesellschaft, -en
correct richtig
(*to*) **cost** kosten
cotton (*die*) Baumwolle
(*to*) **cough** husten
(*to*) **count** zählen
country (*das*) Land, Länder
couple (*das*) Paar, -e
(*to*) **cover** bedecken
cousin (*der*) Vetter, -n, (*die*) Ku-
sine, -n
cow (*die*) Kuh, Kühe
crab die Krabbe, -n, (*der*) Krebs,
-e
crazy verrückt
cream (*die*) Sahne
credit (*der*) Kredit
crime (*das*) Verbrechen, -
criminal (*der*) Verbrecher, -, (*die*)
Verbrecherin, -nen
crisis (*die*) Krise, -n
(*to*) **criticize** kritisieren
crop (*die*) Ernte, -n
cross (*das*) Kreuz, -e
(*to*) **cross** (*the street*)
überqueren
crossing (*die*) Kreuzung, -en
crowd (*die*) Menge
cruel grausam
(*to*) **cry** weinen
culture (*die*) Kultur, -en

cup (*die*) Tasse, -n
(*to*) **cure** heilen
customer (*der*) Kunde, -n
customs office (*der*) Zoll
(*to*) **cut** schneiden
Czech (*person*) (*der*) Tscheche, -n
(*die*) Tschechin, -nen
Czechoslovakia (*die*)
Tschechoslowakei

D

(*to*) **dance** tanzen
danger (*die*) Gefahr, -en
dangerous gefährlich
dark dunkel
darling (*der*) Schatz (see **treasure**)
date (*das*) Datum, Daten
daughter (*die*) Tochter, Töchter
day (*der*) Tag, -e
dead tot
dear lieb
(*my*) **dear** mein Liebling
December (*der*) Dezember
(*to*) **decide** entscheiden
decision (*die*) Entscheidung, -en
deep tief
delay (*die*) Verzögerung, -en
delighted sehr erfreut
delicious köstlich
(*to*) **deliver** liefern
democratic demokratisch
dentist (*der*) Zahnarzt, Zahnärzte
department store (*das*) Kauf-
haus, -häuser
desk (*der*) Schreibtisch, -e
detour (*die*) Umleitung, -en
devil (*der*) Teufel, -

dictionary (*das*) Wörterbuch,
Wörterbücher
different anders; verschieden
difficult schwierig; schwer
(*to*) dine essen; speisen
dining-room (*das*) Speisezimmer,
-; (*das*) Eßzimmer, -
dinner (*das*) Abendessen, -
direction (*die*) Richtung, -en
dirty schmutzig
disagreeable unangenehm
disappointed enttäuscht
discount (*der*) Rabatt, -e
(*to*) discover entdecken
(*to*) discuss besprechen
dish (*der*) Teller, -
dishonest unehrlich
distance (*die*) Entfernung, -en
district (*der*) Bezirk, -e; (*der*)
Kreis, -e
divorced geschieden (*adj. & p.p. of
scheiden*)
dizzy schwindlig
(*to*) do tun; machen
doctor (*der*) Arzt, Ärzte
doctor (*form of address*) Herr
Doktor
dog (*der*) Hund, -e
dollar (*der*) Dollar, -s
done gemacht
door (*die*) Tür, -en
down (*adv., direction*) herunter;
hinunter; herab; nach unten
downtown in der Stadt
dream (*der*) Traum, Träume
(*to*) dream träumen
dress (*das*) Kleid, -er
(*to*) drink trinken (getrunken)

(*to*) drive fahren
driver (*der*) Fahrer, -
driver's license (*der*) Führerschein, -e
drugstore (*die*) Drogerie, -n; (*die*)
Apotheke, -n
drunk betrunken
duck (*die*) Ente, -n
during während
Dutch holländisch
Dutch (*person*) (*der*)
Holländer, (*die*) Holländerin,
-nen
dysentery (*die*) Ruhr

E

each jeder, jede, jedes
eagle (*der*) Adler,—
ear (*das*) Ohr, -en
early früh
earlier früher
(*to*) earn verdienen
earth (*die*) Erde
east Osten
easy mühelos; leicht
(*to*) eat essen (*gegessen*)
egg (*das*) Ei, -er
eight acht
eighteen achtzehn
(*the*) eighth (*der die, das*) achte
eighty achtzig
either ... or entweder ... oder
elbow (*der*) Ellbogen, -
electric elektrisch
elephant (*der*) Elefant, -en
elevator (*der*) Aufzug, Aufzüge
eleven elf

291

else (*adv*) sonst; außerdem; weiter
  anyone else? sonst noch
  jemand?
  anything else? sonst noch
  etwas?
  or else sonst
embassy (*die*) Botschaft, -en
emergency (*die*) Notlage, -n
employee (*der*) (*die*) Angestellte,
  -n
employer (*der*) Arbeitgeber
empty leer
end (*das*) Ende, -n
(*to*) **end** enden
England (*das*) England
English (*adj.*) englisch
English (*person*) (*der*) Engländer,
  -, (*die*) Engländerin, -nen
(*to*) **enjoy** genießen
enough genug
(*to*) **enter** <u>ein</u>treten; betreten
(*to*) **entertain** unterhalten
entertaining unterhaltend
entrance (*der*) Eintritt, -e
error (*der*) Fehler; (*der*) Irrtum,
  Irrtümer
especially besonders
Europe (*das*) Europa
European (*adj*) europäisch
European (*pers.*) (*der*) Europäer,
  (*die*) Europäerin, -nen
even sogar
evening (*der*) Abend, -e
ever je; stets; immer
every jeder, jede, jedes
everybody alle
everything alles
exact genau
exactly genau

excellent ausgezeichnet
except außer
(*to*) **exchange** <u>um</u>tauschen;
  <u>aus</u>wechseln
Excuse me! Entschuldigung!
exit (*der*) Ausgang, Ausgänge
expensive teuer
experience (*die*) Erfahrung, -en
(*to*) **explain** erklären
explanation (*die*) Erklärung, -en
(*to*) **export** exportieren
extra extra
eye (*das*) Auge, -n

F

face (*das*) Gesicht, -er
factory (*die*) Fabrik, -en
fair (*der*) Jahrmarkt, Jahrmärkte
fall (*a drop*) (*der*) Sturz, Stürze
  fall (*autumn*) (*der*) Herbst, -e
  (*to*) **fall** fallen
false falsch
family (*die*) Familie, -n
famous berühmt
far weit
  how far? wie weit?
fare (*der*) Fahrpreis, -e
farm (*der*) Bauernhof,
  Bauernhöfe
farmer (*der*) Bauer, -
fast schnell
fat dick
father (*der*) Vater, Väter
February (*der*) Februar
(*to*) **feel** fühlen
fever (*das*) Fieber
few wenig, wenige
fewer weniger

fifteen fünfzehn
(the) fifth (der, die, das) fünfte
fifty fünfzig
(to) fight kämpfen
(to) fill füllen
film (der) Film, -e
finally endlich
(to) find finden (gefunden)
(to) find out herausfinden
finger (der) Finger, -
(to) finish beenden
fire (das) Feuer, -
(at) first zuerst
(the) first (der, die, das) erste
fish (der) Fisch, -e
   (to) fish fischen; angeln
five fünf
flight (der) Flug, Flüge
floor (of room) (der) Fußboden,
   Fußböden
floor (of building) (der) Stock,
   Stockwerke
flower (die) Blume, -n
(to) fly fliegen
food (das) Essen
foot (der) Fuß, Füße
for für
(to) forbid verbieten (verboten)
foreigner (der) Ausländer, (die)
   Ausländerin, -nen
forest (der) Wald, Wälder
(to) forget vergessen
   Don't forget ...! Vergessen
   Sie nicht...!
fork (die) Gabel, -n
forty vierzig
fountain (der) Springbrunnen, -
four vier
fourteen vierzehn

(the) fourth (der, die, das) vierte
fox (der) Fuchs, Füchse
France (das) Frankreich
free (at liberty) frei
free (no charge) kostenlos
French (adj.) französisch
French (person) (der) Franzose,
   -n, (die) Französin, -nen
frequently oft
fresh frisch
Friday (der) Freitag
fried gebraten (adj. & p.p. of
   braten)
friend (der) Freund, -e, (die)
   Freundin, -nen
from von, aus
front (die) Vorderseite, -n
frozen gefroren
fruit (die) Frucht, Früchte
fuel (der) Treibstoff
full voll
fun (das) Vergnügen, -
funny komisch
fur (der) Pelz, -e
   fur coat (der) Pelzmantel,
   Pelzmäntel
furniture (die) Möbel
future (die) Zukunft

G

gamble spielen
game (das) Spiel, -e
garden (der) Garten, Gärten
gasoline (das) Benzin
gas station (die) Tankstelle, -n
garage (die) Garage, -n
gate (das) Tor, -e
(to) gather sammeln

general allgemein
general (*mil.*) (*der*) General,
  Generäle
generous freigebig
gentle sanft
gentleman (*der*) Herr, -en
genuine echt
German (*adj.*) deutsch
German (*person*) (*der*) Deutsche,
  -n, (*die*) Deutsche, -n
Germany (*das*) Deutschland
(*to*) get bekommen; erhalten
  (*to*) get off aussteigen
  (*to*) get on (*or into*) einsteigen
  (*to*) get up aufstehen
  Get out! Hinaus!
ghost (*das*) Gespenst, -er
gift (*das*) Geschenk, -e
girl (*das*) Mädchen, -
(*to*) give geben (gegeben)
  Give me ... Geben Sie mir
  ..., Gib mir ...
glad froh
glass (*das*) Glas, Gläser
glasses (*die*) Brille, -n
(*to*) go gehen
  go away! Gehen Sie weg!
  (*to*) go away weggehen
  (*to*) go back zurückgehen
  (*to*) go on weitergehen
  go on! Gehen Sie weiter!
goat (*die*) Ziege, -n
God (*der*) Gott, Götter
gold (*das*) Gold
good gut
Goodbye! Auf Wiedersehen!
Good day! Guten Tag!
Good morning! Guten Morgen!
Good evening! Guten Abend!

Good night! Gute Nacht!
goose (*die*) Gans, Gänse
government (*die*) Regierung, -en
grandfather (*der*) Großvater,
  Großväter
grandmother (*die*) Großmutter,
  Großmütter
grape (*die*) Weintraube, -n
grateful dankbar
gray grau
great groß
grave (*noun*) (*das*) Grab, Gräber
Greece (*das*) Griechenland
Greek (*adj.*) griechisch
Greek (*person*) (*der*) Grieche, -n,
  (*die*) Griechin, -nen
green grün
(*to*) greet grüßen
group (*die*) Gruppe, -n
guide (*der*) Reiseführer, -
guitar (*die*) Gitarre, -n

H

hair (*das*) Haar, -e
hairbrush (*die*) Haarbürste, -n
haircut (*der*) Haarschnitt, -e
half halb
hand (*die*) Hand, Hände
handbag (*die*) Handtasche, -n
(*to*) happen geschehen
happy glücklich
hard hart
hat (*der*) Hut, Hüte
(*to*) have haben (gehabt)
  have you ...? Haben
  Sie ...?
he er
head (*der*) Kopf, Köpfe

health (*die*) Gesundheit
(*to*) hear hören (gehört)
heart (*das*) Herz, -en
heat (*die*) Hitze
(*to*) heat heizen
heavy schwer
(*to*) help helfen
Help! Hilfe!
her (*pos.*) ihr
(*to*) her ihr
her (*obj.*) sie
here hier
high hoch
higher höher
highway (*die*) Landstraße, -n
superhighway (*die*) Autobahn, -en
hill (*der*) Hügel, -
him ihn
(*to*) him ihm
his sein
history (*die*) Geschichte
home (*das*) Haus, Häuser
(*at*) home zu Hause
(*to one's*) home nach Hause
(*to*) hope hoffen
hopefully hoffentlich
horse (*das*) Pferd, -e
hospital (*das*) Krankenhaus,
Krankenhäuser
hot heiß
hotel (*das*) Hotel, -s
hour (*die*) Stunde, -n
house (*das*) Haus, Häuser
how wie
however (*conj.*) jedoch; doch;
dennoch
hundred hundert
Hungary (*das*) Ungarn

Hungarian ungarisch
Hungarian (*person*) (*der*) Ungar,
(*die*) Ungarin, -nen
hungry hungrig
(*to be*) hungry Hunger haben
hurry (*die*) Eile
(*to*) hurry eilen, sich beeilen
husband (*der*) Mann, Männer;
(*der*) Ehemann, Ehemänner

I

I ich
ice (*das*) Eis
ice cream (*die*) Eiscreme
idiot (*der*) Idiot, -en
if wenn; falls
ill krank
(*to*) imagine sich vorstellen
(*to*) import importieren
important wichtig
impossible unmöglich
in in
including einschließlich
income (*das*) Einkommen, -
India (*das*) Indien
Indian indisch
Indian (*person*) (*der*) Inder, (*die*)
Inderin, -nen
industry (*die*) Industrie, -n
(*to*) injure verletzen
information (*die*) Auskunft,
Auskünfte
inn (*das*) Wirtshaus, Wirtshäuser
inquiry (*die*) Erkundigung, -en;
(*die*) Anfrage, -n
instead anstatt
inside innen
intelligent klug, intelligent
interested interessiert

interesting interessant
interpreter (*der*) Dolmetscher, -
into in
(*to*) **introduce** (*people*) <u>vor</u>stellen
invitation (*die*) Einladung, -en
(*to*) **invite** <u>ein</u>laden
Ireland (*das*) Irland
Irish irisch
Irish (*person*) (*der*) Ire (*die*) Irin
is ist
island (*die*) Insel, -n
Israel (*das*) Israel
Israeli (*person*) (*der*) Israeli, (*die*)
  Israeli
it es
  it is es ist
  its sein (*neuter*)
Italian (*adj.*) italienisch
Italian (*person*) (*der*) Italiener, -,
  (*die*) Italienerin, -nen
Italy (*das*) Italien

J

jacket (*die*) Jacke, -n
jail (*das*) Gefängnis, -se
January (*der*) Januar
Japan (*das*) Japan
Japanese (*adj.*) japanisch
Japanese (*person*) (*der*) Japaner,
  -, (*die*) Japanerin, -nen
jealous eifersüchtig
jewelry (*der*) Schmuck
Jewish jüdisch
Jew (*der*) Jude, (*die*) Jüdin, -nen
job (*die*) Arbeit, -en; (*die*) Stelle,
  -n
(*to*) **join** <u>hinzu</u>kommen
joke (*der*) Witz, -e

(*to*) **joke** scherzen
journey (*die*) Reise, -n
juice (*der*) Saft, Säfte
July (*der*) Juli
June (*der*) Juni
just (*only*) nur
just (*now*) soeben

K

(*to*) **keep** behalten
  Keep out! Eintritt verboten
  Keep quiet! Seien Sie still!
key (*der*) Schlüssel, -
(*to*) **kill** töten
kind (*adv. & adj.*) liebenswürdig;
  freundlich
king (*der*) König, -e
kiss (*der*) Kuß, Küsse
(*to*) **kiss** küssen
kitchen (*die*) Küche, -n
knee (*das*) Knie, -
knife (*das*) Messer, -
(*to*) **know** (*something*) wissen
  (gewußt)
  (*to*) **know** (*acquainted*
  with) kennen
  (*to*) **know how** können
  Do you know . . . ? Wissen
  Sie . . . ? Kennen Sie . . . ?
  Who knows? Wer weiß?

L

ladies room (*die*) Damentoilette,
  -n
Ladies and gentlemen! Meine
  Damen und Herren!
lady (*die*) Dame, -n
lake (*der*) See, -n

lamb (*das*) Lamm, Lämmer
land (*das*) Land, Länder
language (*die*) Sprache, -n
large groß
last (*adv*) zuletzt
late spät
later später
(*to*) laugh lachen
lawyer (*der*) Anwalt, Anwälte
lazy faul
(*to*) learn lernen
leather (*das*) Leder
(*to*) leave (*a place or
person*) verlassen
   (*to*) leave behind hinterlassen
left links
leg (*das*) Bein, -e
lemon (*die*) Zitrone, -n
(*to*) lend leihen
less weniger
lesson (*die*) Stunde, -n
(*to*) let (*permit*) lassen
   Let's ...! Lassen Sie uns
   ...!, Laßt uns ...!
letter (*der*) Brief, -e
letter (*of alphabet*) (*der*) Buch-
stabe, -n
lettuce (*der*) Kopfsalat, -e
liar (*der*) Lügner, -
liberty (*die*) Freiheit, -en
lieutenant (*der*) Leutnant,
life (*das*) Leben, -
(*to*) lift aufheben
light (weight) leicht
   light (*illumination*) (*das*)
   Licht
like wie
   like this so
   (*to*) like gern haben

limit (*die*) Grenze, -n
linen (*das*) Leinen; (*die*) Wäsche
lion (*der*) Löwe, -n
lip (*die*) Lippe, -n
liquor (*der*) Schnaps, Schnäpse
list (*die*) Liste, -n
(*to*) listen zuhören
   Listen! Hören Sie!
little (*small*) klein
   a little ein bißchen
(*to*) live leben
lived gelebt (*p.p. of leben*)
liver (*die*) Leber, -n
living room (*das*) Wohnzimmer, -
lobster (*der*) Hummer, -
long lang
(*to*) look at ansehen
   Look! Sehen Sie!
   Look out! Vorsicht!
loose locker; los
(*to*) lose verlieren (*verloren*)
lost verloren
(*a*) lot (*much*) viel
loud laut
love (*die*) Liebe, -n
   (*to*) love lieben
lovely lieblich; reizend
low niedrig
luck (*das*) Glück
luggage (*das*) Gepäck
lunch (*das*) Mittagessen, -
lung (*die*) Lunge, -n
luxury (*der*) Luxus
luxurious üppig

M

machine (*die*) Maschine, -n
mad (*crazy*) verrückt

madam (*die*) gnädige Frau
made gemacht (*p.p. of machen*)
magazine (*die*) Illustrierte, -n
maid (*das*) Zimmermädchen, -
mail (*die*) Post
mailbox (*der*) Briefkasten,
   Briefkästen
main (*prefix*) Haupt-
major (*der*) Major, -e
majority (*die*) Mehrzahl
(*to*) make machen (*gemacht*)
male männlich
man (*der*) Mann, Männer
manager (*der*) Geschäftsführer, -;
   (*der*) Betriebsleiter, -
manner (*die*) Art, -en
   good manners gute Manieren
many viele
map (*die*) Karte, -n
March (*der*) März
market (*der*) Markt, Märkte
marriage (*die*) Heirat, -en
married verheiratet (*adj. & p.p. of
   heiraten*)
marvelous wunderbar
match (*for lighting*) (*das*) Streich-
   holz, Streichhölzer
matter (*die*) Sache
   What's the matter? Was ist
   los?
May (*der*) Mai
May I? Darf ich?
maybe vielleicht
me mich
   (*to*) me mir
(*to*) mean meinen; bedeuten
meat (*das*) Fleisch
mechanic (*der*) Mechaniker, -
medicine (*die*) Medizin

Mediterranean (*das*) Mittelmeer
(*to*) meet (*encounter*) treffen
meeting (*das*) Zusammentreffen, -
   business meeting (*die*) Konferenz, -en
member (*person*) (*das*) Mitglied,
   -er
(*to*) mend reparieren
men's room (*die*) Herrentoilette,
   -n
menu (*die*) Speisekarte, -n
message (*die*) Mitteilung, -en
metal (*das*) Metall, -e
Mexico (*das*) Mexiko
Mexican (*person*) (der)
   Mexikaner
middle (*die*) Mitte, -n
midnight (*die*) Mitternacht
mile (*die*) Meile, -n
milk (*die*) Milch
million (*die*) Million, -en
millionaire (*der*) Millionär, -e
minister (*clergy*) (*der*) Geistliche,
   -n
mink (*der*) Nerz, -e
minute (*die*) Minute, -n
mirror (*der*) Spiegel, -
Miss Fräulein, -
   (*to*) miss (*emotion*) vermissen
   (*to*) miss (*a train*) verpassen
mistake (*der*) Fehler, -
Mister Herr, -en
misunderstanding (*das*) Miß-
   verständnis, -se
(*to*) misunderstand mißverstehen
(*to*) mix mischen
mixture (*die*) Mischung, -en
model (*das*) Muster, -
modern modern

modest bescheiden
moment (der) Augenblick, -e
Monday (der) Montag, -e
money (das) Geld, -er
monkey (der) Affe, -n
month (der) Monat, -e
monument (das) Denkmal,
Denkmäler
moon (der) Mond, -e
moonlight (der) Mondschein,
more mehr
more or less mehr oder
weniger
more than mehr als
morning (der) Morgen, -
most das meiste, am meisten
mostly meistens
mother (die) Mutter, Mütter
mother-in-law (die) Schwiegermutter, -mütter
motor (der) Motor, -en
motorcycle (das) Motorrad,
-räder
(to) move bewegen
(to) move (residence)
umziehen
mountain (der) Berg, -e
mouse (die) Maus, Mäuse
mouth (der) Mund, Münder
movie (das) Kino, -s, der Film, -e
much viel
mud (der) Schlamm
(to) murder ermorden
murderer (der) Mörder, -
murderess (die) Mörderin, -nen
muscle (der) Muskel, -n
museum (das) Museum, Museen
mushroom (der) Pilz, -e
music (die) Musik

musician (der) Musiker, -
must müssen
I must go. Ich muß gehen.
moustache (der) Schnurrbart,
-bärte
mustard (der) Senf
my mein, -e, mein
myself mich (acc.) mir (dat.)
mystery (das) Geheimnis, -se

N

name (der) Name, -n
napkin (die) Serviette, -n
narcotics (das) Betäubungsmittel
(das) Rauschmittel
narrow eng
nationality (die) Nationalität, -en
navy (die) Marine; (die) Flotte, -n
near nahe
necessary notwendig; nötig
neck (der) Nacken, -
necktie (die) Krawatte, -n
(to) need brauchen
needle (die) Nadel, -n
neighbor (der) Nachbar, -n
neither ... nor weder ... noch
nephew (der) Neffe, -n
nerve (der) Nerv, -en
nervous nervös
net (das) Netz, -e
net profit (der) Reingewinn,
-e
net weight netto
never nie, niemals
Never mind! Macht nichts!
nevertheless trotzdem
new neu
news (die) Nachrichten

newspaper (*die*) Zeitung, -en
next nächst
    next week nächste Woche
    next time das nächste Mal
nice nett
niece (*die*) Nichte, -n
night (*die*) Nacht, Nächte
    last night vorige Nacht
nightclub (*das*) Nachtlokal, -e
nine neun
nineteen neunzehn
ninety neunzig
(*the*) **ninth** (*der, die, das*) neunte
no (*adj.*) kein
no (*opposite of yes*) nein
nobody niemand
noise (*der*) Lärm
none, not a kein
nonsense (*der*) Unsinn
noon (*der*) Mittag
north (*der*) Norden
North America Nordamerika
northeast (*der*) Nordosten
Norway Norwegen
Norwegian norwegisch
nose (*die*) Nase, -n
not nicht
not at all durchaus nicht
not yet noch nicht
nothing nichts
    nothing at all gar nichts
nothing else sonst nichts
(*to*) **notice** bemerken;
    beobachten;
novel (*der*) Roman, -e
November (*der*) November
now jetzt
nowhere nirgends

number (*die*) Nummer, -n
nurse (*die*) Krankenschwester, -n

O

(*to*) **obey** gehorchen
(*to*) **oblige** zwingen; verpflichten
occasionally dann und wann;
    gelegentlich
occupied besetzt (*adj. & p.p. of*
    besetzen)
ocean (*der*) Ozean, -e; (*das*) Meer,
    -e
o'clock Uhr
October (*der*) Oktober
of (*prep.; origin*) von; aus
    of course natürlich
off weg; ab
(*to*) **offer** anbieten
office (*das*) Büro, -s
officer (*der*) Offizier, -e
official (*der*) Beamte, -n, (*die*)
    Beamtin, -nen
often oft
oil (*das*) Öl, -e
o.k. in Ordhung; gut
old alt
olive (*die*) Olive, -n
omelet (*das*) Omelett, -e-s
on (*prep.*) auf; an; zu; bei; in;
    nach
    on time pünktlich
once einst; einmal
    At once! Sofort!
once more noch einmal
one (*number*) eins
    one (*article*) ein
    one-way street (*die*) Ein-
    bahnstraße, -n

onion (*die*) Zwiebel, -n
only nur
open offen
   (*to*) open öffnen (*geöffnet*)
opera (*die*) Oper, -n
operation (*die*) Operation, -en
opinion (*die*) Meinung, -en
opportunity (*die*) Gelegenheit, -en
opposite gegenüber
or oder
orange (*die*) Apfelsine, -n; (*die*)
   Orange, -n
   orange juice (*der*)
   Orangensaft
orchestra (*das*) Orchester, -
order (*der*) Befehl, -e
   (*to*) order bestellen; befehlen
   in order to um zu
ordinary gewöhnlich
original ursprünglich
orphan (*das*) Waisenkind, -er
other anderer
ought sollte
   You ought to ... Sie sollten ...
our unser
out (*not here*) weg
outside draußen
over (*above*) über
   over (*finished*) vorbei
overcoat (*der*) Mantel, Mäntel
over there dort drüben
(*to*) owe schulden
(*to*) own besitzen
owner (*der*) Eigentümer, -; (*der*)
   Besitzer, -
oxygen (*der*) Sauerstoff
oyster (*die*) Auster, -n

P

(*to*) pack packen
pack (*box*) das Päckchen
package (*das*) Paket, -e
page (*die*) Seite, -n
paid bezahlt (*adj. & p.p. of*
   bezahlen)
pain (*der*) Schmerz, -en
painful schmerzhaft
(*to*) paint malen
painting (*das*) Gemälde, -
pair (*das*) Paar, -e
pajamas (*der*) Pyjama, -s
palace (*das*) Schloß, Schlösser
pan (*die*) Pfanne, -n
pants (*die*) Hose, -n
paper (*das*) Papier, -e
parade (*die*) Parade, -n
   Pardon me! Entschuldigen
   Sie!
parents (*die*) Eltern
(*to*) park parken
park (*der*) Park, -s
part (*der*) Teil, -e
partner (*der*) Teilhaber, -; (*der*)
   Partner, -
party (*die*) Party, Parties
   political party (*die*) Partei,
   -en
(*to*) pass vorbeigehen
passenger (*der*) Fahrgast,
   Fahrgäste; (*der*) Passagier, -e
passport (*der*) Paß, Pässe
past (*die*) Vergangenheit, -en
(*to*) pay zahlen, bezahlen
peace (*der*) Friede (*n*)
pedestrian (*der*) Fußgänger, -
pen (*die*) Feder, -n

pencil (*der*) Bleistift, -e
people (*die*) Leute
pepper (*der*) Pfeffer
percent (*das*) Prozent, -e
perfect vollkommen
perfume (*das*) Parfüm, -e
perhaps vielleicht
permanent dauernd
(*to*) permit gestatten; erlauben
permitted erlaubt (*adj. & p.p. of erlauben*)
person (*die*) Person, -en
personality (*die*) Persönlichkeit, -en
(*to*) persuade überreden
pharmacy (*die*) Apotheke, -n
phone (*das*) Telefon, -e
photo (*das*) Photo, -s
piano (*das*) Klavier, -e
picture (*das*) Bild, -er
piece (*das*) Stück, -e
pier (*der*) Pier, -e
pig (*das*) Schwein, -e
pill (*die*) Pille, -n
pillow (*das*) Kissen, -
pin (*die*) Nadel, -n
pipe (*smoking*) (*die*) Pfeife, -n
pistol (*die*) Pistole, -n
place (*der*) Platz, Plätze
plan (*der*) Plan, Pläne
plane (*das*) Flugzeug, -e
planet (*der*) Planet, -en
plant (*garden*) (*die*) Pflanze, -n
plant (*factory*) (*die*) Fabrik, -en
plate (*der*) Teller, -
(*to*) play spielen
play (*theatre*) (*das*) Schauspiel, -e
plastic plastisch
pleasant angenehm

Please! Bitte!
(*to*) please gefallen
pleasure (*das*) Vergnügen, -
pocket (*die*) Tasche, -n
poem (*das*) Gedicht, -e
(*to*) point out zeigen
poison (*das*) Gift, -e
poisonous giftig
Poland (*das*) Polen
Pole (*person*) (*der*) Pole, -n; (*die*) Polin, -nen
police (*die*) Polizei
policeman (*der*) Polizist, -en
policewoman (*die*) Polizistin, -nen
police station (*die*) Polizeiwache, -n
Polish polnisch
polite höflich
pool (*swimming*) (*das*) Schwimmbecken, -
poor arm
pope (*der*) Papst, Päpste
popular beliebt
pork (*das*) Schweinefleisch
portrait (*das*) Porträt, -s
Portugal (*das*) Portugal
position (*die*) Stellung, -en
positive (*or*) positively bestimmt
(*to*) possess besitzen; haben
possible möglich
postcard (*die*) Postkarte, -n
post office (*das*) Postamt, Postämter
pot (*der*) Topf, Töpfe
potato (*die*) Kartoffel, -n
pound (*weight*) (*das*) Pfund, -e
power (*die*) Macht, Mächte
powerful mächtig
practical praktisch

(to) practice üben
(to) praise loben
(to) pray beten
precious kostbar
(to) prefer vorziehen
pregnant schwanger
(to) prepare vorbereiten
present (time) (die) Gegenwart
present (gift) (das) Geschenk, -e
president (der) Präsident, -en
(to) press (clothes) bügeln
pretty hübsch
(to) prevent verhindern
previously vorher
price (der) Preis, -e
priest (der) Priester, -
prince (der) Prinz, -en
princess (die) Prinzessin, -nen
prison (das) Gefängnis, -se
prisoner (der/die) Gefangene, -n
private privat
prize (der) Preis, -e
probable (or) probably
  wahrscheinlich
problem (das) Problem, -e
(to) produce produzieren,
  herstellen
production (die) Produktion; (die)
  Herstellung; (der) Gewinn, -e
profession (der) Beruf, -e
professor (der) Professor, -en
profit (der) Profit, -e
program (das) Programm, -e
progressive progressiv
promise (das) Versprechen
  (to) promise versprechen
prompt pünktlich
(to) pronounce aussprechen

pronunciation (die) Aussprache,
  -n
proof (der) Beweis, -e
propaganda (die) Propaganda
property (der) Besitz, -e
prosperity (der) Wohlstand
(to) protect schützen
protection (der) Schutz
(to) protest protestieren
protestant protestant, -isch
proud stolz
(to) prove beweisen
psychiatrist (der) Psychiater, -
public öffentlich
publicity (die) Publizität;
  Werbung
publisher (der) Verleger, -
publishing firm (der) Verlag
(to) pull ziehen
pure rein
(to) purchase kaufen
purse (der) Geldbeutel, -; (das)
  Portemonnaie, -s
(to) push schieben
(to) put down hinlegen
  (to) put on anlegen; anziehen
  (to) put up aufstellen

Q

quality (die) Qualität, -en
quantity (die) Menge, -n
quarrel (der) Streit, -e
queen (die) Königin, -nen
question (die) Frage, -n
quick (or) quickly schnell
quiet still
  Keep quiet! Ruhig!
quite ganz

German Step by Step

R

rabbit (*das*) Kaninchen, -
race (*human*) (*die*) Rasse, -n
race (*contest*) (*das*) Rennen, -
radiator (*die*) Heizung, -en
radio (*das*) Radio, -s
railroad (*die*) Eisenbahn, -en
rain (*der*) Regen
(*to*) rain regnen
raincoat (*der*) Regenmantel,
-mäntel
rapid (*or*) rapidly rasch
rarely selten
rat (*die*) Ratte, -n
rate (*of exchange*) (*der*) Kurs, -e
rather lieber
I would rather .... Ich
würde lieber ...
razor (*der*) Rasierapparat, -e
razorblade (*die*) Rasierklinge, -n
(*to*) read lesen
ready bereit; fertig
real, really wirklich
reason (*der*) Grund, Gründe
receipt (*die*) Quittung, -en
(*to*) receive erhalten
recent (*or*) recently kürzlich
recipe (*das*) Rezept, -e
(*to*) recognize erkennen
(*to*) recommend empfehlen
red rot
refrigerator (*der*) Kühlschrank,
-schränke
(*to*) refund zurückzahlen,
zurückerstatten
(*to*) refuse abschlagen;
verweigern

(*my*) regards to ... (*meine*) Grüße
an ...
(*to*) regret bedauern
regular regelrecht
reliable zuverlässig
religion (*die*) Religion, -en
relatives (*die*) Verwandten
(*to*) remain bleiben
remedy (*die*) Arznei
(*to*) remember sich erinnern
(*to*) rent mieten
rent (*die*) Miete, -n
(*to*) repair reparieren
(*to*) repeat wiederholen
Repeat please! Wiederholen
Sie, bitte!
reply (*die*) Antwort, -en
report (*der*) Bericht, -e
(*to*) represent repräsentieren,
vertreten
representative (*der*) Repräsen-
tant, -en, (*die*) Repräsentantin,
nen; (*der*) Vertreter,- (*die*) Ver-
treterin, -en
(*to*) rescue retten
responsible verantwortlich
(*the*) rest (*der*) Rest; (*der*) Über-
rest; (*das*) übrige
(*to*) rest sich ausruhen
restaurant (*das*) Restaurant, -s
return (*come back*)
zurückkommen
(*to*) return (*give back*) wiedergeben
revolution (*die*) Revolution, -en
reward (*die*) Belohnung, -en
rice (*der*) Reis
rich reich
(*to*) ride (*a horse*) reiten
(*to*) ride (*in a vehicle*) fahren (*mit*)

304

right (*direction*) rechts
right (*correct*) richtig
Right away! Sofort!
ring (*der*) Ring, -e
riot (*der*) Aufruhr
risk (*das*) Risiko, -s
river (*der*) Fluß, Flüsse
road (*der*) Weg, -e
(*to*) rob rauben; stehlen
roof (*das*) Dach, Dächer
room (*das*) Zimmer, -
room (*space*) (*der*) Raum, Räume
room service (*die*)
Zimmerbedienung
rope (*das*) Seil, -e
round trip hin und zurück
route (*der*) Weg, -e
rug (*der*) Teppich, -e
(*to*) run laufen; rennen
Run! Laufen Sie!
Russia (*das*) Rußland
Russian (*person*) (*der*) Russe, -n,
(*die*) Russin, -nen
Russian (*adj.*) russisch

S

sad traurig
safe sicher
said gesagt (*p.p. of sagen*)
sail (*das*) Segel, -
sailor (*der*) Seemann, Seeleute
saint (*der*) Heilige, -n (*die*) Heilige, -n
salad (*der*) Salat, -e
salary (*das*) Gehalt, Gehälter
sale (*der*) Verkauf, -käufe
Ausverkauf; -käufe
salesman (*der*) Verkäufer, -

saleswoman (*die*) Verkäuferin,
-nen
salt (*das*) Salz
same derselbe, dieselbe, dasselbe
sandwich (*das*) Butterbrot, -e
Saturday (*der*) Sonnabend; (*der*)
Samstag
sauce (*die*) Soße, -n
sausage (*die*) Wurst, Würste
savage wild
(*to*) save sparen
(*to*) say sagen (gesagt)
scarf (*der*) Schal, -s
scenery (*die*) Landschaft, -en
school (*die*) Schule, -n
science (*die*) Wissenschaft, -en
scissors (*die*) Schere, -n
Scotland (*das*) Schottland
Scotch schottisch
Scotsman (*der*) Schotte, -n
Scotswoman (*die*) Schottin, -nen
sea (*die*) See, -n; (*das*) Meer, -e
(*to*) search suchen
season (*die*) Jahreszeit, -en
seat (*der*) Sitz, -e
(*the*) second (*der, die, das*) zweite
secret (*das*) Geheimnis, -se
secretary (*der*) Sekretär, -e (*die*)
Sekretärin -nen
section (*die*) Abteilung, -en
(*to*) see sehen
(*to*) seem scheinen
It seems ... Es scheint ...
seen gesehen (*p.p. of sehen*)
seldom selten
(*to*) sell verkaufen
(*to*) send schicken
(*to*) send for holen lassen

separate getrennt (*adj. & p.p. of*
trennen)
September (*der*) September
series (*die*) Serie, -n
servant (*male*) (*der*) Diener, -,
servant (*female*) (*das*)
Dienstmädchen
service (*der*) Dienst, -e
seven sieben
seventeen siebzehn
seventh siebte
(*the*) seventh (*der, die, das*) siebte
seventy siebzig
several mehrere
(*to*) sew nähen
shade, shadow, (*der*) Schatten, -
shampoo (*das*) Shampoo, -s
shape (*die*) Form, -en
shark (*der*) Haifisch, -e
sharp scharf
(*to*) shave rasieren
she sie
sheep (*das*) Schaf, -e
sheet (*paper*) (*das*) Blatt, Blätter
sheet (*bed*) (*das*) Laken, -; (*das*)
Bettuch, Bettücher
shell (*egg, nut*) (*die*) Schale, -n
(*to*) shine scheinen
(*to*) shine (*shoes*) putzen
ship (*das*) Schiff, -e
(*to*) ship senden; schicken
shirt (*das*) Hemd, -en
shoe (*der*) Schuh, -e
shop (*der*) Laden, Läden
short kurz
should (*I, he, she, it*) (*ich er, sie, es*
sollte)
should (*you, we, they*) (*Sie*
wir, sie sollten)

shoulder (*die*) Schulter, -n
show (*theater* (*die*) Vorstellung,
-en
show (*exhibition*) (*die*) Ausstel-
lung, -en
(*to*) show zeigen
Show me! Zeigen Sie mir!
shower (*die*) Dusche, -n (*die*)
Brause, -n
shrimp (*die*) Krabbe, -n
(*to*) shut schließen
shy scheu
sick krank
side (*die*) Seite, -n
sight (*das*) Gesicht; (*das*)
Augenlicht
sign (*das*) Zeichen, -
(*to*) sign unterschreiben
signature (*die*) Unterschrift, -en
silence (*die*) Ruhe; (*das*)
Schweigen
silent ruhig
silk (*die*) Seide
silly albern
silver (*das*) Silber
similar ähnlich
simple, simply einfach
since seit
sincerely (*in a letter*)
hochachtungsvoll
sincere aufrichtig
(*to*) sing singen
singer (*der*) Sänger, (*die*)
Sängerin
sir mein Herr
sister (*die*) Schwester, -n
sister-in-law (*die*) Schwägerin,
-nen

(*to*) **sit** sitzen
Sit down! Setzen Sie sich!
six sechs
sixteen sechzehn
(*the*) **sixth** (*der, die, das*) sechste
sixty sechzig
size (*die*) Größe, -n
skin (*die*) Haut, Häute
skirt (*der*) Rock, Röcke
sky (*der*) Himmel
(*to*) **sleep** schlafen
slow langsam
small klein
(*to*) **smoke** rauchen
snow (*der*) Schnee
so so
soap (*die*) Seife, -n
sock (*die*) Socke, -n
sofa (*das*) Sofa, -s
soft weich
soldier (*der*) Soldat, -en
some (*a little*) etwas
some (*a few*) einige
somebody jemand
something etwas
sometimes manchmal
somewhere irgendwo
somewhere else sonst irgendwo
son (*der*) Sohn, Söhne
son-in-law (*der*) Schwiegersohn,
-söhne
song (*das*) Lied, -er
soon bald
(*I am*) **sorry.** Es tut mir leid.
soup (*die*) Suppe, -n
south (*der*) Süden
South America (*das*) Südamerika
souvenir (*das*) Andenken, -
Spain (*das*) Spanien

Spanish (*adj.*) spanisch
Spanish (*person*) (*der*) Spanier,
(*adj.*) (*die*) Spanierin, -nen
(*to*) **speak** sprechen (*gesprochen*)
special besonders
(*to*) **spend** (*money*) ausgeben
(*to*) **spend** (*time*) verbringen
spoon (*der*) Löffel, -
sport (*der*) Sport, Sportarten
spring (*season*) (*der*) Frühling, -e
stairs (*die*) Treppe, -n
stain (*der*) Fleck, -en
stamp (*die*) Briefmarke, -n
(*to*) **stand** stehen
star (*der*) Stern, -e
(*to*) **start** anfangen
state (*der*) Staat, -en
station (*railway*) (*der*) Bahnhof,
Bahnhöfe
statue (*das*) Standbild, -er; (*die*)
Statue, -n
(*to*) **stay** bleiben
steak (*das*) Steak, -s
(*to*) **steal** stehlen
steel (*der*) Stahl, Stähle
stenographer (*der*) Stenograph,
-en; (*die*) Stenographin, -nen
still (*adj.*) ruhig
still (*adv.*) noch (*immer*)
stock (*share*) (*die*) Aktie, -n
stocking (*der*) Strumpf, Strümpfe
stockmarket (*die*) Börse, -n
stone (*der*) Stein, -e
(*to*) **stop** halten
Stop! Halt!
Stop it! Aufhören!
store (*der*) Laden, Läden
storm (*der*) Sturm, Stürme
story (*die*) Geschichte, -n

straight gerade
straight ahead geradeaus
strange (*odd*) sonderbar
stranger (*der*) Fremde, -n
street (*die*) Straße, -n
strike (*der*) Streik, -s
string (*der*) Bindfaden, Bindfäden
strong stark
student (*der*) Student, -en, (*die*) Studentin, -nen
(*to*) **study** studieren
stupid dumm
submarine (*das*) Unterseeboot, -e
suburb (*der*) Vorort, -e
subway (*die*) Untergrundbahn, -en
success (*der*) Erfolg, -e
such solch
suddenly plötzlich
(*to*) **suffer** leiden
sugar (*der*) Zucker
(*to*) **suggest** vorschlagen
suggestion (*der*) Vorschlag, Vorschläge
suit (*clothes*) (*der*) Anzug, Anzüge
suitcase (*der*) Koffer, -
summer (*der*) Sommer, -
summons (*die*) Vorladung, -en
sun (*die*) Sonne
Sunday (*der*) Sonntag, -e
supper (*das*) Abendessen, -
sure sicher
surely sicherlich
surprise (*die*) Überraschung, -en
(*to*) **surround** umgeben
surroundings (*die*) Umgebung, -en
sweater (*der*) Sweater, -; (*der*) Pullover, -

sweet süß
(*to*) **swim** schwimmen
swimming pool (*das*) Schwimmbad, -bäder
Swiss (*adj.*) schweizerisch
Swiss person (*der*) Schweizer, -, (*die*) Schweizerin, -nen
Switzerland (*die*) Schweiz
sympathy (*das*) Mitleid
symphony (*die*) Symphonie, -n
symptom (*das*) Symptom, -e
system (*das*) System, -e

T

table (*der*) Tisch, -e
tablecloth (*das*) Tischtuch, -tücher
tail (*der*) Schwanz, Schwänze
tailor (*der*) Schneider, (*die*) Schneiderin, -nen
(*to*) **take** nehmen
    (*to*) **take along** mitnehmen
    (*to*) **take away** wegnehmen
    (*to*) **take a walk** spazierengehen
    (*to*) **take a ride** herumfahren
talent (*das*) Talent, -e
talented begabt
(*to*) **talk** reden; sprechen
tall groß
tame zahm
tape (*das*) Band, Bänder
tape recorder (*das*) Tonbandgerät, -e
taste (*der*) Geschmack, Geschmäcker
(*to*) **taste** schmecken; versuchen
tax (*die*) Steuer, -n

taxi Taxi, -s, (*die*) Taxe, -n
tea (*der*) Tee, -s
(*to*) **teach** lehren
teacher (*der*) Lehrer, (*die*)
  Lehrerin, -nen
team (*die*) Mannschaft, -en
(*to*) **tear** reißen
telegram (*das*) Telegramm, -e
telephone (*das*) Telefon, -e
television (*das*) Fernsehen
(*to*) **tell** sagen
  Tell him (*her*). . . . Sagen Sie
  ihm (*ihr*) . . .
temperature (*die*) Temperatur,
  -en
temporary vorübergehend
ten zehn
tenant (*der*) Mieter, -
tender zart
tennis (*das*) Tennis
(*the*) **tenth** (*der, die, das*) zehnte
terrace (*die*) Terrasse, -n
terrible furchtbar
(*to*) **test** prüfen
than als
(*to*) **thank** danken
thanks danke
that (*conj.*) daß
that das
  That's all. Das ist alles.
  That's fine. Das ist gut.
that (*one*) jener
the der (*m*), die (*f.*), das (*n.*); die
  (*pl.*)
theater (*das*) Theater, -
their ihr
theirs (*der*) ihre, (*die*) ihre, (*das*)
  ihre, (*die*) ihren

them sie
  (*to*) **them** ihnen
themselves sie selbst; sich
then dann
there dort
there is, there are es gibt
these diese
they sie
thick dick
thief (*der*) Dieb, -e
thin dünn
thing (*das*) Ding, -e, (*die*) Sache
(*to*) **think** (*cogitate*) denken
(*to*) **think** (*believe*) glauben
  I think of you. Ich denke an
  dich.
(*the*) **third** der, (*die, das*) dritte
thirsty durstig
thirteen dreizehn
thirty dreißig
this das
this one dieser
  What is this? Was ist das?
those (*adj.*) jene
those (*pron*) die, solche
thousand (*das*) Tausend, -e
thread (*der*) Faden, Fäden
three drei
throat (*die*) Gurgel, -n, (*der*) Hals,
  Hälse
through durch
(*to*) **throw** werfen
thunder (*der*) Donner
Thursday (*der*) Donnerstag, -e
ticket (*railroad etc.*) (*die*) Fahr-
  karte, -n
ticket (*theater*) (*die*) Eintrittskarte, -n
tiger (*der*) Tiger, -

tight eng
till bis
time (*die*) Zeit, -en
tip (*das*) Trinkgeld, -er
tire (*der*) Reifen, -
tired müde
to (*direction*) nach
    to (*in order to*) um zu
toast (*bread*) (*der*) Toast, -e/-s
tobacco (*der*) Tabak, -e
today heute
toe (*die*) Zehe, -n
together zusammen
toilet (*die*) Toilette, -n
tomato (*die*) Tomate, -n
tomb (*die*) Grabstätte, -n; (*das*)
    Grab, Gräber
tomorrow morgen
tongue (*die*) Zunge, -n
tonight heute abend (*evening*);
    heute nacht (*night*)
too (*also*) auch
too (*excessive*) allzu
tool (*das*) Werkzeug, -e
tooth (*der*) Zahn, Zähne
toothbrush (*die*) Zahnbürste, -n
toothpaste (*die*) Zahnpasta
total (*adj.*) gesamt
total (*sum*) (*der*) Gesamtbetrag,
    -beträge
(*to*) touch berühren
tough hart; zäh
tour (*die*) Rundreise, -n
tourist, (*der*) Tourist, -en
toward zu, zum (*m. & n.*) zur (*f*)
towel (*das*) Handtuch,
    Handtücher
tower (*der*) Turm, Türme
town (*die*) Stadt, Städte

toy (*das*) Spielzeug, -e
trade fair (*die*) Handelsmesse, -n
traffic (*der*) Verkehr
train (*der*) Zug, Züge
tragedy (*die*) Tragödie, -n
tragic tragisch
(*to*) translate übersetzen
translation (*die*) Übersetzung, -en
translator (*der*) Übersetzer, -
transportation (*der*) Transport, -e
(*to*) travel reisen
travel agency (*das*) Reisebüro, -s
traveler (*der*) Reisende, -n
treasure (*der*) Schatz, Schätze
tree (*der*) Baum, Bäume
trip (*long*) (*die*) Reise, -n
    trip (*short*) (*die*) Fahrt, -en
trouble (*die*) Mühe, -n
truck (*der*) Lastwagen, -
true wahr
truth (*die*) Wahrheit, -en
(*to*) try versuchen
    (*to*) try on <u>an</u>probieren
Tuesday (*der*) Dienstag
Turkey (*die*) Türkei
Turkish türkisch
Turkish person (*der*) Türke, -n
    (*die*) Türkin, -nen
(*to*) turn around <u>um</u>drehen
    (*to*) make a turn <u>um</u>kehren
    (*to*) turn off <u>ab</u>stellen
    (*to*) turn on <u>an</u>stellen
twelve zwölf
twenty zwanzig
twice zweimal
twin (*der*) Zwilling, -e
two zwei
type (*sort*) (*die*) Art, -en

typewriter (*die*) Schreibmaschine, -n
typical typisch
typist (*die*) Stenotypistin, -nen

U

ugly häßlich
umbrella (*der*) Regenschirm, -e
uncle (*der*) Onkel, -
uncomfortable unbequem
unconscious unbewußt
under, underneath unter
(*to*) **understand** verstehen
(*verstanden*)
Do you understand? Verstehen Sie?
I don't understand. Ich verstehe nicht.
underwear (*die*) Unterwäsche
unemployed arbeitslos
unfortunately leider
unfair unfair
uniform (*die*) Uniform, -en
United Nations (*die*) Vereinigten Nationen
United States (*die*) Vereinigten Staaten
university (*die*) Universität, -en
unless es sei denn
until bis
up hinauf
urgent dringend
us, to us uns
(*to*) **use** gebrauchen
used to (*accustomed to*) gewöhnt an
useful nützlich
useless nutzlos
usually gewöhnlich

V

vacant frei
vacation (*die*) Ferien; (*der*) Urlaub, -e
vaccination (*die*) Schutzimpfung, -en
valley (*das*), Tal, Täler
valuable wertvoll
value (*der*) Wert, -e
variety (*die*) Abwechslung, -en
vegetables (*das*) Gemüse, -
verb (*das*) Zeitwort, Zeitwörter
very sehr
very well sehr gut
vest (*die*) Weste, -n
vicinity (*die*) Nähe
victory (*der*) Sieg, -e
view (*die*) Aussicht
village (*das*) Dorf, Dörfer
vinegar (*der*) Essig
vineyard (*der*) Weinberg, -e
violence (*die*) Gewalt
visit (*der*) Besuch, -e
(*to*) **visit** besuchen
voice (*die*) Stimme, -n
vote (*die*) Stimme, -n
voyage (*die*) Reise, -n
vulgar ordinär; vulgär

W

wages (*der*) Lohn, Löhne
waist (*die*) Taille, -n
(*to*) **wait** warten
waiter (*der*) Kellner, -
waitress (*die*) Kellnerin, -nen
(*to*) **wake up** aufwachen
(*to*) **walk** gehen
walk (*take a walk*) spazierengehen

walk (*to go on foot*) zu Fuß gehen
wall (*die*) Wand, Wände
wallet (*die*) Brieftasche, -n
(*to*) want wollen
war (*der*) Krieg, -e
warm warm
was war
    there was es gab
(*to*) wash waschen
(*to*) waste verschwenden
watch (*die*) Uhr, -en
(*to*) watch <u>auf</u>passen
    Watch out! Passen Sie auf!,
    Paß auf!
water (*das*) Wasser
way (*manner*) (*die*) Art, -en
way (*road*) (*der*) Weg, -e
we wir
weak schwach
weapon (*die*) Waffe, -n
(*to*) wear (*clothes*) tragen
weather (*das*) Wetter
wedding (*die*) Hochzeit, -en
Wednesday (*der*) Mittwoch
week (*die*) Woche, -n
weekend (*das*) Wochenende, -
(*to*) weigh wiegen
weight (*das*) Gewicht, -e
Welcome! Willkommen!
    You are welcome! Bitte sehr!
well gut
    He is well. Es geht ihm gut.
were waren
    (*there*) were es gab (*plural*)
west (*der*) Westen
wet naß
what was
what else? was sonst (*noch*)?

What's the matter? Was ist
los?
wheel (*das*) Rad, Räder
when wann
where wo
where else? wo anders?
whether ob
which der, die, das; welcher, -e,
    -es
while während
white weiß
who? wer?
    who der, die, das, die
who else? wer sonst?
whole ganz
whom den (*acc*), die
whom? wen?
why? warum?
    Why not? Warum nicht?
wide breit
widow (*die*) Witwe, -n
widower (*der*) Witwer, -
wife (*die*) Frau, -en
wife (*die*) Ehefrau, -en
wild wild
I will (*fut.*) Ich werde & (*the
    infinitive*)
    he, (*she, it*) will... er, (*sie, es*)
    wird...
    you, (*they*) will ... Sie, (*sie*)
    werden...
    we will ... wir werden...
(*to*) win gewinnen
wind (*der*) Wind, -e
window (*das*) Fenster, -
wine (*der*) Wein, -e
winter (*der*) Winter
wise weise; klug
(*to*) wish wünschen (*gewünscht*)

with mit
without ohne
witness (*der*) Zeuge, -n, (*die*) Zeu-
  gin, -nen
wolf (*der*) Wolf, Wölfe
woman (*die*) Frau, -en
(*to*) wonder sich fragen
wonderful wunderbar
wood (*das*) Holz, Hölzer
woods (*der*) Wald, Wälder
wool (*die*) Wolle
word (*das*) Wort, Wörter
work (*die*) Arbeit, -en
(*to*) work arbeiten
world (*die*) Welt, -en
(*to*) worry Sorgen haben
worried besorgt
worse schlimmer
I (*he, she, it*) would ich (*er, sie, es*)
  würde + the infinitive
you (*they*) would Sie (*sie*) würden
(*to*) wrap einpacken
wrist (*das*) Handgelenk, -e
(*to*) write schreiben (*geschrieben*)
writer (*der*) Schriftsteller, -, (*die*)
  Schriftstellerin, -nen
wrong falsch

X

X-rays (*die*) Röntgenstrahlen

Y

(*to*) yawn gähnen
yacht (*die*) Jacht, -en
year (*das*) Jahr, -e
yellow gelb
yes ja
yesterday gestern
yet (*adv.*) noch
  not yet noch nicht
yet (*however*) doch
you (*formal*) Sie
  you (*informal*) du
young jung
your (*formal*) Ihr
  your (*informal*) dein
youth (*die*) Jugend

Z

zero (*die*) Null
zipper (*der*) Reißverschluß, -üsse
zone (*die*) Zone, -n
zoo (*der*) Zoo, -s